THE
PERSONAL
HANDBOOK ON
PRAYER

Guideposts®

CARMEL, NEW YORK 10512

CONTENTS

CONTRIBUTORS

General Editor
James C. Wilhoit, PhD
Price-LeBar Professor of Christian Formation and Ministry
Wheaton College

Volume Editor
Mark Fackler, PhD
Professor of Communications
Calvin College

Writing and Development Team
Joshua S. Benton
Amanda Black
Elizabeth Brady
Philip Christman
Jay Collier
Dean Kladder
Steve Luchies
J. David Muyskens
Erica Schemper
Michael Wagenman

Editorial Team
Bruce Barton
Paige Drygas
Linda K. Taylor

Interior Design
Mark Wainwright

Production Team
Carol Barnstable
Kirk Luttrell
Ashley Taylor

INTRODUCTION

Come and feast! That is the invitation of the Bible, an invitation to prayer. From Isaiah's call, "Every one who thirsts, come to the waters" (Isaiah 55:1), to Jesus' invitation, "If anyone thirsts, let him come to Me and drink" (John 7:37), the pages of Scripture are filled with invitations to come and be refreshed, filled, comforted, and healed. George Herbert said it well: "Prayer, the church's banquet." God has prepared a banquet for His people. Today we can come and feast at God's table. Young and old, rich and poor, women and men are all invited to attend, and prayer is one of the ways that we can come to this banquet. It is in prayer that we feel His embrace and hear Him rejoice over us "with singing" (Zephaniah 3:17).

P. T. Forsyth began his volume on prayer with these wise words: "It is a difficult and even formidable thing to write on prayer, and one fears to touch the Ark."[1] Prayer is central to the spiritual life, and a writer must be careful not to be presumptuous in describing this amazing divine-human interaction. I am helped when I remember that prayer makes sense only when it is seen as an aspect of a vital divine-human relationship. The heart of prayer lies in God's desire to enter into relationship with humankind. It is His self-revelation, divine attributes, and work of redemption that cause Him to invite us to pray, "Our Father in heaven" (Matthew 6:9). The redeemed divine-human relationship of mutual love, trust, and commitment provides the context for our praying.

This relationship excludes any attempt to use magic or formulas to control or placate God. In 1 Kings, we see Elijah offering a simple, straightforward prayer clearly rooted in his relationship with God—"I am Your servant"—while the priests of Baal vainly seek to win the favor of deity through crying aloud and cutting themselves (1 Kings 18:16–38). Jesus reminds us that true prayer is a matter of the heart and must be free of show and self-glorification. This volume is not only about techniques of prayer, but more important, it is about how to live in relationship with God fostered by prayer.

Prayer is virtually a universal phenomenon in our country. Today, over 90 percent of

Americans report, as they have for the past 50 years, that they pray. More people pray than watch sports on television, follow the stock market, jog, worry about their weight, or are sexually active. While prayer is very common, we are intensely private and tight-mouthed when it comes to talking about how we pray. In part, this reticence to talk about our prayer lives is prudent. Jesus warned about the dangers of "showing off" our praying, and we learn from Mary the value of quietly treasuring in our hearts our deep spiritual experiences.

We have designed this handbook to explore the mystery of prayer by taking a closer look at the Person to whom we pray, the person praying, the power of prayer, and the process of prayer. We want you, the reader, to hear from others and to get a glimpse into the patterns of praying that have sustained others. We have sought to include topics and authors who can speak to the range of places where readers are as they seek direction through these pages. So far as we can determine, all the articles are written by people of genuine prayer whose authenticity is corroborated by others. Not all the authors share my angle of vision on their subject, but the writings are always sincere, clear, and optimistic about God's power and purpose in the world through our prayers.

Some years ago I discovered the prayers of the Bible. When I began to realize that I could pray the prayers of Paul or David or Jesus, it was almost as if I were reading them for the first time. These prayers provided a road map for my praying that I had been desperately seeking. I found a new confidence in my praying when I prayed what Jesus had prayed for others (see John 17). During this time, I had the opportunity to speak in the former Soviet Union, and I spoke about the need for us to turn our Bibles into our prayer books. I remember being humbled by a pastor as he told me how the biblical prayers had sustained him during the dark days of state-sponsored persecution. We have built in this handbook an emphasis on the prayers of the Bible, and I urge you to use these prayers to shape and guide your praying.

In addition, we have collected classic prayers and quotations from various sources. For years I had little interest in written prayers. Then I found some historic prayers that gave voice to my deepest needs in words that I had yearned to pray but had eluded me. Well-crafted prayers that we learn to use in our sunny days can sustain us during the dark nights.

Prayer is not an optional activity for those who are especially spiritual. To pray is a frontal attack on our pride. When we pray, we turn to God and thereby acknowledge there is something more important to bring to bear on a task than just our creativity and work—namely the wisdom and power of God. Prayer also is the chief means of deepening our relationship with God. I appreciate Forsyth's analogy that "prayer is for the religious life what original research is for science—by it we get direct contact with reality."[2] Science could not go on without research, and Christianity cannot go on in a vibrant way without prayer. It is in prayer that we "taste and see that the LORD is good" (Psalm 34:8).

As you read these pages, please remember that you will not find the key to prayer here. You will find good advice, inspiration, and wisdom, but the key to praying is bigger than any technique or belief about prayer. Prayer involves so much more than just asking. In fact, it is much more than words. It is first and foremost a way of life before God marked by living in a humble and loving relationship with God. If there is a key to prayer it is not, as is so often said, faith, but righteousness.

Jesus' life is a powerful testimony to the effectiveness of prayers borne out of a life lived in submission and love before the Father. His prayers did not merely bounce off the ceiling and limply fall back into His lap; they were a powerful force for good. Because His life was marked by such integrity, His life of obedience and His praying testified to the same things. "In the days of His flesh, when He had offered up prayers and supplications . . . [He] was heard because of His godly fear" (Hebrews 5:7). There is a deep and necessary connection between our praying and our living. James wrote, "The effective, fervent prayer of a righteous man avails much" (James 5:16).

I trust this volume helps draw you closer to our Father's heart. May it enable you to serve others through prayer, discern more clearly God's call on your life, and engage in the work of God's kingdom through intercession.

—*Dr. James C. Wilhoit*

HOW TO USE THIS BOOK

This is a book to help you pray. The elements that comprise this book are all designed to make talking to God and listening to God a stronger and more effective part of your life.

Normally, we don't ask a book for this kind of help. Rather, trouble of some sort pushes us toward prayer. Someone close to us gets sick or loses a job. Or sometimes it's not trouble but gratitude for a particularly big blessing—a clean bill of health, a marriage, a birth. Quickly we go to our knees. We pray when moved by life's great ups and downs. But if we prayed only at these times, prayer would be a rare experience—merely part of our response to the major events of life, forgotten altogether in the mundane of the everyday.

This book is for the great days, the bad days, and the normal days—with all their pressures, time crunches, and even boredom. Most days are not spent dealing with great highs and lows but the steady in-between. To make prayer a regular habit, a daily discipline, part of our "walk with God"—that's the point of this book.

You will find plenty of help here. Read what Christian leaders have said about prayer in the various articles on prayer excerpted from excellent books on the topic. They have struggled, too—the life of leadership is not easy—and prayer has strengthened them. Meditate on some of the Bible's key teachings on prayer in the section of devotions on many of the prayers of the Bible. These short essays explain the passage and encourage your personal application of its truth. Use the section of heartfelt prayers to launch your daily contact with God. Prayer is *always* the right thing to do, and these prayer starters should help infuse new energy into your communication with God.

Books cannot solve the mystery of prayer: how God hears, why God listens, what's effective. We don't seek to give you all the answers; we seek to help you dig in and discover the Person, the Power, and the Process of this mystery called prayer. This book begins with three assumptions of faith: God is good, His Word is true, and Christians should pray. We do not set out to prove these assumptions. People of faith worldwide will understand that. A bad-hearted god (many have been worshiped) could still require prayers, but the overwhelmingly wonderful fact is that our God invites prayer as part of an intimate relationship with Him. That very communication becomes the most important channel for God's blessing into your life. A lying god (many of these have been worshiped, too) could still require prayer, if only to try to trick us into believing his lies. But the Word of God is true. Prayer to the true God is not cunning, but open communication to a Person; not a maneuver, but a sharing of your deepest hurts and hopes with your loving, merciful Father. If you have not yet found these things to be true, your first prayer should be the eager acceptance of God as your best Friend, your only Lord, your Source of every truth.

Now you're ready to pray.

So here's a warning.

If reading this book consumes the time you would have spent praying, all of us who have worked to prepare this book have labored for naught. We would rather you pray than read. So if you're in a bit of a hurry, now is a good time to set this volume aside and just do it. Let our wonderful God hear your heart. Let His Word comfort yours. Build a relationship that brings strength for today's journey and hope for tomorrow. God invites you to speak with Him right now. Find a quiet place where the phone cannot interrupt you. Take your Bible and . . . okay . . . this Handbook too, to help you get going. Now start in: Praise God for your life, thank God for the tender mercies you enjoy today, and ask God for the help you need. You have begun a wonderful discipline. Be assured that God is listening, glad for your attention, and ready to enrich your life beyond your wildest expectations.

—*Dr. Mark Fackler*

THE PERSON TO WHOM WE PRAY

[focus on the God to Whom we are praying]

HOW DOES THE BIBLE DESCRIBE GOD?

Give to the LORD the glory due His name;

Bring an offering, and come before Him.

Oh, worship the Lord in the beauty of holiness!

(1 Chron. 16:29 NKJV)

O Lord, our Lord, how majestic is Your name in all the earth (Ps. 8:1 NIV)! I delight in You, the King of glory. You are strong and mighty in battle (Ps. 24:7–8), and Your kingdom is built on righteousness and justice (Ps. 89:14). You have given all authority to Your Son Jesus (Matt. 28:18), the Prince of Peace (Isa. 9:6). Jesus, I rejoice that at Your name, every knee will bow—both in heaven, on earth, and under the earth—and every tongue will confess that Jesus Christ is Lord, to the glory of God the Father (Phil. 2:10–11).

Almighty God, there is no king like *my* King. There is no god like *my* God. All the nations are but a drop in the bucket compared to Your power and might (Isa. 40:15). Your reign extends from human events and the change in seasons (Dan. 2:21) through eternity (Dan. 7:14). The powers of death, sin, and hell are no match for You. I can't help but sing and shout for my King. You reign (1 Chron. 16:31)!

To look upon Your face in all Your fullness would mean certain death (Ex. 33:20). Yet You allow me—laden with sin that I am—to enter into Your presence through the blood of Jesus Christ (Heb. 4:16). And as I approach Your throne, I am enamored with Your beauty. The grandeur and splendor of Your presence astounds me.

My heart trembles at the thought that I am privileged to enter into the courts of the almighty God who reigns above the heavens and holds the destiny of earthly kingdoms in His hands (Dan. 2:21). So I build a throne of worship and praise for You to take Your rightful place (Ps. 22:3)—in my hardships (James 1:2); in my successes (Ps. 115:1); in my thoughts (Col. 3:2); in everything I do (1 Thess. 5:16–18).

Your holiness describes Your beauty. You are perfect in all Your ways (Deut. 32:4), devoid of all evil (Ps. 5:4), and unrighteousness (Ps. 92:15). There is no one like You (Isa. 40:25). Jesus, You are the manifestation of God's beauty (Isa. 4:2). The beauty of this world reflects the essence of who You are. Lord, let Your beauty be upon me (Ps. 90:17).

Only those with clean hands and a pure heart may enjoy Your presence (Ps. 24:3–4). Thank You for giving me Your Holy Spirit so that I may have the power to be holy just as You are holy (Lev. 11:45).

The one thing I desire is that I may dwell in Your house all the days of my life, to behold Your beauty, and to seek You in Your temple (Ps. 27:4). "Better is one day in your courts than a thousand elsewhere" (Ps. 84:10 NIV). As I see You in all Your beauty and splendor, I fall in love with You all over again.

> PRAYER REFLECTION
>
> *Set our hearts on fire with love to you, Christ our God, that in its flame we may love you with all our heart, mind, soul, and strength and love our neighbors as ourselves, so that, keeping your commandments, we may glorify you, the giver of all good gifts.*
>
> —Eastern Orthodox Prayer
> (adaptation)

So I pledge my allegiance to You my King and join the four living creatures surrounding Your throne who cry "Holy, holy, holy/Lord God Almighty,/Who was and is and is to come!" (Rev. 4:8 NKJV).[1]

—*from* Prayers to Move Your Mountains

WHO IS THIS GOD TO WHOM I AM PRAYING?

These are just a few of the names of God which describe his character. Study them, for in a given day, you may need each one of them . . .

When you are confused about the future, go to your *Jehovah-raah,* your caring shepherd. When you are anxious about provision, talk to *Jehovah-jireh,* the Lord who provides. Are your challenges too great? Seek the help of *Jehovah-shalom,* the Lord is peace. Is your body sick? Are your emotions weak? *Jehovah-rophe,* the Lord who heals you, will see you now. Do you feel like a soldier stranded behind enemy lines? Take refuge in *Jehovah-nissi,* the Lord my banner.

Meditating on the names of God reminds you of the character of God. Take these names and bury them in your heart.

God is

>   the shepherd who guides,
>
>   >   the Lord who provides,
>   >
>   >   >   the voice who brings peace in the storm,
>   >   >
>   >   >   >   the physician who heals the sick, and
>   >   >   >
>   >   >   >   >   the banner that guides the soldier.

And most of all, he . . . is.[2]

—*Max Lucado*

HOW CAN I TALK TO A HOLY GOD?

On Wednesday nights my family piled into the car and drove dutifully to church for prayer meeting. Even in grade school, I would sit among the adults, listening quietly, sometimes even praying. Prayer was formal. In those heads-bowed-eyes-closed moments I heard a basketful of *thees, thous,* and *shouldests,* and I concluded that prayers were said with a certain language. (We certainly didn't talk that way at home.)

Another misconception of prayer, but related to the first, is that it only takes place in church or some other "holy" spot. I knew this wasn't totally true because we prayed a lot at home, but for many people this is a real issue.

The Bible provides two "bookend" concepts of prayer. On one end we read that prayer is communication with a holy God, an infinite, eternal Being, the Sovereign of the universe (Colossians 1:15–18) against whom we have sinned. Our response, therefore, should be reverence (2 Corinthians 7:1), honoring, and praising God for who he is and what he does.

At the other end is the truth that because of what Christ has done, we may come boldly into God's presence (Hebrews 4:16), asking him for anything in Christ's name (John 14:13, 14).

In the middle of these two biblical truths lies the practical reality. Because God is sovereign and holy, we must come to him with reverence and respect, rejecting casualness and flippancy. He is *not* our "big buddy in the sky." At the same time, however, we need not fear him if we are his children through faith in Jesus Christ. We can indeed talk to God about anything, at any time, in any place. And, because we have an intimate relationship with him, we can discuss matters as with our closest friend, using our own words.

There is another application from this tension between "holiness" and "familiarity." We should build into our lives times of deep communication and worship. This is a necessary part of being Christ's disciple, and a church building or other "holy" place may set the atmosphere where this can take place. Sometimes it just means sitting there, listening, and meditating on God's goodness and love.

The Bible also tells us, however, to "pray continually" (1 Thessalonians 5:17). This implies a constant chattering, talking to him about everything, all day long. God wants us to be totally honest with him, telling him about our deepest needs and committing every decision to his control. These prayers can be aloud or silent, with head bowed or with eyes wide open, at home or at work.

The fact is that we need to understand both ends to live in the middle. God wants us to know that he is holy and in control; but he also wants us to be confident in our love relationship with him.

Don't reserve your prayers for church. Prayer must be central in our lives—it is our lifeline, our vital communication link with God.[3]

—*Dave Veerman*

> **PRAYER REFLECTION**
>
> *My Lord God, I have no idea where I am going. I do not see the road ahead of me, I cannot know for certain where it will end. Nor do I really know myself, and the fact that I think I am following your will does not mean that I am actually doing so. But I believe that the desire to please you does in fact please you. And I hope I have that desire in all that I am doing. . . . And I know that if I do this you will lead me by the right road, though I may know nothing about it. Therefore I will trust you always though I may seem to be lost and in the shadow of death. I will not fear, for you are ever with me, and you will never leave me to face my perils alone.*
>
> —*Thomas Merton*

DO I NEED TO KNOW GOD IN ORDER TO PRAY?

If you've ever been on a blind date, you probably have a few horror stories of your own. After all, what's more awkward than trying to make conversation with someone you don't know very well, especially when it's just the two of you?

You can't really talk about anything deep or meaningful—you're practically strangers. You also have to worry about saying the wrong thing or giving the wrong impression. Even worse, you don't know which topics are off-limits or what might set the other person off and ruin the whole experience.

So usually what happens is that you end up talking about nothing and waiting for the whole thing to be over.

Strange as it may seem, the same thing can happen with prayer if you're not careful.

If you don't know—really know—the One you're communicating with when you pray, you may find yourself talking about nothing and waiting for the whole thing to be over. Your prayer time may not be as awkward as a bad blind date, but it probably won't mean much to you. You may even feel that you're just going through the motions. And what's worse, your prayers probably won't accomplish much.

That's not the kind of prayer life you want, is it? . . .

No, what you want is to experience dynamic prayer—the kind of prayer that changes lives and makes a difference in the world. But to develop that kind of prayer life, you have to get to know the One you're talking to. And not just in a casual, "Hey, God, how's it going?" way, either.

If you want maximum power from your prayer life, you've got to put maximum effort into it. That means you have to get to know God better than you know your best friend, better than you know your family—even better than you know yourself. Your goal is to understand who God is, what He's capable of, why He does what He does, and what's important to Him.

If that doesn't seem like a monster responsibility to you, then you probably don't have the complete picture of what we're talking about. Think about how long it took you to get to know your best friend. What kinds of things did you have to learn about him or her? What mistakes did you make on your way to best friendship? How long was it before you were comfortable sharing your most private thoughts and feelings with each other?

Now think about how that same process might work with God. Keep in mind that

> ## PRAYER REFLECTION
>
> *O Lord, you represent everything good. So who am I that I dare to talk to you? I am your poorest and most minor servant, a vile worm, much more poor and worthy of despising than I have courage to say. You know I am nothing—need I remind you?—I have nothing, and I can do nothing. But you— that is a different matter! Only you are good, without fault, and holy. You can accomplish everything, you give all things, you fill to the brim everything. Only the wretched sinner do you leave with hands empty of heavenly joys.*
>
> *Please, then, remember your kind mercies and fill my heart with your grace. . . . How else can I bear the hardships and stresses unless you bring mercy and grace? Do not turn your face from me. Do not be slow in coming. Do not hold back your comfort, or my soul will become arid like the desert.*
>
> —*Thomas à Kempis*

He's been around forever. He's had His hand in every moment of human history. He sees everything and knows everything.

This isn't Someone you're going to get to know overnight.

You can start to gather bits of information about Him—information that you can use like pieces of a jigsaw puzzle as you try to put together the big picture of who God is.[4]

—*Randy Southern*

DID JESUS REALLY TELL ME TO PRAY?

In our Lord's last discourse to His loved ones, just before the most wonderful of all prayers, the Master again and again held out His kingly golden scepter and said, as it were, "What is your request? It shall be granted unto you, even unto the whole of My kingdom!"

Do we believe this? We must do so if we believe our Bibles. Shall we just read over very quietly and thoughtfully one of our Lord's promises, reiterated so many times? If we had never read them before, we should open our eyes in bewilderment, for these promises are almost incredible. From the lips of any mere man they would be quite unbelievable. But it is the Lord of heaven and earth Who speaks; and He is speaking at the most solemn moment of His life. It is the eve of His death and passion. It is a farewell message. Now listen!

"Verily, verily I say unto you, he that believeth on Me, the works that I do shall he do also; and greater works than these shall he do: because I go unto the Father. And whatsoever ye shall ask in My name, that will I do, that the Father may be glorified in the Son. If ye shall ask anything in My name, that will I do" (John 14:13, 14). Now, could any words be plainer or clearer than these? Could any promise be greater or grander? Has anyone else, anywhere, at any time, ever offered so much?

How staggered those disciples must have been! Surely they could scarcely believe their own ears. But that promise is made also to you and to me.

And, lest there should be any mistake on their part, or on ours, our Lord repeats Himself a few moments afterwards. Yes, and the Holy Spirit bids St. John record those words again. "If ye abide in Me, and My words abide in you, ask whatsoever ye will, and it shall be done unto you. Herein is My Father glorified, that ye bear much fruit; and so shall ye be My disciples" (John 15:7, 8).

These words are of such grave importance, and so momentous, that the Savior of the world is not content even with a threefold utterance of them. He urges His disciples to obey His command "to ask." In fact, He tells them that one sign of their being His "friends" will be the obedience to His commands in all things (verse 14). Then He once more repeats His wishes: "Ye did not choose Me, but I chose you, and appointed you, that ye should go and bear fruit, and that your fruit should abide: that whatsoever ye shall ask the Father, in My name, He may give it you" (John 15:16).

> **PRAYER REFLECTION**
>
> *Satan's no fool. He knows that prayer is your lifeline to God. He also knows that if he can interfere with that connection, he has a good chance of stalling your spiritual growth.*
>
> —*Randy Southern*

One would think that our Lord had now made it plain enough that He wanted them to pray; that He needed their prayers, and that without prayer they could accomplish nothing. But to our intense surprise He returns again to the same subject, saying very much the same words.

"In that day ye shall ask Me nothing"—i.e., "ask Me no question" (R.V., marg.)—"Verily, verily I say unto you, if ye ask anything of the Father, He will give it you in My name. Hitherto have ye asked nothing in My name: ask, and ye shall receive, that your joy may be fulfilled" (John 16:23, 24).

Never before had our Lord laid such stress on any promise or command—never! This truly marvelous promise is given us six times over. Six times, almost in the same breath, our Savior commands us to ask whatsoever we will. This is the greatest—the most wonderful—promise ever made to man. Yet most men—Christian men—practically ignore it! Is it not so?

The exceeding greatness of the promise seems to overwhelm us. Yet we know that He is "able to do exceedingly abundantly above all that we ask or think" (Phil. 3:20). So our blessed Master gives the final exhortation, before He is seized, and bound, and scourged, before His gracious lips are silenced on the cross, "Ye shall ask in My name . . . for the Father Himself loveth you" (John 16:25, 26). We have often spent much time in reflecting upon our Lord's seven words from the cross. And it is well we should do so. Have we ever spent one hour in meditating upon this, our Savior's seven-fold invitation to pray?

Gracious Savior, pour out upon us the fullness of the Holy Spirit, that we may indeed become Kneeling Christians.[5]

—*Anonymous*

When Jesus ascended back to heaven, one of the main reasons He sent the Holy Spirit was because He knew we would need help in our praying.

The well-known reasons for the Holy Spirit's being sent by Jesus—providing supernatural power, giving us boldness, recalling what Jesus had said to us, convicting of sin, and comforting us—would determine the direction and content of our A.D. praying. But needing the Holy Spirit to help in our praying is an often-overlooked reason in our "I-can-do-it-myself,-God" modern culture.

However, when we are confused or devastated by circumstances, not only at a loss as to the answer we desire, but even *what* to pray, it is the Holy Spirit who takes our prayers to the Father—according to His will. This is the omniscient Father, who never makes a mistake, who knows the what-ifs of every possible solution, and who knows how to answer while He works out everything for *our* good.

Romans 8:26–27 explains the Holy Spirit's role in prayer:

> And in the same way the Spirit also helps our weakness; for we do not know how to pray as we should, but the Spirit Himself intercedes for us with groanings too deep for words; and He who searches the hearts knows what the mind of the Spirit is, because He intercedes for the saints according to the will of God.

Many times when life has crashed in around me, I have found myself utterly unable to see a light at the end of the dark tunnel. Incapable of even thinking of any possible solution to what had happened, I was not capable of suggesting to God what His remedy might be. It is at those times I have cried out in agony to the Holy Spirit, "Please pray for me. I can't pray!"

The Holy Spirit is the member of the Godhead for whom Jesus told His followers to wait as He was leaving them to go back to heaven. Their waiting for the promised Holy Spirit in their ten-day prayer meeting before Pentecost began their A.D. praying. Jesus kept His word with the Holy Spirit's coming in His new A.D. way to them with the sound of a mighty rushing wind and sitting as tongues of fire on each of them. And the Holy Spirit remains their prayer helper—and ours—until Jesus comes back in person again.

The Holy Spirit is the in-residence intercessor in my life—and yours—at all times. He helps us to pray when we can't, assuring us that our feeble prayers are reaching the Father in heaven according to His all-knowing will![6]

—*Evelyn Christenson*

WHAT ROLE DOES THE HOLY SPIRIT PLAY IN MY PRAYERS?

Jesus said, "God is spirit, and his worshipers must worship in spirit and in truth" (John 4:24). The Holy Spirit's role in worship is to bring us into the presence of the Father, wrapped in the righteousness of Christ.

The Spirit presents us much as the priests presented the Old Testament sacrifices. The Israelites themselves did not prepare the offering for the altar; instead the priests slaughtered the animals and laid them upon the altar before God. In the same way, the Holy Spirit presents us as living sacrifices before the Father. It is not through our own action or desire or initiative that we are presented—the Spirit himself becomes the agent and the executor of our prayers.

Paul said in Romans 8:26, 27: "The Spirit helps us in our weakness. We do not know what we ought to pray, but the Spirit himself intercedes for us with groans that words cannot express. And he who searches our hearts knows the mind of the Spirit, because the Spirit intercedes for the saints in accordance with God's will."

Though the Holy Spirit intercedes for us in several ways, I believe this passage focuses specifically on the prayer that goes beyond conscious understanding. I call this the "above-and-beyond prayer." It may be, as some New Testament scholars maintain, that Paul is referring here to speaking in tongues.

The Scriptures clearly indicate the unique power of the spoken word. In fact, its power transcends the limits of our finite understanding. The gift of tongues allows a wider frame of reference for the release of God's power. One blessing this gift brings is an increased ability to release my concerns to God.

I don't just pray, "God, you take care of this situation. You understand it better than I do." Instead I pray, "Lord, I'm going to pray beyond the limits of my understanding. I'm going to trust the Spirit to articulate this prayer."

The Scriptures indicate that the Spirit accomplishes this prayer "in accordance with God's will." We are moved in this prayer toward the will and purpose of God. This is not a static or predictable movement. The Spirit is flexible; his work can't be nailed down to a specific method-ology.

I discovered this when I first got involved with a healing ministry in a California congregation. We experienced a dramatic healing of cancer. We thought we had discovered a right method of prayer. The Holy Spirit disabused us of this notion quickly—the next time we tried the method, it didn't work. It was the Spirit we had to take hold of, not a method.

Every situation is different. We are continually driven to seek God anew. We must constantly ask the Father, What do I do now?

That's the difference between walking in the Spirit and walking in the flesh. In the flesh we can learn certain practices and become skillful in them. In the Spirit, however, our only skill is our ability to hear the Spirit and to follow his leadings.

> PRAYER REFLECTION
>
> *Our good Lord showed that it is God's great pleasure that a soul come to God naked, plainly, and humbly. For this is the natural yearning of the soul [through] the touching of the Holy Spirit. . . . God, of your goodness, grant me your self, for you are enough for me, and nothing less that I might ask would be worthy of you. And if I ask for anything less, I still want more. But only in you do I have all.*
>
> *—Julian of Norwich*

If we do not cultivate this humble, listening attitude, the Spirit will force it upon us. He will not let us manipulate him. We must be brutally honest with ourselves. If something does not work out as we had hoped, we must ask ourselves if we have truly received the Lord's Word in that situation. We must go daily in prayer before the Lord, seeking anew his will and his direction. That is what is meant by praying "in spirit and in truth."[7]

—*Larry Christenson*

HOW DID JESUS TEACH HIS FOLLOWERS TO PRAY?

Fortunately, God has not left us to muddle through on our own. In a teaching recorded by both Matthew and Luke, Jesus Himself gave us clear directions. . . .

We can imagine Jesus up on the hillside with His Father. Down in the valley the disciples were tidying up the camp and watching from a distance. They were probably thinking, *What does He do all that time?* They were mystified and intrigued. So when Jesus came down for breakfast, they said to Him, "Lord, teach us to pray, just as John taught his disciples" (Luke 11:1 NIV).

The first thing Jesus advised them was not to make the same mistake as the Pharisees. You don't win brownie points, He said, by praying ostentatiously in a public place. You're better off seeking out a quiet corner and praying where no one can see you. Also, there's no virtue in using fifty words when ten will do the job. God knows what you need before you ask Him. What matters is to pray—not to frame your requests in pretty speech. . . .

But then Jesus came out with one of the most familiar—and one of the most difficult and abused—statements in the Bible:

This is how you should pray:

"Our Father in heaven,
hallowed be your name,
your kingdom come,
your will be done
on earth as it is in heaven.
Give us today our daily bread.
Forgive us our debts,
as we also have forgiven our debtors.
And lead us not into temptation,
but deliver us from the evil one." (Matt. 6:9–13 NIV)

The New King James Version adds this phrase to verse 13:

"For Yours is the kingdom and the power and the glory forever. Amen."

I believe these few short verses contain a gold mine of wisdom about prayer . . . But to learn these lessons, we must first avoid some elementary mistakes. And the first mistake we make is thinking we know the Lord's Prayer just because we have it memorized. . . .

The mistake is not as dumb as it sounds. What we commonly call the Lord's Prayer really isn't the *Lord's* prayer at all. Jesus never prayed using these words. If anything deserves the title "Lord's Prayer," it is the prayer uttered by Jesus at the Last Supper in John 17. A better name for Matthew 6:9–13 would be the Disciples' Prayer. . . .

Jesus never meant for us to repeat these verses mechanically. Still less should we treat them as a magic charm. The words themselves have no power. And in saying "This is how you should pray," Jesus certainly did not mean for us to recite the Lord's Prayer as we would recite a Shakespearean sonnet.

This is clear from the context. First, Jesus had just taken the Pharisees to task for using meaningless and repetitious prayers, so He would hardly have told His disciples to follow the same practice. And second, nowhere in the New Testament do we find an instance of the Lord's Prayer being reproduced verbatim by the apostles. Had Jesus told them to, His closest followers would surely have taken heed. But no. The early church had no place for this kind of superstitious ritual—nor should we.

Now, if the Lord's Prayer was never intended to be a rote prayer, then what is its purpose?. . .

The Lord's Prayer lays out the curriculum for biblical teaching on prayer. It lists the study course and pulls together the major themes. It tells us what we will have to learn if we wish to master the art of praying. In drafting this curriculum, Jesus set out to keep things simple. We are not expected to have a previous degree or to have done a stack of background reading. Nor do we have to worry about being clever enough to learn, for the Holy Spirit, the third person of the Trinity, will always be on hand for personal instruction. As Paul told us in Romans 8:26 NASB, "We do not know how to pray as we should, but the Spirit Himself intercedes for us with groanings too deep for words." . . .

Most modern teaching deals with the "how" of prayer. We want to know how to

> ### PRAYER REFLECTION
>
> *I need thee ev'ry hour,*
> *most gracious Lord;*
> *No tender voice like thine*
> *can peace afford.*
> *I need thee, Oh I need thee,*
> *ev'ry hour I need thee!*
> *Oh bless me now, my Savior;*
> *I come to thee.*
>
> *I need thee ev'ry hour, in joy*
> *or pain;*
> *Come quickly, and abide,*
> *or life is vain.*
> *I need thee, Oh I need thee;*
> *ev'ry hour I need thee!*
> *Oh bless me now my Savior,*
> *I come to thee.*
>
> *I need thee ev'ry hour; teach me*
> *thy will,*
> *And thy rich promises in me fulfill.*
> *I need thee, Oh I need thee;*
> *ev'ry hour I need thee!*
> *Oh bless me now, my Savior,*
> *I come to thee.*
> *—Annie Hawks*

pray, just as we want to know how to access the Internet or use a cellular phone. Internalizing that information, we think, is the secret of lobbying God successfully and getting our prayers answered.

But Jesus' perspective was radically different. In the Lord's Prayer, He focused not on *how* we pray, but on *what* we pray. Jesus' curriculum gave little room to technique. So, first we must learn to pray for the *right thing*—because that is God's central purpose in having us pray. . . .

> **PRAYER REFLECTION**
>
> *The one concern of the devil is to keep the saints from prayer. He fears nothing from prayerless studies, prayerless work, prayerless religion. He laughs at our toil, mocks at our wisdom, but trembles when we pray.*
>
> —*Jonathan Edwards*

Throughout biblical history, God's people have known not just *how* to pray, but *what* to pray. They were inspired to see the outcomes that would give God the greatest glory—because the "purpose of all purposes" in prayer is for God to be glorified. The act of praying may bless us out of our socks, but that is not why God asks us to pray. Prayer is God's opportunity to reveal His goodness and power, and to be glorified and magnified. Why else did Jesus say to the disciples, "And whatever you ask in My name, that I will do, *that the Father may be glorified*" (John 14:13 NKJV)?

Unless we understand *what* to pray to achieve the glory of God, our prayers will be ineffectual. The prayer that God will answer is one that we pray in a deepening awareness of God's agenda, not our own. It is one that we pray not from the urgency of our need (urgent as that may be!), but in surrender to His will and purpose.[8]

—*Michael Youssef*

WHAT DO I MEAN WHEN I SAY, "THY KINGDOM COME" IN THE LORD'S PRAYER?

Jesus tells how to begin. "When you pray, pray like this. 'Our Father who is in heaven, hallowed be thy name. Thy kingdom come.'"

When you say, "Thy kingdom come," you are inviting the Messiah himself to walk into your world. "Come, my King! Take your throne in our land. Be present in my heart. Be present in my office. Come into my marriage. Be Lord of my family, my fears, and my doubts." This is no feeble request; it's a bold appeal for God to occupy every corner of your life.

Who are you to ask such a thing? Who are you to ask God to take control of your world?

You are his child, for heaven's sake! And so you ask boldly. "So let us come boldly to the very throne of God and stay there to receive his mercy and to find grace to help us in our times of need" (Heb. 4:16).[9]

—*Max Lucado*

WHAT DOES JESUS' PARABLE OF THE UNJUST JUDGE TEACH ABOUT PRAYER?

It is my firm conviction that our Lord never used a fictitious story when giving a parable. When Jesus told this story about the unjust judge and the widow, it probably was well known to the hearers of that day. They knew exactly the situation He was talking about. The story began like this:

> There was in a certain city a judge who did not fear God
> nor regard man. Now there was a widow in that city; and
> she came to him, saying, "Get justice for me from my
> adversary." (Luke 18:2–3 NKJV)

We're told that this judge was a godless fellow. He was an unscrupulous, scheming, cold, and calculating politician. Everything he did had to minister to his own advancement and satisfy his own ambition. He did not fear God. God had no place in this man's thinking. And since he did not fear God, he had no regard for man. He had no respect for this widow who was being treated unjustly and forced out of her little home. So the widow went to this prominent judge for help. She asked his secretary if she might talk to the judge, but the secretary told her, "He's very busy. If you will just tell me the nature of your complaint . . ."

So the widow told her, "I'm just a poor widow. I live out here at the edge of town, and I'm about to lose my place. It is unfair and unjust, and I want to appeal to the judge."

The secretary went into the judge's office and said, "There is a widow out there who wants to see you."

"Well," he said, "I can get rid of her in three minutes. I'm a politician, I know how to handle her. Let her come in." So she came in, he listened to her for three minutes, and then he said, "I'm sorry, but that's out of my realm. I'd love to do something for you, but I am unable to do anything. Good day."

The next day when he came into the office, there was the widow. He hurried into his office, called his secretary in, and asked, "What's that widow doing back?"

"She says she wants to see you."

"You go back and tell her I am busy until lunchtime."

"I've already told her that. But she brought her lunch. She says she will stay here as long as necessary."

The widow stayed all that day and didn't get to see him. He thought he had gotten rid of her. But the next morning when he came in, there she was! She did that for several days, and finally he said, "I'll have to do something about this. I can't go on like this."

Notice that our Lord recorded what the judge said to himself:

> But afterward he said within himself, "Though I do not
> fear God nor regard man, yet because this widow troubles
> me I will avenge her, lest by her continual coming she
> weary me." (Luke 18:4–5 NKJV)

The word *weary* is a very poor translation. I only wish it were translated literally. What he said was this: "I must see her lest she give me a black eye!" I don't know if he meant a literal black eye—we are not told that the widow had threatened him—but the very fact that a widow is sitting in the judge's office every day doesn't look good. You see, he was thinking of himself. He had gotten into office by saying, "I'm thinking of the poor people," but he wasn't—he was thinking of himself. "And lest she give me a black eye, I'd better hear her."

So he told his secretary to let the widow in. This time he said to the widow, "I'll give you legal protection." He called up his man in her area and told him to take care of the matter. I imagine the man out there, who was also a politician, said, "But she has no vote! She has no influence!"

"I know it," the judge says.

"Then why are you doing it?"

"*I have been coming into my office every day for a week, and she's sat here every day!* She is giving me a black eye. I've got to help her." . . .

A parable is a story our Lord told to illustrate divine truth. There are two ways He can do this: one is by comparison, but the other is by *contrast*.

This parable that our Lord gave on prayer is a very simple story, yet it has been greatly misunderstood. I have heard many Bible teachers say that this parable teaches the value of importunate prayer. Although I don't like to disagree with men who are greater than I, that isn't so. This is not a parable on the persistency of prayer—as though somehow God will hear if you hold on long enough. This is a parable by *contrast,* not by comparison.

Listen to what our Lord had to say about this parable:

> Hear what the unjust judge said. And shall God not avenge His own elect who cry out day and night to Him, though He bears long with them? (Luke 18:6–7 NKJV)

He is saying, "When you come to God in prayer, do you think that God is an unjust judge? When you come to Him in prayer, do you think He is a cheap politician? Do you think God is doing things just for political reasons?" My friend, if you think this, you are wrong. God is not an unjust judge.

Why are God's people today so discouraged in their prayer life? If this *unjust* judge would hear a poor widow because she kept coming continually, then why do you get discouraged going to God who is *not* an unjust judge but who actually *wants* to hear and answer prayer? Don't you know, my friend, He is not unjust? We act as if we have to hold on to Him or He will not hear us at all. We don't have to hang on to His coattail and beg and plead with Him. God *wants* to act in our behalf! If we would come into His presence with an attitude of knowing that He *wants to hear, it would transform our prayer lives.*[10]

—*J. Vernon McGee*

WHAT DOES THE PARABLE OF THE PERSISTENT FRIEND TEACH ABOUT PRAYER?

> And He said to them, "Which of you shall have a friend, and go to him at midnight and say to him, 'Friend, lend me

three loaves; for a friend of mine has come to me on his journey, and I have nothing to set before him'; and he will answer from within and say, 'Do not trouble me; the door is now shut, and my children are with me in bed; I cannot rise and give to you'? I say to you, though he will not rise and give to him because he is his friend, yet because of his persistence he will rise and give him as many as he needs."

(Luke 11:5–8 NKJV)

Let's bring this parable up-to-date. Imagine it's midnight and you are standing on your neighbor's front step, ringing the doorbell. He calls out, "Who's there?"

"It's me—your neighbor next door."

"What do you want?"

"I'm in grave difficulty. Remember I told you my aunt from Iowa and my uncle from Texas were coming out to visit? I didn't know they were going to arrive here at the same time, but they both drove in tonight! Now, I was going down to the market tomorrow to lay in a supply of food to feed these folk because my aunt from Iowa and my uncle from Texas are accustomed to *eating!* I really wanted to feed them well. But I don't have anything. Would you mind getting up and letting me have a loaf of bread and maybe a little butter? If you've got a little bacon or ham there, would you let me have it?"

"Look, I've already gone to bed! My children are in bed, and I don't want to disturb my household. So go on back and put your aunt from Iowa and your uncle from Texas to bed, and we'll feed them in the morning." Then your neighbor turns over in his bed and pulls the covers up over his head.

But you put your finger down on the doorbell, and you begin to kick at the door.

By that time the baby is crying. He says, "Look, go home! Let us alone!"

"But I've got to feed my aunt from Iowa and my uncle from Texas. I wouldn't *dare* go back over there without some food for those hungry folks who have just come in from a long drive!"

> **PRAYER REFLECTION**
>
> *Christ be with me,*
> *Christ be in me,*
> *Christ before me,*
> *Christ behind me,*
> *Christ beside me,*
> *Christ to win me,*
> *Christ to comfort,*
> *And restore me.*
>
> —*Celtic Blessing*

Finally, your neighbor says to his wife, "Well, it sounds like our neighbor is going to kick the door down unless I do something." So, he gets out of bed, half awake and half asleep, goes to the refrigerator, digs out what he's got, brings it to the door, and hands it to you.

Perhaps you are saying, "I've been knocking at the door of heaven, but there has been no answer. God has not come to the door." My friend, do you think that God is asleep when you pray? He is not. "Behold, He who keeps Israel shall neither slumber nor sleep" (Psalm 121:4 NKJV). Do you believe that He does not want to answer your prayers? God does want to answer your prayers and He will. That is what this parable is saying. It is another parable by contrast and not by comparison. You do not have to knock down the door of heaven in order to attract God's attention. God is not reluctant to hear and answer you. He told us in Isaiah 65:24, "Before they call, I will answer; and while they are still speaking, I will hear." He knows what is in your heart before you ever put it into words.

Perhaps you are saying, "But He said no." Well, then, that's His answer. Our problem is that we do not like to take no for an answer. God *always* hears and answers the prayers of His own, but when He says no, it is because we are not praying for that which is best for us. You have been answered. The difficulty was that you asked for ice cream, and when He came to the door He gave you corn bread. It wasn't what you wanted, but corn bread was the best thing for you.

When you go to the door of heaven and knock—and He says to come and knock—you are not coming as a neighbor from next door. You are a child who has come to your Father. We come to God as a *child* comes to a father. My friend, He is hearing only the prayers of His children. Are you a child of God? You can attend church, you can be religious, and not be His child. How do you become His child?

> But as many as received Him, to them He gave the right
> to become children of God, to those who [do no more nor
> less than simply] believe in His name. (John 1:12 NKJV)

When you have received Him as your own personal Savior, then you become His child. And when you pray to Him you are knocking at your *Father's* door. That changes prayer. You are not going to a God who is reluctant. You are going to a Father who wants to answer and *will* answer. You do not have to storm the gate of heaven to get God to answer your prayer. God has not gone to bed. The door is wide open, and He says, "Knock, seek, and ask." Take everything to God in prayer, and He will give you His very best.

But I say this very carefully: when we come into His presence we need to realize it is the Father's will that must prevail. When we come we must recognize that God is holy, that we are sinners, and that the most important thing in our prayers is not that we get something but that God's will might prevail. If you are His child and you desire the Father's will, He graciously opens the door and gives you your request.[11]

—*J. Vernon McGee*

WHAT DOES THE PARABLE OF FATHERHOOD TEACH ABOUT PRAYER?

We come now to the picture of a son:

> If a son asks for bread from any father among you, will he
> give him a stone? Or if he asks for a fish, will he give him
> a serpent instead of a fish? Or if he asks for an egg, will he
> offer him a scorpion? (Luke 11:11–12 NKJV)

Our Lord looked around at the crowd that day—there were many fathers there—and He said, "You, you're a father. If your boy came to you and asked for bread, would you give him a stone?" Of course no father would do that! So where did we get the idea that we are better than God? If earthly fathers want to be good to their children, don't you know that the One who put a parent's heart in us has Himself a father's heart? When you go to Him, you can expect Him to do the very best thing for you.

Before the Day of Pentecost, our Lord stated it this way:

> If you then, being evil, know how to give good gifts to
> your children, how much more will your heavenly Father
> give the Holy Spirit to those who ask Him! (Luke 11:13
> NKJV)

Our Lord is saying here that the highest gift that any person can receive is the Holy Spirit. And in order for the Holy Spirit to be able to come and indwell every believer, God had to give His own Son to die for us. The Lord Jesus died, not only for our sins, but He died because you and I have an awful sin nature. Writing to the Corinthians—and they were carnal folk—Paul said:

> Or do you not know that your body is the temple of the
> Holy Spirit who is in you, whom you have from God, and
> you are not your own? (1 Corinthians 6:19 NKJV)

Everyone who trusts Christ—that is, becomes a child of God—is *indwelt* by the Spirit of God today. He dwells *within* us! This wonderful transaction began in believers on the Day of Pentecost.

God today has already done for you the best that He possibly can do. To the Romans Paul said again:

> He who did not spare His own Son, but delivered Him up
> for us all, how shall He not with Him also freely give us all
> things? (Romans 8:32 NKJV)

He will give us *all* things that are needful in our Christian life. He didn't say He would give you everything you *wanted,* but everything that you *needed.* Listen, my friend, if God gave His Son to die for you—and now has given you the highest gift, the Holy Spirit, to indwell you—do you think He will withhold from you *any* good thing? No, sir! He has already done the best.

Dwight L. Moody, in his inimitable way, used to illustrate this verse something like this: "Suppose I went to Tiffany's in New York, and Mr. Tiffany called me to the back of the store, opened the safe where he kept his most valuable jewels, brought out the biggest diamond he had, laid it on the showcase, and said, 'It's yours!'; I would say, 'It's mine? You mean I don't have to pay you for it?' And he would say, 'I'm giving it to you.'" Then Mr. Moody would close his illustration by asking, "Do you think if he gave me that diamond that I would hesitate to ask him for a little piece of brown wrapping paper to take it home in?"

> ### PRAYER REFLECTION
> *What then is the prayer ministry of the church? It is God telling the church what He wants to do and the church praying on earth what God wants to do. This prayer is not asking God to accomplish what we want Him to do, but asking God to accomplish what He Himself wants to do.*
> —*Watchman Nee*

Don't you know that if God has given His Son to die for you, and if He indwells you by the Holy Spirit, He will not withhold from you any good thing? Do you believe that? Not many Christians believe that. They say, "Well, He's sort of holding out on me." My friend, if you are His child, He will do for you the very best He can. And the best He can do is the best![12]

—J. Vernon McGee

WHAT DOES THE PARABLE OF THE PHARISEE AND THE TAX COLLECTOR TEACH ABOUT PRAYER?

We now look at our final picture. Oh, what trenchant and biting satire our Lord uses here! But He didn't do it to hurt them; He did it to help them,

> Also He spoke this parable to some who trusted in them-
> selves that they were righteous, and despised others: "Two
> men went up to the temple to pray, one a Pharisee and the
> other a tax collector." (Luke 18:9–10 NKJV)

You could not get any two as far apart as these two men were. The tax collector was at the bottom of the religious ladder; the Pharisee was at the top. Tax collectors were grouped right down there with the sinners; the Pharisees were considered to be the most acceptable ones to God.

This Pharisee went into the temple to pray and make his sacrifice. As he stood and prayed, his priest was yonder in the Holy Place putting incense on the altar. In other words, this old Pharisee had it made. But listen to how he prayed:

> The Pharisee stood and prayed thus with himself, "God,
> I thank You that I am not like other men—extortioners,
> unjust, adulterers, or even as this tax collector." (Luke
> 18:11 NKJV)

Isn't that an awful way to begin a prayer? Yet that is the way many of us do it. You say, "I don't do that." Yes, you do! Oh, we don't say it exactly that way—we've learned to say it better than that. But we have our own way of putting it: "Lord, I thank You I can give You my time and my service." How often I hear that! What a compliment that is for the

Lord! Friend, we don't get anywhere in prayer when we pray like that. God doesn't need our service.

The Pharisee said, "I thank You that I am not like other men," and then he began to enumerate what he *wasn't*. "I'm not an extortioner"—evidently there was somebody around who was an extortioner. "I am not unjust. I am not an adulterer." Then he spied that tax collector way outside the temple, and he said," And, believe me, Lord, I'm not like that tax collector! I'm not like that sinner out there." Then he began to tell the Lord what he did do:

> I fast twice a week; I give tithes of all that I possess. (Luke
> 18:12 NKJV)

My, isn't he a wonderful fellow? Wouldn't you love to have him in your church?

Our Lord said he "prayed thus *with himself.*" . . . This old Pharisee was in the temple talking to himself—he thought he was talking to God, but his prayer never got out of the rafters. All he did was give himself a pep talk. He patted himself on the back and went out proud as a peacock. But God never heard that prayer.

Then there was the tax collector. Oh, he was a rascal! He was a sinner; he was as low as they come. When he became a tax gatherer, he denied his nation. When he denied his nation, as a Jew, he denied his religion. He turned his back on God. He took a one-way street, never intending to come back to God. Why did he do it? It was lucrative. He said, "There's money down this way." He became rich as a tax collector, but it did not satisfy his heart. We know from the story of Zacchaeus in Luke 19 that a tax collector's heart was *empty*.

> And the tax collector, standing afar off, would not so much
> as raise his eyes to heaven, but beat his breast, saying, "God,
> be merciful to me a sinner!" (Luke 18:13 NKJV)

This poor man, in his misery and desperation, knowing that he had no access to the mercy seat in the temple, cried out to God. "God, be merciful to me a sinner" does not

23

adequately express it. Let me give it to you in the language that he used: "Oh, God, I'm a poor tax collector. I have no access to that mercy seat, yonder in the temple. Oh, if You could only make a mercy seat for *me!* I want to come."

> I tell you, this man went down to his house justified rather
> than the other; for everyone who exalts himself will be
> humbled, and he who humbles himself will be exalted.
> (Luke 18:14 NKJV)

Our Lord said that man was heard. Do you know why he was heard? Because Jesus Christ right there and then was on His way to the cross to make a mercy seat for him. John wrote:

> And He Himself is the propitiation for our sins, and not
> for ours only but also for the whole world. (1 John 2:2
> NKJV)

Propitiation means *mercy seat.* Christ is the mercy seat for our sins, and not for ours only, but for the sins of the *whole world.*

The tax collector's prayer has been answered. Actually, today you don't have to ask God to be merciful. He is merciful. Many people say, "We have to beg Him to be merciful." My friend, what else do you want Him to do? He already gave His Son to die for you. He says to the very worst sinner, *"You* can come. There is a mercy seat for you." I have to admit to you that I had to come to that mercy seat. And if you want to be God's child, you'll have to come to that mercy seat where He died on the cross for your sins and my sins.[13]

—*J. Vernon McGee*

I CAN'T SEE GOD, SO HOW CAN I TALK TO HIM?

First, a lively earnest realization that His Presence is universal; that is to say, that He is everywhere, and in all, and that there is no place, nothing in the world, devoid of His Most Holy Presence, so that, even as birds on the wing meet the air continually, we, let us go where we will, meet with that Presence always and everywhere. It is a truth which all are ready to grant, but all are not equally alive to its importance. A blind man when in the presence of his prince will preserve a reverential demeanour if told that the king is there, although unable to see him; but practically, what men do not see they easily forget, and so readily lapse into carelessness and irreverence. Just so, my child, we do not see our God, and although faith warns us that He is present, not beholding Him with our mortal eyes, we are too apt to forget Him, and act as though He were afar: for, while knowing perfectly that He is everywhere, if we do not think about it, it is much as though we knew it not. And therefore, before beginning to pray, it is needful always to rouse the soul to a steadfast remembrance and thought of the Presence of God. This is what David meant when he exclaimed, "If I climb up to Heaven, Thou art there, and if I go down to hell, Thou art there also!" And in like manner Jacob, who, beholding the ladder which went up to Heaven, cried out, "Surely the Lord is in this place and I knew it not," meaning that he had not thought of it; for assuredly he could not fail to

> PRAYER REFLECTION
>
> *I thank Thee, my Creator and Lord, that Thou has given me these joys in Thy creation, this ecstasy over the works of Thy hands. I have made known the glory of Thy works to men as far as my finite spirit was able to comprehend Thy infinity. If I have said anything wholly unworthy of Thee, or have aspired after my own glory, graciously forgive me. Amen.*
>
> —*Johann Kepler*

know that God was everywhere and in all things. Therefore, when you make ready to pray, you must say with your whole heart, "God is indeed here."

The second way of placing yourself in this Sacred Presence is to call to mind that God is not only present in the place where you are, but that He is very specially present in your heart and mind, which He kindles and inspires with His Holy Presence, abiding there as Heart of your heart, Spirit of your spirit. Just as the soul animates the whole body . . . but abides especially in the heart, so God, while present everywhere, yet makes His special abode with our spirit. Therefore David calls Him "the Strength of my heart;" and Paul said that in Him "we live and move and have our being." Dwell upon this thought until you have kindled a great reverence within your heart for God Who is so closely present to you.

The third way is to dwell upon the thought of our Lord, Who in His Ascended Humanity looks down upon all men, but most particularly on all Christians, because they are His children; above all, on those who pray, over whose doings He keeps watch. Nor is this any mere imagination, it is very truth, and although we see Him not, He is look-ing down upon us. . . .

The fourth way is simply to exercise your ordinary imagination, picturing the Savior to yourself in His Sacred Humanity as if He were beside you just as we are wont to think of our friends, and fancy that we see or hear them at our side. . . .

Make use of one or other of these methods for placing yourself in the Presence of God before you begin to pray—do not try to use them all at once, but take one at a time, and that briefly and simply.[14]

—*St. Francis of Sales*

WHEN SHOULD I PERSIST IN PRAYER, AND WHEN SHOULD I TAKE NO FOR AN ANSWER?

I want to suggest to you that you pray something through until one of the following three things occurs. Pray it through . . .

Until you know it is not God's will

> **PRAYER REFLECTION**
>
> *We wait with patience and submission until God gives us what we request—or something more.*
>
> —*David Roper*

Since God speaks to you through His Word and your circumstances, you should pray it through until God affirms to you that it is just not His will for your life. If the Word is not for it, do not bother to even pray about it. You must remember: God's Spirit will never lead you opposite of God's Word.

Some years ago, I was asked to consider taking a position away from the pastorate in the evangelical world. This position was a position of great influence and vision. As soon as I was approached about this position, I felt God wanted me to draw aside in fasting and prayer in order to pray it through. The position was highly visible, so I did not want even to be considered if I knew God did not want me to do it. I prayed it through until I knew for certain that it was not God's will for my life. I called the person who wanted me to talk with this search committee and with con-fidence informed him that I really sensed it was not God's will for my life, so I would not let my name be considered for the position.

For those seven days, I was persistent before God in prayer. By praying it through,

God affirmed me as a pastor and confirmed that the position was not His will for me. I was committed to go on with God in prayer until I prayed it through. God does not always answer that quickly, but I am thankful that He did.

I want to encourage you to pray your burden through until you know it is not God's will for your life. Pursue your dream. Activate your passion. Get before God and stay there until you know it is just not right in the eyes of God. If it is God's will, you will soon know. If you do not know, do not do it. When in doubt, don't! This is an important rule to follow in your life. Pray it through until you know it is not God's will.

You should also pray it through . . .

Until God answers your prayer

Pray it through until you know the doors are shut tightly. Pray it through until you know it is just not right. Pray it through until God says no or until God says yes. Sometimes it is difficult to let it go when you know God says no. Yet when He says no, walk away. The worst place you can be spiritually is somewhere God does not want you to be in your life. Pray it through until God says yes. Thank God for the times in life when your persistence in prayer resulted in God saying yes. What an encouragement! What faith is created through God saying yes to our persistent praying.

If you are praying for someone who does not know Christ, then claim God's expressed desire in 2 Peter 3:9: "The Lord . . . is patient toward you, not wishing for any to perish but for all to come to repentance."

God is willing for all persons to repent of their sin and be saved. He does not want anyone to perish. Therefore, upon the authority of God's Word, you know it is God's will for this lost person to be saved. So pray it through! Claim this verse before God. Hang on to it! Remind God of what He said. Pray with confidence, believing that God will save this person. . . .

Whatever you are facing today, pray it through until God gives you the answer. Do not stop! Hang in there and pray. Pray with persistence. Pray with faith! You may be praying for your house to sell, but it has not sold. Keep praying until God gives you the answer. You may be praying for a new job. Keep praying until God gives you the answer. You may be praying for a financial breakthrough. Keep praying until God gives you the answer. You may be praying for someone's salvation. Keep praying until God comes through. Yes, pray it through! Pray with persistency.

How long should you pray something through? Pray it through . . .

Until God releases you

Many times what you pray about is a burden to you. I believe a burden is something that you go to bed with, wake up with, and live with all through the day. (No, I am not talking about your spouse!) I am talking about something that is very heavy on your heart. I have learned recently that you should pray that burden through until God releases you. If He does not release you from that burden, then keep on praying persistently about it. . . .

The burden that God gives you is a wake-up call. If God gives you the burden, it signifies He is active in the situation. Therefore, you keep praying it through until He releases you. How do you know when He releases you? He releases you when the situation is answered just the way you have prayed for it. He releases you when the situation is irreparable. He releases you when He removes your burden and replaces it with His peace. You will know when He releases you. Until then, pray persistently!

Do not give up in prayer. Keep on praying until God releases you. Sometimes that burden may last one year, ten days, or even forty years. Yet pray until God releases you. Persistent prayer is effective prayer.

Persistency in your prayer life demonstrates that you have great faith in God. It does not indicate a lack of faith. Persistency in prayer develops your character. It does not show you are inferior or prone to worry. Persistency in prayer guarantees God's activity—not in the sense that He will answer it the way you want it answered or even that He will answer it at all—but by indicating that God is active in the situation as long as He wants you to pray it through. Stay involved in prayer until God speaks to you in the situation.

Do you want to move to a new level in your prayer life? I hope so. One of the great ways that you can move to a new level in your prayer life is to learn to pray things through. Remember, you have a perfect Father in heaven who is willing to meet your needs. So pray them through! Give God the opportunity to receive the glory when you can announce to others that He answered your prayer as you prayed it through. I promise you, this will help you take a quantum leap in your prayer life.[15]

—*Ronnie W. Floyd*

I'M NOT GETTING THE ANSWER I WANTED.

Sometimes circumstances don't work out at all as we'd like. People we pray for die. Husbands leave their wives and never come back. Children wreck and ruin their lives in spite of the influence of godly parents. Businesses go bankrupt. Christians lose their jobs. And thousands of women *do* have abortions.

But God is no less faithful in these events than He is in the others. His faithfulness, however, takes a different form. Nevertheless, many Christians are quick to doubt God when adversities are not resolved the way they deem appropriate. As a result, they doubt God. Some become angry and turn their back on Him completely. I cannot tell you how many men and women I have counseled who lived for years in rebellion toward God over this very issue. God did not do things the way *they* thought He should, so they wrote Him off as unfaithful and walked away.

God is *always* faithful to His promises. Nowhere, however, did He promise to always work things out the way we think they should be. If that were the case, He would be no more than a magic genie. God's ways are not our ways. And in the same vein, His goals are oftentimes not our goals. But He is always faithful.

God's faithfulness does not always take the form of deliverance *from* adversity. Many times God demonstrates His faithfulness by sustaining us *through* adversity. Take, for instance, a man marooned on a deserted island. As he explores the island looking for food, he discovers a speedboat washed up on shore. Upon further examination he finds that the tank is full of gas. He cranks the engine, and away he goes. He is delivered from being stranded.

Let's take the same example again. Only this time he does not discover a boat; he discovers a deserted house and fruit orchard. Inside the house he finds all the tools he will need to cultivate the orchard. Although he is still stranded on the island, he has what he needs to survive. He will be able to carry on.

No doubt we would all agree that the first set of circumstances sounds much better. Yet the man in the second scenario could have been much worse off. In both illustrations the man was provided for; the difference was in the form of the provision.

Oftentimes God demonstrates His faithfulness in adversity by providing for us what we need to survive. He does not change our painful circumstances. He sustains us through them. This is what the writer of Hebrews was referring to when he wrote,

> Let us therefore draw near with confidence to the throne
> of grace, that we may receive mercy and may find grace to
> help in time of need. (Hebrews 4:16)

The writer makes an interesting promise. When we are in need, God will provide us with mercy and grace. This verse does not promise us a change of circumstances, freedom from pain, or deliverance from our enemies. It simply states that when we have a need, God will shower us with mercy and grace. Granted, we would rather have God relieve us of pain than sustain us through it. But He is under no obligation to do so. And He is no less faithful either way.

Paul certainly did not lack confidence in God's faithfulness. Yet God opted not to remove his thorn in the flesh. He chose instead to sustain Paul through it. When Paul asked for relief, the answer he received was simply, "My grace is sufficient for you" (2 Cor. 12:9). In other words, "Paul, you will continue to suffer, but if you hang in there with Me, you will make it."[16]

—*Charles Stanley*

I DON'T REALLY THINK GOD HEARS MY PRAYERS.

"But I want to believe in God. I want to know that there is a God that answers prayer, that I may believe in him. There was a time when I believed in him. I prayed to him in great and sore trouble of heart and mind, and he did not hear me. I have not prayed since."

How do you know that he did not hear you?

"He did not give me what I asked, though . . . my soul hung on it."

In your judgment. Perhaps he knew better.

"I am the worse for his refusal. I would have believed in him if he had heard me."

Till the next desire came which he would not grant, and then you would have turned your God away. A desirable believer you would have made! . . . You would accept of him no decision against your desire! . . . This only I will say: God has not to consider his children only at the moment of their prayer. Should he be willing to give a man the thing he knows he would afterwards wish he had not given him? If a man be not fit to be refused, if he be not ready to be treated with love's severity, what he wishes may perhaps be given him in order that he may wish it had not been given him; but . . . to give a man what he wants because he wants it, and without farther purpose of his good, would be to let a poor ignorant child take his fate into his own hands—the cruelty of a devil. Yet is every prayer heard; and the real soul of the prayer may require, for its real answer, that it should not be granted in the form in which it is requested.

"To have a thing in another shape might be equivalent to not having it at all."

If you knew God, you would leave that to him. . . . He knows you better than you know yourself, and would keep you from fooling yourself. He will not deal with you as the child of a day, but as the child of eternal ages. You shall be satisfied, if you will but let him have his way with the creature he has made. The question is between your will and the will of God. He is not one of those who gives readiest what they prize least. He does not care to give anything but his best, or that which will prepare for it. Not many years may pass before you confess, "Thou art a God who hears prayer, and gives a better answer." . . . That God should, as a loving father, listen, hear, consider, and deal with the request after the perfect tenderness of his heart, is to me enough; it is little that I should go without what I pray for. If it be granted that any answer which did not come of love, and was not for the final satisfaction of him who prayed, would be unworthy of God; that it is the part of love and knowledge to watch over the wayward, ignorant child; then the trouble of seemingly unanswered prayers begins to abate, and a lovely hope and comfort takes its place in the child-like soul. To hear is not necessarily to grant—God forbid! but to hear is necessarily to attend to—sometimes as necessarily to refuse.

"Concerning this thing," says St. Paul, "I besought the Lord thrice, that it might depart from me. And he hath said unto me, My grace is sufficient for thee; power is made perfect in weakness." God had a better thing for Paul than granting his prayer and removing his complaint: he would make him strong; the power of Christ should descend and

> **PRAYER REFLECTION**
>
> *When God places an urgent need in someone else's life upon your heart, commit yourself to pray for that person daily.*
>
> —*Ronnie W. Floyd*

remain upon him; he would make him stronger than his suffering, make him a sharer in the energy of God. Verily, if we have God, we can do without the answer to any prayer.[17]

—*George MacDonald*

WHAT SHOULD I DO WHEN MY PRAYERS AREN'T BEING ANSWERED?

There will be times that your prayers will not be answered—at least not exactly the way you prayed them or according to your timetable. If that happens, trust that God knows what is best.

Until Diane died, I and all who knew her never stopped praying for her healing. Hundreds of strong believers in two different congregations prayed for her continually. If her healing depended on prayer and faith, she was covered. But those specific prayers were not answered, at least not the way we wanted them to be.

We all have lived through the painful consequences of unanswered prayer. Sometimes what seems like unanswered prayer is actually a matter of waiting on God. Other times the prayers are answered so differently from what we expect that we can't even see they've been answered until much later. Sometimes our prayers are never answered at all as we have prayed them. The key is standing strong in the Lord whether we see that our prayers are answered or not.

When getting an answer to prayer takes a long time, we sometimes lose hope. We become discouraged and fear the Lord has forgotten us. We stop praying, stop going to church, stop reading the Bible, stop obeying God's rules because we think *What's the point?* Sometimes we get mad at God. We don't like waiting the two weeks, two months, two years, or as long as it takes for the answer to come. And what if the answer never comes? That's miserable and we don't like to suffer. . . .

So what do you do when you've believed and praised and prayed but are still disillusioned and afraid your dreams and hopes are gone? First of all, don't be consumed with guilt. Don't feel that this is all your fault and therefore God won't answer your prayer. If your prayers are unanswered because of sin, confess it, stop doing it, and pray. God will turn things around.

Second, allow no situation to make you turn your back on Him. Know that He sees where you are, He has not forgotten you, and He will sustain you through it. Rest in the fact that He is in control and more powerful than your problems. It's at this time that we either turn away from the Lord's ways or determine to live them even more diligently. We can give up too soon and say, "This obviously isn't working so why bother doing it this way?" We can choose to try to ride the storm out by ourselves, or we can align with the God who either calms the storm or sets our feet on solid ground in the center of it where we won't be harmed. Far too many people have given up when the answer to their prayer was just around the corner.

Part of standing strong in times of unanswered prayer is waiting, and waiting produces patience. The Bible says, "In your patience possess your souls" (Luke 21:19). When you are patient, you're able to take control of your very being and place yourself in God's hands. He, then, is in control whether it is night or day

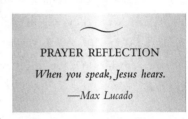

PRAYER REFLECTION
When you speak, Jesus hears.
—*Max Lucado*

in your soul. He becomes God to you in every season of your life—the good and the bad. And because you know Him that way, you become unshakable.

Since we have no choice but to wait, our attitude makes a lot of difference. We can either shake our fist at God and scream, "Why me?" Or we can open up our hearts to God and pray, "Lord, change this situation. Perfect Your life in me as I wait on You. Help me to do the right thing, and let it all work out for my greatest good."

You may have to wait for God to move, but you don't have to sit twiddling your thumbs until it happens. The best way to sustain a good attitude while you wait is to spend much time in praise and worship of God. Say, "Lord, I praise You in the midst of this situation. I confess I'm afraid that my prayers may never be answered. I'm weary and discouraged from the waiting, and feel I'm losing the strength to fight. Forgive me, Lord, for not trusting You more. I pray my weariness would end and there would be renewed hope in my spirit. Help me to feel Your presence and Your love, and help me to hear Your voice and follow Your lead. Thank You that You are in full control."

Don't stop praying even if you've been doing it for a long time and it seems as if God must not be listening. God hears your every prayer. You may feel like nothing is going on, but you are tapping into God's love, healing, and redemption when you pray and surrender yourself and your life to Him daily.[18]

—*Stormie Omartian*

WHAT ROLE DO ANGELS HAVE WHEN WE PRAY?

Asking our Lord to provide angels to watch over us

Another wonderful means of protection is the ministry of the Lord's angels. The psalmist wrote that He commissions angels to watch over us. "If you make the Most High your dwelling—even the LORD, who is my refuge—then no harm will befall you, no disaster will come near your tent. For he will command his angels concerning you to guard you in all your ways; they will lift you up in their hands, so that you will not strike your foot against a stone" (Ps. 91:9–12).

Prayer unleashes the ministry of guardian angels in ways we perhaps never fully comprehend. Frequently we are like Elisha's servant; he could see clearly the large Aramean army surrounding the city but could not see the Lord's horses and chariots of fire (2 Kings 6:17). Similarly perhaps we too fail to realize how often the Lord has commanded His angels to guard us. Sometimes, however, He gives us a glimpse of His protection.

> **PRAYER REFLECTION**
>
> *Talking to God and listening to what God is saying to you. This is what prayer is all about.*
>
> —*Ronnie W. Floyd*

That has happened to me several times. One of those dramatic experiences took place several years ago when my two sons, Dan and Mark, and I were returning home on New Year's Day from a Rose Bowl game. We left the game a few minutes early to beat the traffic. As we were driving on the freeway, I commented on how light the traffic was and how fortunate we were to get away before the rush began.

Suddenly, without warning, a car just ahead of us careened out of control. In a matter of seconds it crashed into the center divider and literally flew through the air, stopping abruptly in our lane and then exploding into flames. I instinctively cried out, "Lord, help us!" as I braced for the crash. I knew it was humanly impossible for me to stop the car in time to avoid the flaming wreckage, and it was impossible to change lanes because of other traffic. I was certain we were going to hit the other car.

Inexplicably, an opening appeared in the midst of the wreckage. We were guided through the fire and debris by an unseen guide. I sensed I was no longer in control of the car. We did not hit anything, nor were we injured in any way. It was absolutely amazing. In fact, it was humanly impossible.

I am convinced the Lord provided one or more angels to guide us. I will always be grateful for the Lord's protection that day. And I give God thanks for the many times His angels have protected us from harm, whether we were aware or unaware of their presence or involvement. Only eternity will reveal fully just how many times our Lord has protected us from harm and even death.

Our Lord's protection

He who dwells in the secret place of the Most High will abide under the protective shadows of the Almighty. This is not "pie-in-the-sky" theology. This is practical Christianity.

We need to ask our Lord to lead us each day as we commit ourselves to follow Him. He will guide us in the paths of righteousness if we but ask Him to do so. And we need to ask Him not to allow us to be led into temptation, and to deliver us from the evil one. Our Lord wants to protect us from harm.

We are wise to follow His instruction to "put on the whole armor" of God as we begin each day, and to use the sword of the Spirit as our offensive weapon. To triumph over the devil we must use the shield of faith to extinguish his fiery arrows, that is, his repeated temptations.

And let us not forget to take advantage of the protection our loving God gives us under the shelter of His wings, and to thank our Lord for the angels He lovingly and quietly provides to watch over us as silent sentinels.[19]

—*Paul Cedar*

DOES GOD REALLY ANSWER PRAYER?

Let's clarify one thing now, so there's no confusion. God answers prayer. The Bible is very clear about that fact:

> Ask, and it will be given to you; seek, and you will find;
> knock, and it will be opened to you. For everyone who
> asks receives, and he who seeks finds, and to him who
> knocks it will be opened. Or what man is there among
> you who, if his son asks for bread, will give him a stone?
> Or if he asks for a fish, will he give him a serpent? If you

then, being evil, know how to give good gifts to your children, how much more will your Father who is in heaven give good things to those who ask Him! (Matt. 7:7–11)

You are My friends if you do whatever I command you. No longer do I call you servants, for a servant does not know what his master is doing; but I have called you friends, for all things that I heard from My Father I have made known to you. You did not choose Me, but I chose you and appointed you that you should go and bear fruit, and that your fruit should remain, that whatever you ask the Father in My name He may give you. These things I command you, that you love one another. (John 15:14–17) Now this is the confidence that we have in Him, that if we ask anything according to His will, He hears us. And if we know that He hears us, whatever we ask, we know that we have the petitions that we have asked of Him (1 John 5:14–15).

These are all inspiring, heartwarming, and encouraging passages, especially when God is answering your prayers in an obvious way. But when it seems that you're not getting any response from Him, you may chime in with David when he asked,

How long, O LORD? Will You forget me forever? How long will You hide Your face from me? (Ps. 13:1)

> **PRAYER REFLECTION**
>
> *When God says "yes," it is because He loves us. When God says "no," it is because He loves us.*
>
> —O. Hallesby

Even with all of the biblical assurance available, life can be pretty frustrating when it seems that you're being ignored by God. That's where faith and silence come in handy.

Faith is necessary because you must believe that God answers all prayers. Sometimes He answers, "Yes." Sometimes He answers, "No." Sometimes He answers, "Not yet." But He always answers. It's also important to believe that God's "no" and "not yet" responses are ultimately just as beneficial to us as His yeses. We have to learn to cling to the promise of Romans 8:28: "We know that all things work together for good to those who love God, to those who are the called according to His purpose."

What often happens, though, is that people fail to recognize God's "no" or "not yet" responses and they assume that He's not listening to them or not answering them for some reason. To put it another way, some people confuse not getting what they want with not having their prayers answered.[20]

—*Randy Southern*

IF I'M REALLY SPIRITUAL, SHOULDN'T I ALWAYS GET A "YES" FROM GOD?

Getting a "yes" response from God has nothing to do with who you are or how spiritual you are. Paul, for example, would likely finish in the top five Christians of all time.

But consider what he said about his prayer life in 2 Corinthians 12:7–10:

> Lest I should be exalted above measure by the abundance of the revelations, a thorn in the flesh was given to me, a messenger of Satan to buffet me, lest I be exalted above measure. Concerning this thing I pleaded with the Lord three times that it might depart from me. And He said to me, "My grace is sufficient for you, for My strength is made perfect in weakness." Therefore most gladly I will rather boast in my infirmities, that the power of Christ may rest upon me. Therefore I take pleasure in infirmities, in reproaches, in needs, in persecutions, in distresses, for Christ's sake. For when I am weak, then I am strong.

Many people think Paul's "thorn in the flesh" was an eye problem. Perhaps he even had problems seeing. Whatever the affliction was, Paul prayed to be healed of it. And God said... "No." He wanted Paul to rely on Him for his strength. He also wanted people to recognize His work in Paul's life.[21]

—*Randy Southern*

HOW CAN WE DETERMINE GOD'S ANSWER?

Christians believe that they should carefully obey God's will. But how can we know what His will is? How should we go about making decisions that honor the Lord?

The example of Gideon is frequently cited as a model for godly decision making. Before acting, Gideon carefully considered whether the Lord wanted him to rally an army and attack the Midianites. Twice he set out a fleece (a clump of wool) to make sure of God's intentions (Judg. 6:36–40). On this basis, some have argued that before Christians make major decisions with long-range consequences, they should "put out a fleece before the Lord," seeking some tangible sign that indicates His will with certainty.

Is that an appropriate way to know God's will? In considering the questions, it is important to note that this is the only occasion in the Bible when God revealed His will through a fleece. It is also worth noting Gideon's extreme hesitation, doubt, and fear. The Lord had already told him what to do through the Angel of the Lord (6:11–16). In fact, the Angel had already given Gideon a confirming sign (6:17–22).

> PRAYER REFLECTION
>
> *Neglect prayer. Neglect God.*
>
> —O. Hallesby

In light of these facts, Gideon's use of the fleece would appear to demonstrate a *lack of faith* more than any zeal to be certain of God's will. Fortunately, God was very patient with him and granted his request for a confirming sign. But it seems that using a fleece to determine God's will was the exception rather than the rule, and thus does not serve as the beast pattern for how we can depend on God for guidance.

Is there a more reliable way? Yes, God has clearly and objectively told us what He wants throughout the Bible. For example, the Ten Commandments give straightforward instructions to guide our behavior in numerous areas of life. Likewise, one of the New Testament letters to the Thessalonians says plainly, "This is the will of God" (1 Thess. 4:3). The passage then goes on to outline some of God's will in regard to sexuality.

Thus when it comes to making choices in life, God calls us to clear thinking—thinking that is based on our relationship with Him and our allegiance to His values, which are clearly spelled out in Scripture. God has made us to be thinking, discerning, analytical persons who assume responsibility for working our way through life in accordance with His general plans and purposes. He challenges us to learn all that we can about any situation, relationship, responsibility, or opportunity that we have, weigh it in light of His precepts and principles, and then act. As we act, we can take comfort from the fact that He is at work within us, "both to will and to do for His good pleasure" (Phil. 2:13).[22]

—*from* The Word in Life Study Bible

HOW SHOULD I APPROACH GOD?

One of the dangers of our frenzied culture is that we tend to hurry into the presence of God, share our list of wants with Him, then rush back to our hectic lives and overcrowded schedules for the rest of the day. What a sad thing that is, and how foolish. David wrote, "The Lord reigns, let the nations tremble; he sits enthroned between the cherubim, let the earth shake. Great is the LORD in Zion; he is exalted over all the nations. Let them praise your great and awesome name—he is holy ... Exalt the Lord our God and worship at his holy mountain, for the LORD our God is holy" (Ps. 99:1–3, 9).

There is no one like the Lord—awesome in holiness, power, and love. No wonder He is to be worshiped and exalted!

In our humanness we frequently enter His presence with words we speak or sing. But sometimes, when we sense the presence of God, it is good to be silent before the Lord. It is not easy for most of us to be silent. But God has encouraged it. He has said, "Be still, and know that I am God; I will be exalted among the nations, I will be exalted in the earth" (46:10).

I believe it is an insult to come into God's presence, verbalize what is on our minds in an attempt to get what we want, and then rush back to our busy lives expecting God to take care of our requests. I need not point my finger at others. That has been my own experience at times—and I have discovered that God is not pleased with that approach.

That truth has been illustrated to me a number of times over the years as I have been involved in pastoral counseling. I have found that people would get entangled in major problems and crises through their own sin and disobedience. Then, when they could no longer endure the situation, they would make an appointment to see their pastor. They would often come to the counseling situation expecting me to straighten things out within an hour so they could return to their lives as normal. Seldom would a husband or wife come with a mind open to resolving failure in their own lives. Inevitably, they came so I could help straighten out the weaknesses and failures of their mate.

Often without realizing it, we tend to do the same thing with God. Many of us come to Him in prayer to resolve a situation or straighten out another person so we can enjoy life once again in the comfort zone.

Several years ago a Christian leader from Africa was visiting the church I was pastoring. He was impressed with how much time I spent counseling. It was difficult for him to understand, since such counseling was not offered in his church. With simple and uncritical logic, he concluded, "I think I see the difference between our churches. In America, you counsel Christians who are having problems. In Africa, we ask them to repent."

He was not suggesting that there was not a place for legitimate pastoral counseling. Nor am I. In fact, I have given much of my life to that important ministry. However, without fully realizing it he was being used of God to remind me of the great need for authentic and deep repentance in the lives of Christians from every culture of the world. Prayers of repentance can bring us into the awesome presence of God.

In short, self-centered prayers focus on ourselves. God-centered prayers bring us into the very presence of God. We would do well to approach God with a deep sense of awe. This is where meaningful prayer begins. Only then are we prepared to consider our physical posture as it relates to our praying. When the posture of our hearts is what it should be, when we come to God with a spirit of humility and the recognition of our utter helplessness, then we are ready to employ the most meaningful and appropriate physical posture for our times of prayer.[23]

—*Paul Cedar*

THE PERSON

[focus on the person praying]

HOW DOES PRAYER HELP ME TO KNOW GOD BETTER?

The joy of eye contact with God

God not only inclines His ear to us, but He also looks us in the eye. We are not praying to "Someone up there" who is so high above us that He cannot see or hear. Through the power of His Holy Spirit, He sees, hears, and is very present in our hearts.

What does God see? He sees our hearts. He sees the vanity of the hypocrite or the desire of His child who wants to sit at His feet. Jesus tells us that He sees our needs: "Your Father knows what you need before you ask Him" (Matt. 6:8 AMPLIFIED). The knowledge that God is ever-present and all-knowing encourages me to flee to Him often. He knows everything anyway, so why not talk it all over with Him and leave my closet with His guidance and peace?

How it pleases our Father when we take time to enter His presence, desiring secret communion with Him. He has provided everything necessary for our intimacy with Him. He waits for us to go into a private room, shut the door, and lift up our hearts to Him.

When we come to God secretly, He rewards us openly. Sometimes the reward is renewed strength in the spirit. Sometimes it includes a direct answer to prayer. Often it is the assurance of His presence and guidance. What a great reward it is just to be met by the Lord, knowing that He cares and that we are worthy to be loved and listened to. This is an honor in itself.

The Pharisees were rewarded publicly by the praise of men in the synagogue. Our ultimate reward will be granted before all the world on that great day when every knee shall bow and every tongue confess that Jesus Christ is Lord. What a joy to be among those who deepened their intimacy with the Father through rich times of secret prayer.

It is no use to ask what those who love God do with Him.

There is no difficulty in spending our time with a friend
we love; our heart is always ready to open to Him; we do
not study what we shall say to Him, but it comes forth
without premeditation; we can keep nothing back—even
if we have nothing special to say, we like to be with Him.
—François Fenelon[1]

—*Cynthia Heald*

HOW DOES PRAYER DRAW ME CLOSER TO GOD?

When we sit before the Lord, it's like the experience we had when we met that special
person for the first time. As we talked and shared our hearts, our joys, and our hurts, we
grew intimately interested in each other.

As time passed, we realized that we could live with
that person for the rest of our lives. It's the same with
God. He never wants us to think of Him as distant or
detached. Through the Holy Spirit, God lives intimately with each of us. He is embedded within the deepest

> PRAYER REFLECTION
> *God needs time with us. If we
> would only give him time . . .*
> —Andrew Murray

core of our lives, and He desires fellowship with us so that He can pour His life into us.
But, He can't do that if we fail to spend time meditating upon Him and learning who
He is.[2]

—*Charles Stanley*

HOW DO I GET ALONE WITH GOD?

In contrast to the practices of the Pharisees, the Lord taught His disciples how to give, to
pray, and to fast. When He began teaching on prayer, He started by saying, "When you
pray you must not be like the hypocrites, for they love to pray standing in the synagogues
and on the corners of the streets, that they may be seen by people. Truly, I tell you, they
have their reward—in full already" (Matt. 6:5 AMPLIFIED). How tragic to be used as a negative example, especially in the appropriate way to pray!

Until Jesus came, however, there really were no other religious role models. The
Pharisees were the leaders and teachers. In the "How to Pray Effectively as a Pharisee"

course, you were taught to stand in the most public places so that others could see your piety and reward you with their praise and honor. The Pharisees prayed to be heard by people, not by God.

All Jesus could say in response to the Pharisees' prayer life was, "Don't do it the way they do—do the opposite! Pray privately. Prayer is communion, not a performance." Jesus does not say it is wrong to pray publicly, but He teaches that the rewards for praying in secret are far greater than those for praying in public.

Jesus taught that if you wish to draw close to your Father in prayer, then go into your private room, your closet, any place you can be by yourself. Only when you are alone can you discover the treasure of speaking to your Father in secret. In private, you can be yourself, a child who converses with her Father. It is hard to be pretentious or artificial because no one else is there to watch; you need not maintain a particular posture or pray in a certain prescribed way. Praying in secret allows you to be honest, to cry, to talk out loud, and to listen.

Perhaps you are asking, "Do *private* rooms really exist? There are none in my home!" Some rooms are private only at certain times—mostly early in the morning or late at night. Hudson Taylor, missionary to China, often had his time of communion at 2:00 a.m. He would retire at a reasonable hour, wake at 2:00, and after a time of Scripture reading and prayer, continue his sleep until morning.

> ### PRAYER REFLECTION
> *Lord,*
> *Make me an instrument*
> *of Thy peace;*
> *Where there is hatred,*
> *let me sow love;*
> *Where there is injury, pardon;*
> *Where there is doubt, faith;*
> *Where there is despair, hope;*
> *Where there is darkness, light; and*
> *Where there is sadness, joy.*
> *Divine Master,*
> *Grant that I may not so much seek*
> *to be consoled as to console;*
> *To be understood as to understand;*
> *To be loved as to love;*
> *For it is in giving that we receive;*
> *It is in pardoning*
> *that we are pardoned;*
> *And it is in dying*
> *that we are born to eternal life.*
> *—St. Francis of Assisi*

Sometimes the "closet" can be outside. Mark recorded that Jesus "got up and went out to a deserted place, and there He prayed" (1:35 AMPLIFIED). Jesus didn't even have a place to lay His head, and everywhere He went He was surrounded by people. Yet prayer was such a necessity for Him that He found gardens, hillsides, any deserted places to be with His Father.

My closet is often the neighborhood when I am taking a walk—just the Lord and me. There are no interruptions and very few distractions. If your life is one continual demand after another, then you know that your private room can be any place you choose to quiet your heart and enter the presence of the Lord. Susanna Wesley, who had nineteen children, withdrew into her closet by putting her apron over her head!

In reality, our prayer closet is in our hearts. John Chrysostom counseled, "No one should give the answer that it is impossible for a man occupied with worldly cares to pray always. You can set up an altar to God in your mind by means of prayer. And so it is fitting to pray at your trade, on a journey, standing at a counter or sitting at your handicraft." A particular place is not as essential as a pure heart and the desire to be alone with God, wherever that place might be.[3]

—*Cynthia Heald*

HOW IMPORTANT IS PRIVATE PRAYER?

The first thing the Lord teaches His disciples is that they must have a secret place for prayer; every one must have some solitary spot where he can be alone with his God. Every teacher must have a schoolroom. We have learnt to know and accept Jesus as our only teacher in the school of prayer. . . . He wants each one to choose for himself the fixed spot where He can daily meet him. That inner chamber, that solitary place, is Jesus' schoolroom. That spot may be anywhere; that spot may change from day to day if we have to change our abode; but that secret place there must be, with the quiet time in which the pupil places himself in the Master's presence, to be by Him prepared to worship the Father. There alone, but there most surely, Jesus comes to us to teach us to pray.

A teacher is always anxious that his schoolroom should be bright and attractive, filled with the light and air of heaven, a place where pupils long to come, and love to stay. In His first words on prayer in the Sermon on the Mount, Jesus seeks to set the inner chamber before us in its most attractive light. If we listen carefully, we soon notice what the chief thing is He has to tell us of our tarrying there. Three times He uses the name of Father: "Pray to *thy Father*"; "*Thy Father* shall recompense thee;" "*Your Father* knoweth what things ye have need of." The first thing in closet-prayer is: I must meet my Father. The light that shines in the closet must be . . . the light of the Father's countenance. The fresh air from heaven with which Jesus would have it filled, the atmosphere in which I am to breathe and pray, is . . . God's Father-love, God's infinite Fatherliness. Thus each thought or petition we breathe out will be simple, hearty, childlike trust in the Father. This is how the Master teaches us to pray: He brings us into the Father's living presence. What we pray there must avail. Let us listen carefully to hear what the Lord has to say to us.

First, *"Pray to thy Father which is in secret."* God is a God who hides Himself to the carnal eye. As long as in our worship of God we are chiefly occupied with our own thoughts and exercises, we shall not meet Him who is a Spirit, the unseen One. But to the man who withdraws himself from all that is of the world and man, and prepares to wait upon God alone, the Father will reveal Himself. As he forsakes and gives up and shuts out the world, and the life of the world, and surrenders himself to be led of Christ into the secret of God's presence, the light of the Father's love will rise upon him. The secrecy of the inner chamber and the closed door, the entire separation from all around us, is an image of, and so a help to that inner spiritual sanctuary, the secret of God's tabernacle, within the veil, where our spirit truly comes into contact with the Invisible One. And so we are taught, at the very outset of our search after the secret of effectual prayer, to remember that it is in the inner chamber, where we are alone with the Father, that we shall learn to pray aright. . . . Just because your heart is cold and prayerless, get you into the presence of the loving Father. As a father pitieth his children, so the Lord pitieth you. Do not be thinking of how little you have to bring God, but of how much He wants to give you. Just place yourself before, and look up into, His face; think of His love, His wonderful, tender, pitying love. . . .

"And thy Father, which seeth in secret, will recompense thee." Here Jesus assures us that secret prayer cannot be fruitless: its blessing will show itself in our life. We have but in secret, alone with God, to entrust our life before men to Him; He will reward us openly; He will see to it that the answer to prayer be made manifest in His blessing upon us. Our Lord would thus teach us that as infinite Fatherliness and Faithfulness is that with which God meets us in secret, so on our part there should be the childlike simplicity of faith, the confidence that our prayer does bring down a blessing. "He that cometh to God must believe that *He is a rewarder* of them that seek Him." Not on the strong or the fervent feeling with which I pray does the blessing of the closet depend, but upon the love and the power of the Father to whom I there entrust my needs.[4]

—*Andrew Murray*

Several years ago a precious, godly couple had a special-needs baby. They had prayed for a healthy child, but their prayer was not answered in the way they had wanted. The major-ity of couples we know have healthy children; we had four ourselves. I know that our prayers and our faith were no different from that of others who love God. Why is this so? Why are we told to pray in faith, and assured that our petition will be answered, when that is not always the case?

I think this issue does have everything to do with faith. What is the character of the God in whom we place our faith? What does He desire? To venture to pray requires our trust in the goodness of God. For He is lov-ing, trustworthy, all-wise, all-knowing, full of grace and mercy. He delights that I trust Him and come to Him in faith, believing that He hears and responds.

My prayer of faith is based on wholehearted trust that I have perfect freedom to ask anything, as a child who has faith in her Father, because I love to abide in Him and His Word. However, that same faith rests in His good purpos-es regarding the answer I receive. It is not the amount of my faith that matters, but where my faith is placed—in a God who makes no mistakes, who is always working for the highest and best for His children. Because I seek His will and want to please Him, I want what He wants. And what He wants is that I reflect His image and depend on Him for the direction of my life.

> ### PRAYER REFLECTION
>
> *Equip me today, O God, with*
> *The humility which will keep me*
> *from pride and from conceit;*
> *The graciousness and the gentleness*
> *which will make me*
> *both easy to live with and a*
> *joy to meet;*
> *The diligence, the perseverance, and*
> *the reliability*
> *which will make me a good work-*
> *man; The kindness which will give*
> *me a quick eye*
> *to see what I can do for others,*
> *and a ready hand to do it;*
> *The constant awareness of your*
> *presence, which will make me*
> *do everything as unto you.*
> *So grant that today people may*
> *see in me a glimpse of the life of*
> *my blessed Lord.*
> *This I ask for your love's sake.*
> *Amen.*
>
> —William Barclay, 1907–1978

Our friends with the special-needs child, who is now in elementary school, are fac-ing a new test. The husband has just been diagnosed with an aggressive form of cancer. While I was visiting with the wife she commented, "I thought I could never handle hav-ing a baby who would demand so much care, but as I look back over the years I see how

God has provided and given strength in such amazing ways. Now that we face this difficult trial, all I know is that God is faithful, and He will provide and sustain us."

A purified faith is a stronger faith—able to pray boldly, humbly, and submissively. Sometimes our faith can move mountains; sometimes it can only reach out and touch the hem of His garment; sometimes it simply cries out for mercy—but in all prayers of faith, in some measure, the true healing is that our eyes are opened and we see the Lord.[5]

—*Cynthia Heald*

HOW DO I LISTEN TO GOD?

We, as believers, often weary and worried, need to hear just one thing to refresh, encourage, and strengthen us in our service of the King—God's *voice*. Whatever our situation may call for—guidance, comfort, assurance, strength, perseverance, faith, joy, peace—God's Voice will supply.

> **PRAYER REFLECTION**
>
> *The whole field of prayer, and praying as laying hold on unlimited power, is unexplored, with the result that spiritual laws still lie undiscovered by the average believer.*
>
> —*Peter Marshall*

The answer will not be found in the noise and rumble (earthquake, wind, and fire) of the world or religion. It is seldom that we will hear accurately from God in the rush of traffic, the din of the office, or the clatter of friends. God wishes to speak to us individually, and for that we must be committed to seek solitude, however brief.

How many times have we waited in line to hear a particularly noted orator speak of religion or politics or sports? How often have we patiently waited in front of a television to tune into the "important news of the day" (apartment fires and floods) or stayed glued to the radio for changes in the weather? How many (literally) thousands of hours have we invested in listening to things that make no eternal difference?

Only a few minutes of sitting before the God who speaks can transform a life, metamorphose a mind, and reset purpose and direction for eternity. The sad heart is cheered, the confused mind is ordered, the pessimistic outlook is eliminated, the lonely spirit is befriended, the rebellious will is subdued, and the drifting seeker is made steadfast.

Wherever Jesus went and taught, He said, "He who has ears let him hear." To those who heard, He called "blessed." To those who rejected His truth, He condemned to further unbelief.

Two thousand years later, we are equipped with everything necessary to confidently hear from God. We are the repositories of the Holy Spirit, who teaches us all things and brings to our remembrance everything Jesus said. We have at our fingertips His completed Word, which is the magnificent sum of God's character, nature, truth, and principles. In a nation that abounds with sincere believers, we have unhindered access to the wise counsel of people who know and love God.

Therefore, we can go "boldly to the throne of grace, that we may obtain mercy and find grace" (Heb. 4:16). What could be a fuller, richer expression of such grace and mercy than our Father's clear communication to His children?

Laying aside our fears, we can come expectantly, not to a mountain consumed by fire (Mount Horeb) but "to Mount Zion and to the city of the living God" (Heb. 12:22) where He delights to instruct and encourage His people. We will never be disappointed, even if reproof or admonishment is given, for everything God speaks is for our welfare.

Like Mary, we should learn to listen to the Lord's Word, seated at His feet (see Luke 10:39). Through quiet, disciplined prayer and interaction with His Word and people, we can become men and women who fruitfully learn to distinguish the speaking Voice from amid the clamor of our environs.

When we do, we too can trust and we have "chosen that good part, which will not be taken away" (Luke 10:42). For when once we have heard God speak, nothing else compares. Everything else pales beside the priceless experience of hearing God. Above all, absolutely nothing—no trouble, no tribulation, no circumstance, no uncertainty—can displace the wonderful peace and assurance that result from definitely being on the receiving end of God's communication.

The man who has heard from God has the enduring power to engage adversaries, confront tragedy, and surmount any problem that lies in his path, because upon what God has spoken, he can steadfastly rest. God fulfills His promises and guarantees His Word.

God is still speaking. Let us choose the "good part" of listening obediently to Him. He has great and mighty things in store for each of us.[6]

—*Charles Stanley*

WHY IS PRAYER SOMETIMES SO DIFFICULT FOR ME?

The Bible teaches us that, in some way or other, Satan can hinder our prayers and delay the answer. Does not St. Peter urge certain things upon Christians, that their "prayers be not hindered"? (I Peter 3:7) Our prayers can be hindered. "Then cometh the evil one and snatcheth away that which hath been sown in the heart" (Matt. 13:19, R.V.).

. . . We are comforted by the fact that "the Spirit helpeth our infirmities: for we know not how to pray as we ought" (Rom. 8:26). How does the Spirit "help" us, teach us, if not by example as well as by precept? How does the Spirit "pray"? "The Spirit Himself maketh intercession for us with groanings which cannot be uttered (Rom. 8:26). Does the Spirit "agonize" in prayer as the Son did in Gethsemane?

If the Spirit prays in us, shall we not share His "groanings" in prayer? . . . "But," one asks, "may not a godly sorrow for sin and a yearning desire for the salvation of others induce in us an agonizing which is unnecessary, and dishonoring to God?"

May it not reveal a lack of faith in God's promises? Perhaps it may do so. But there is little doubt that St. Paul regarded prayer—at least sometimes—as a conflict (see Rom. 15:30). In writing to the Colossian Christians he says: "I would have you know how greatly I strive for you . . . and for as many as have not seen my face in the flesh; that their hearts may be comforted" (Col. 2:1, 2). . . . Again, he speaks of Epaphras as one who is "always striving for you in his prayers, that ye may stand perfect, and fully assured in all the will of God" (Col. 4:12). The word for "strive" is our word "agonize," the very word used of our Lord being "in an agony" when praying Himself (Luke 22:44).

The apostle says again, Epaphras "hath much labor for you," that is, in his prayers. St. Paul saw him praying there in prison, and witnessed his intense striving as he engaged in a long, indefatigable effort on behalf of the Colossians. How the Praetorian guard to whom St. Paul was chained must have wondered—yes, and have been deeply touched—to see these men at their prayers. Their agitation, their tears, their earnest supplications as

> ### PRAYER REFLECTION
>
> *There is not in the world a life more pleasing and more delicious than a life of continual conversation with God; only those can understand it who practice it and experience it. If I were a preacher, I would preach above everything else the practice of the presence of God. I strive only to swell in His holy presence, and do that by a simple attention and loving gaze constantly fixed upon Him, which I am able to call a real presence of God; or to say it better, a secret conversation, silent and habitual, of the soul with God.*
>
> —from the letters of
> Brother Lawrence

they lifted up chained hands in prayer must have been a revelation to him! What would they think of our prayers?

No doubt St. Paul was speaking of his own custom when he urged the Ephesian Christians and others "to stand," "with all prayer and supplication, praying at all seasons in the Spirit, and watching thereunto in all perseverance and supplication for all saints, and on my behalf . . . an ambassador in chains." (Eph. 6:18–20). That is a picture of his own prayer-life, we may be sure.

So then prayer meets with obstacles, which must be prayed away. That is what men mean when they talk about praying through. We must wrestle with the machinations of Satan. It may be bodily weariness or pain, or the insistent claims of other thoughts, or doubt, or the direct assaults of spiritual hosts of wickedness. With us, as with St. Paul, prayer is something of a "conflict," a "wrestle," at least sometimes, which compels us to "stir" ourselves up "to lay hold on God" (Isa. 64:7). . . .

The very word used for "striving" in prayer means "a contest." The contest is not between God and ourselves. He is at one with us in our desires. The contest is with the evil one, although he is a conquered foe (I John 3:8). He desires to thwart our prayers.

"We wrestle not against flesh and blood, but against principalities, against the world-rulers of this darkness, against the spiritual hosts of wickedness in the heavenly places" (Eph. 6:12). We, too, are in these "heavenly places in Christ" (Eph. 1:3); and it is only in Christ that we can be victorious. Our wrestling may be a wrestling of our thoughts from thinking Satan's suggestions, and keeping them fixed on Christ our Savior—that is, watching as well as praying (Eph. 6:18); "watching unto prayer."[7]

—*Anonymous*

WHAT TYPES OF ATTITUDES CAN GET IN THE WAY OF MY PRAYER LIFE?

Pride

Pride is one of the major reasons we do not pray. Why does pride keep us from praying? **Pride keeps us from praying because it overestimates the power of self. . . .**

Would you take an inventory of your life right now? Pride is the "self-life." Pride always leads you to point fingers at others. Pride never takes the blame for anything. Pride leads you to think more of yourself than you do of God. Do you have any pride? . . .

Force yourself to pray. Make yourself go down on your knees. Do whatever it takes to get before God daily. You will never be stronger and your enemy will never be weaker than when you pray. . . .

Unbelief

. . . There are moments when we just cannot believe. Even though we know about Jesus' ability, we are just not certain that He is willing to intervene in our situation. Rather than choosing to pray, we choose to trust in ourselves. Our unbelief keeps us from praying.

Unbelief is another major reason we do not pray. Why does our unbelief keep us from praying? **Unbelief underestimates the power of God.**

Whereas pride overestimates the power of self, unbelief underestimates the power of God. The result of each of these sins is prayerlessness. . . .

When we pray we must first believe that God is. What does it mean to believe that God is? It means to believe that God is who He says He is and that He can do whatever He says He can do.

When you do not believe that God is who He says He is and that God can do whatever He says He can do, then you do not have faith in God. Without faith, prayer will not occur. Remember: Unbelief underestimates the power of God. Unbelief is a major obstacle to prayer.

Satan wants you to think that God is too busy to listen to your prayers. Your enemy places into your imagination the false idea that God is limited in His power. I trust that you know better. God is who He says He is and He can do whatever He wants to do. He is God! . . .

Ignorance

. . . Ignorance is one of the major reasons we do not pray. How does ignorance keep us from prayer? **Ignorance overestimates the difficulty of talking to God.**

God is not difficult to talk to in prayer. Just as I once overestimated the difficulty of talking to influential people, I used to overestimate the difficulty of talking to God. What I know now is that God is easier to talk to than any person. God wants you to talk to Him. He wants you to come to Him anytime, anywhere, and about anything. He wants to fellowship with you.

Forget trying to impress God with your language. He is not interested in your words.

He is interested in your heart. Share your heart with God. Real prayer occurs when you share your heart with God. Ignorance can no longer be a reason why you do not pray. . . .

Time

. . . One of the major reasons people do not pray is time. How does time keep you from talking with God? **Time underestimates the value of being with God.**

Remember, each person has the same amount of time. Time only becomes the problem when you underestimate the value of being with God. . . .

Time with God is essential for life. Whenever you do not take the time to pray, you have a problem with your values. You just do not deem God as important and worthy of your time. Make time to talk to God. Time with God is critical to a successful Christian life.

When my schedule becomes cramped with many demands, I always make sure that the first thing I do every day is spend time with God. However, there have been times in the past when my schedule has seemed to force me to cut short my time with God. This has never been beneficial to my day. Rushing my time with God is never advantageous to my spiritual health.

When you take time for God, He will meet with you. Invest your time wisely with God, and He will make your effort worthwhile, Remember what Hebrews 11:6 says: "He is a rewarder of those who seek Him."

> ## PRAYER REFLECTION
> ### More Like Jesus
> *May God the Father, and the eternal high priest Jesus Christ, build us up in faith and truth and love, and grant to us our portion among the saints with all those who believe on our Lord Jesus Christ. We pray for all saints, for kings and rulers, for the enemies of the cross of Christ, and for ourselves we pray that our fruit may abound and we be made perfect in Christ Jesus our Lord. Amen.*
>
> —*St. Polycarp*
> *(Prayers Across the Centuries)*

Take time for God today. Do not put Him off, He is the King of kings and Lord of lords, He is more prominent than any person you will ever meet in life. No one is like Him. . . .

Prayer is your means of spending time with God. It is the way that you express yourself to Him. Never underestimate the value of spending time with God. All God needs with you is a moment. In that moment, He can transform you. He can fill you with hope. God can do more in a moment than you can do in a lifetime.

What is keeping you from praying? Pride? Unbelief? Ignorance? Time? Now is the time to identify what is standing in the way of your becoming a great prayer warrior for God. None of these obstacles are too big to be conquered.[8]

—Ronnie W. Floyd

WHAT IF I CAN'T BELIEVE GOD HEARS MY PRAYERS?

And to call forth . . . faith, Christ Himself has said, Mark 9: "Therefore I say unto you, What things soever ye desire, when ye pray, believe that ye receive them, and ye shall surely have them." And Luke 1:9: "Ask, and it shall be given you; seek, and ye shall find; knock, and it shall be opened unto you; for every one that asketh receiveth; and he that seeketh findeth; and to him that knocketh it shall be opened. Or what father is there of you, who, if his son shall ask bread, will he give him a stone? or if he ask a fish, will he give him a serpent? or if he ask an egg, will he give him a scorpion? But if you know how to give good gifts to your children, and you yourselves are not naturally good, how much more shall your Father which is in heaven give a good spirit to all them that ask Him!"

Who is so hard and stone-like, that such mighty words ought not to move him to pray with all confidence! . . . For where this faith and confidence is not in the prayer, the prayer is dead, and nothing more than a grievous labor and work. . . . One who prays aright never doubts that his prayer is surely acceptable and heard, although the very thing for which he prays be not given him.

> ### PRAYER REFLECTION
>
> *We sin against the Lord when we stop praying for others. When once we begin to see how absolutely indispensable intercession is, just as much a duty as loving God or believing in Christ, and how we are called and bound to it as believers, we shall feel that to cease intercession is grievous sin.*
> *Let us ask for grace to take up our place as priests with joy, and give our life to bring down the blessing of heaven.*
> —*Andrew Murray*

But if you say: "What if I cannot believe that my prayer is heard and accepted?" I answer: For this very reason faith, prayer and all other good works are commanded, that you shall know what you can and what you cannot do. And when you find that you cannot so believe and do, then you are humbly to confess it to God, and so begin with a weak spark of faith and daily strengthen it more and more by exercising it in all your living and doing. For as touching infirmity of faith . . . there is no one on earth who does not have his good share of it. For even the holy Apostles in the Gospel, and especially St. Peter, were weak in faith, so that they also prayed Christ and said: "Lord, increase our faith"; and He very frequently rebukes them because they have so little faith.

Therefore you shall not despair, nor give up, even if you find that you do not believe as firmly as you ought and wish, in your prayer or in other works. Nay, you shall thank God with all your heart that He thus reveals to you your weakness, through which He daily teaches and admonishes you how much you need to exercise yourself and daily strengthen yourself in faith. For how many do you see who habitually pray, sing, read, work, and seem to be great saints, and yet never get so far as to know where they stand in respect of the chief work, faith; and so in their blindness they lead astray themselves and others; think they are very well off, and so unknowingly build on the sand of their works without any faith, not on God's mercy and promise through a firm, pure faith.[9]

—*Martin Luther*

WHAT KINDS OF THINGS COULD HINDER MY PRAYER LIFE?

10 common prayer killers

The best way to keep from having spiritual junk hinder your prayer life is to avoid it. But when you haven't, the best thing to do is clean it up as soon as possible. I've found that there are ten very common blocks to effective prayer. I call them prayer killers because they take away all power from our prayers and hinder our relationship with God. . . .

Prayer Killer #1: Unconfessed Sin
Unconfessed sin is probably the most common prayer killer. Psalm 66:18 says, "If I regard wickedness in my heart, the Lord will not hear" (NASB). When the Scripture talks about regarding wickedness, it's referring to unconfessed sin. God is perfect and can't abide sin in us. If we knowingly tolerate sin in our lives, it pushes God away from us. As a result, it makes our prayers powerless.

The good news is that when we confess sin, God forgives it, and it's gone. The slate is clean and we are no longer held accountable. Jeremiah 31:34 says, "For I will forgive their wickedness and will remember their sins no more." Not only are we forgiven, but God chooses to truly forget our sins of the past. At that point our relationship is restored, and our prayers regain their power. Our past actions may still have consequences, but the sin itself is forgiven. . . .

Prayer Killer #2: Lack of Faith
Lack of faith has an incredibly negative impact on a Christian's life. Without faith, prayer has no power. Even Jesus was powerless to perform any miracles in Nazareth because of the people's lack of faith (Mark 6:1–6).

Jesus' brother James gives some insight into the effect that faithlessness has on prayer. James 1:5–8 says:

> If any of you lacks wisdom, he should ask God, who gives
> generously to all without finding fault, and it will be given
> to him. But when he asks, he must believe and not doubt,
> because he who doubts is like a wave of the sea, blown and
> tossed by the wind. That man should not think he will
> receive anything from the Lord; he is a double-minded man,
> unstable in all he does.

What incredible insight this is into the mind of the unfaithful person. The word double-minded speaks of a condition where a person is emotionally divided, almost as if he had two souls. That condition makes a person unstable and incapable of hearing from God or receiving His gifts. . . .

Prayer Killer #3: Disobedience
. . . If we are to grow in our relationship with God and become strong people of prayer, we must learn to obey. Keeping free from sin is not enough. Neither is faith. If our mouths say that we believe, but our actions don't back up that belief with a strong display of obedience, it shows the weakness of our belief. Obedience should be a natural outgrowth of faith in God. He that obeys God, trusts Him; he that trusts Him, obeys Him. . . .

Prayer Killer #4: Lack of Transparency with God and with Others
. . . James 5:16 says, "Therefore, confess your sins to one another, and pray for one another, so that you may be healed" (NASB). James is sharing a truth about God: When we confess our sins to one another, which requires us to be absolutely transparent, God is able

to heal and cleanse us. We experience a spiritual, physical, and emotional restoration. In addition, our transparency helps others, because it shows them that they are not alone in their difficulties. . . .

Transparency is a difficult thing for a lot of people. Many pastors I know have an especially hard time with it. But openness with others can have a profound effect on you. Transparency with God when you pray puts you on His agenda instead of your own. And it also releases other believers to pray for you strategically and specifically.

Prayer Killer #5: Unforgiveness

You may remember the Scripture passage in which Peter asked Jesus about forgiveness. He asked, "Lord, how many times shall I forgive my brother when he sins against me? Up to seven times?" (Matt. 18:21). Hebrew law required a person to forgive a person three times for an offense. Peter, by suggesting seven, thought he was being very lenient and forgiving. He was probably shocked when he heard Jesus' answer: "Not seven times, but seventy-seven times" (Matt. 18:22).

Jesus was trying to teach Peter that forgiveness is not a matter of mathematics. Nor is it a choice of words. It is an attitude of the heart, and it is the Holy Spirit who empowers us to forgive. Why is forgiveness so important? The answer is found in Matthew 6:14–15, "For if you forgive men when they sin against you, your heavenly Father will also forgive you. But if you do not forgive men their sins, your Father will not forgive your sins." . . .

Prayer Killer #6: Wrong Motive

. . . God makes no mistakes about our motives. When they're not right, our prayers have no power. James 4:3 says, "When you ask, you do not receive, because you ask with wrong motives."

Sometimes even knowing our own motives can be difficult. In my experience, I've observed two things that quickly expose wrong motives:

> ### PRAYER REFLECTION
>
> *O God, we thank you for this earth, our home; for the wide sky and the blessed sun, for the salt sea and the hills and the never-resting winds, for trees and the common grass underfoot.*
>
> *We thank you for our senses by which we hear the songs of birds, and see the splendors of the summer fields, and taste of the autumn fruits, and rejoice in the feel of the snow, and the smell of the breath of spring.*
>
> *Grant us a heart wide open to all the beauty; and save our souls from being so blind that we pass unseeing when even the common thornbush is aflame with your glory, O God our creator, who lives and reigns for ever and ever.*
>
> —*Walter Rauschenbusch, 1861–1918*

1. *A project greater than ourselves:* Big projects—ones that put us in way over our heads—force us to examine why we are doing them. And that process exposes our motives. . . .

2. *Prayer:* When we pray, God speaks to us and shows us our motives. If we are acting out of pride, fear, possessiveness, self-satisfaction, convenience, etc., God will show it to us, if only we are willing to listen. And if we are willing, He will change those motives. . . .

Prayer Killer #7: Idols in our Lives

. . . Ezekiel 14:3 clearly shows the negative effect of anything that comes between a person and God. It says, "Son of man, these men have set up idols in their hearts and put wicked stumbling blocks before their faces. Should I let them inquire of me at all?" The distaste that God has for idols should be clear from this passage. He doesn't even want an idol worshiper to talk to Him. On the other hand, when we remove idols from our lives, we become ripe for a personal revival.

Take a look at your own life. Is there anything that you're putting ahead of God? Sometimes it's hard to tell. One of the ways to know that something in your life is an idol is to ask yourself, "Would I be willing to give this thing up if God asked me to?" Look honestly at your attitude toward your career, possessions, and family. If there are things you wouldn't release to God, then they're blocking your access to Him.

Prayer Killer #8: Disregard for Others

Psalm 33:13 says, "From heaven the Lord looks down and sees all mankind." God's perspective is expansive. He loves everyone, and His desire is that we care for others in the same way. When we disregard others, it grieves Him.

Scripture is full of verses supporting God's desire for unity among all believers—between Christian brothers and sisters, husbands and wives, laypeople and pastors. For example, in John 13:34, Jesus said, "A new command I give you: Love one another. As I have loved you, so you must love one another." First Peter 3:7 exhorts husbands and wives to be considerate to one other. Otherwise, it says, their prayers will be hindered. And 1 Peter 2:13 says, "Submit yourselves for the Lord's sake to every authority instituted among men."

One of the added benefits of prayer is that it helps you learn to love others. It's impossible for a person to hate or criticize someone they're praying for. Prayer breeds compassion, not competition. . . .

Prayer Killer #9: Disregard for God's Sovereignty

I believe very strongly in the sovereignty of God. I think that's one of the things that has helped me remain positive during difficult times over the years. I know that God knows me completely and knows what's best for me. Jeremiah 1:5 says, "Before I formed you in the womb I knew you, before you were born I set you apart."

When Jesus showed the disciples how to pray, the first thing He did was teach them to honor God for who He is, "Our Father in heaven, hallowed be your name, your kingdom come, your will be done on earth as it is in heaven" (Matt. 6:9–10). That is a clear acknowledgment that God is in charge, that He is sovereign. And it establishes our relationship to Him: that of a child under the authority of his Father. Any time we disregard the divine order of things, we're out-of-bounds, and we hinder our relationship with our heavenly Father.

Prayer Killer #10: Unsurrendered Will

. . . The ultimate purpose of prayer is not to get what we want, but to learn to want what God gives. But that will never happen if we don't surrender our will and put ourselves on God's agenda instead of our own. . . .

There are great benefits to surrendering your will to God. One is that God promises to answer your prayers and grant your requests. Another is that we get to receive the power of Christ through the Holy Spirit. Just

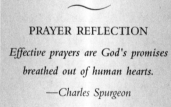

PRAYER REFLECTION

Effective prayers are God's promises breathed out of human hearts.

—*Charles Spurgeon*

as with the vine and the branches, He flows through us, gives us power, and produces fruit.

Developing an effective prayer life depends on keeping your relationship with God strong and uncluttered by sin and disobedience. First Peter 3:12 says, "The eyes of the Lord are on the righteous and his ears are attentive to their prayer, but the face of the Lord is against those who do evil." If we strive for righteousness and confess our errors, we can remain close to God. But maintaining our relationship with Him is an ongoing process. A Christian can't simply pray once through a list like these ten prayer killers and expect to be done with it. Every day we need to go to God and ask Him to reveal anything that may be hindering our progress.[10]

—*from* Partners in Prayer

I'M SUCH A SINNER. HOW CAN I POSSIBLY PRAY?

If there be a God, and I am his creature, there may be, there should be, there must be some communication open between him and me. If any one allow that there is a God, but one not good enough to care about his creatures, I will yield him that it were foolish to pray to such a God; but the notion that, with all the good impulses in us, we are the offspring of a cold-hearted devil, is so horrible in its inconsistency, that I would ask that man what hideous and cold-hearted disregard to the truth makes him capable of the supposition!

If I find . . . that I can neither rule the world in which I live nor my own thoughts or desires; that I cannot quiet my passions, order my likings, determine my ends, will my growth, forget when I would, or recall what I forget; that I cannot love where I would, or hate where I would; that I am no king over myself; that I cannot supply my own needs, do not even always know which of my seeming needs are to be supplied, and which treated as impostors; if, in a word, my own being is everyway too much for me; if I can neither understand it, be satisfied with it, nor better it—may it not well give me pause—the pause that ends in prayer? When my own scale seems too large for my management; when I reflect that I cannot account for my existence, have had no . . . hand in it, neither, should I not like it, can do anything towards causing it to cease; when I think that I can do nothing to make up to those I love, any more than to those I hate, for evils I have done them and sorrows I have caused them; that in my worst moments I disbelieve in my best, in my best loathe my worst; that there is in me no wholeness, no unity; that life is not a good to me, for I scorn myself—when I think all or any such things, can it be strange if I think also that surely there ought to be somewhere a being to account for me, one to account for himself . . . one whose very being accounts and is necessary to account for mine; whose presence in my being is imperative, not merely to supplement it, but to make to myself my existence a good? . . . He that is made in the image of God must know him or be desolate: the child must have the Father! Witness the dissatisfaction, yea desolation of my soul—wretched, alone, unfinished, without him! It cannot act from itself, save in God; acting from what seems itself without God, is no action at all, it is a mere yielding to impulse. All within is disorder and spasm. There is a cry behind me, and a voice before; instincts of betterment tell me I must rise above my present self—perhaps even above all my possible self: I see not how to obey, how to carry them out! I am shut up in a world of consciousness, an unknown I in an unknown world: surely this world of my unwilled, unchosen, compelled existence, cannot be shut out from him, cannot be unknown to him, cannot be impenetrable, impermeable, unpresent to him from whom I am! nay, is it not his thinking in which I think? is it not by his consciousness that I am conscious? Whatever passes in me must be as naturally known to him as to me, and more thoroughly, even to infinite degrees. My thought must lie open to him: if he makes me think, how can I elude him in thinking? "If I should spread my wings toward the dawn, and sojourn at the last of the sea, even there thy hand would lead me, and thy right hand would hold me!" If he has determined [my] being, how shall any [part] of that being be hidden from him? If I speak to him, if I utter words ever so low; if I but think words to him; nay, if I only think to him, surely he, my original, in whose life and will and no otherwise I now think concerning him, hears, and knows, and acknowledges! Then shall I not think to him? Shall I not tell him my troubles . . . how unfit I am to be that which I am?—that my being is not to me a good thing yet?—that I need a law that shall . . . reveal to me how I am to make it a good—how I am to be a good, and not an evil? Shall I not tell him that I need him to comfort me? his breath to move upon the face of the waters of the Chaos he has made? Shall I not cry to him to be in me rest and strength? to quiet this uneasy motion called life, and make me live indeed? to deliver me from my sins, and make me clean and glad? Such a cry is of the child to the Father: if there be a Father, verily he will hear, and let the child know that he hears!"

> PRAYER REFLECTION
>
> *It's Yours, God. It's not mine.*
>
> —*Richard Kriegbaum*

—*George MacDonald*

I FEEL SO UPSET. GOD DOESN'T WANT TO HEAR ME COMPLAIN, DOES HE?

> In the day when I cried out, You answered me,
> And made me bold with strength in my soul.
> (Psalm 138:3 NKJV)

Have you ever left a message for your doctor to call you and then waited all day for his reply? You can't leave the house because you might miss him, and every time the phone rings, you're disappointed when it's not him. When the doctor does call, it's such a relief to get an answer or some advice from him.

With today's automated technology, speaking to a real person is a rarity! No matter what our needs, it can be frustratingly difficult to get a response to our request. We live in a quick-fix society, but we don't always have quick access to those who can give us the answers we need.

Easy access and a listening ear are blessings offered by the Father to His obedient child. He is always on call. David knew that well, and he took full advantage of his loving relationship with the Lord in calling upon Him continually. In Psalm 138:3, he expressed his gratitude for the Lord's answer.

David had no trouble crying out to the Lord. He never hesitated; he easily and confidently lifted his voice to the One he knew could help. He poured out his heart; he wept; he pleaded for the Lord's intervention. Listen to this vivid cry:

> My enemy has chased me.
> He has knocked me to the ground.
> He forces me to live in darkness like those in the grave.
> I am losing all hope;
> I am paralyzed with fear.
> (Ps. 143:3–4 NLT)

There was no soft-pedaling; David forthrightly and honestly cast his burden upon the Lord. He cried because he knew God heard, cared, and answered.

I struggle with feeling I have to be strong when I speak with the Lord. I think I'm supposed to exhibit all the fruit of the Spirit even when I'm in great distress. I think I should be joyful, patient, kind toward any enemy that might assail me. I want to show the Lord what a "big girl" I am. I want to be strong in my own strength!

In truth, I am the Father's imperfect child who will always be in the process of growing. So what should I do with these feelings of desperation, this sense of a crushed spirit? Our

Father wants us, His children, to share freely our whole hearts with Him. My relief always lies in being honest with Him.

David is a wonderful role model for how to cast your burden upon the Lord and find relief for your soul. How refreshing it is to read his prayers. He truly lifted up his soul to his Father: "God, here is what's going on, and this is how I feel. I'm losing all hope, and I'm paralyzed with fear. I need you!" David easily became the child seeking refuge and solace from his Father. He admitted his inability to save himself, his total dependence on God. His intimate knowledge of God enabled him to say, "I will call on the Lord, who is worthy of praise, for he saves me from my enemies" (Ps. 18:3 NLT). David did not try to do for himself what he knew only God could do. What David did well was cry. What God did well was answer—and He still does![12]

—*Cynthia Heald*

WHEN I PRAY, I FEEL GUILTY.

As an expression of His love and devotion to us, God will often put His finger on areas of our lives that are conspicuously wrong. Because He loves us, He wants to cleanse us so that we might be filled with His life and joy.

That is when we either run away or develop our relationship with Him. When we are willing to sit before Him and let Him expose our hearts, something happens. He prunes from our lives what isn't clean. However, if we rationalize our problems when He points them out, we will spend less and less time meditating, because we won't want to face God in that area of our lives.

If we don't want to be alone with God, it may be because He is dealing with particular points in our lives that we simply don't want exposed. We will not let Him love us.

When two people who live together intimately have something wrong in their relationship, they don't really have to tell each other. Both of them know it. When we are quiet before the Lord, and He wants to do something in our lives and things are not right, we stymie our growth by not yielding to Him. We work against the very God who is on our side, working for us, encouraging us, building us up. So whatever He brings to mind, the best thing is to admit it, confess it, repent of it, and deal with it. That is the only way to keep the sweet fellowship of meditation.

Ongoing personal purification was one of the chief attributes that made David a man after God's own heart. We all know that he was far from perfect. His record as a murderer and adulterer would eliminate him from any pulpit in America, yet Jesus referred to Himself as the "Offspring of David" (see Rev. 22:16). How could David commit such gross iniquity and still obtain such divine affirmation?

I believe it was because David was zealous to confess and repent whenever God pinpointed David's sin and confronted him with it. Psalm 51 has been the soulful prayer of many a believer who has willfully or blindly offended God, as David's remorse was laid open before God.

When he wrongfully numbered the children of Israel in a census, he quickly admitted his wrongdoing. "And David's heart condemned him after he had numbered the people. So David said to the Lord, 'I have sinned greatly in what I have done; but now, I pray, O LORD, take away the iniquity of Your servant, for I have done very foolishly'" (2 Sam. 24:10). Rather than run from God's searching, probing light, David humbled himself before the Lord, confessing his transgressions and asking God to cleanse him. [13]

—*Charles Stanley*

I WANT GOD TO CHANGE ME . . . BUT I'M NOT SURE HOW MUCH I REALLY WANT TO CHANGE.

Desires and intentions are two different things, although many believe they are one and the same. You can have very good or godly intentions, but they may not be your true desires. Several people have told me that they desired to walk away from the influences of the world and press into God, yet they don't follow through. They are out of touch with their true desires, for James declares that "each one is tempted when he is drawn away by his own desires and enticed" (James 1:14 NKJV). Desire is the path that a person will take, no matter how good his intentions may be. For this reason, James goes on to say, "Do not be deceived, my beloved brethren" (James 1:16 NKJV). (Of course, there is a positive aspect of desire, but in this case we are dealing with the negative side.)

A comedian, not God, is the one who said, "The devil made me do it." The devil can't make a believer do anything. He can only entice, but you cannot be enticed with something you don't desire. If a line of cocaine or a few hits of LSD were offered to most believers, they would without hesitation refuse them, because they have no desire for them; therefore, they cannot be enticed by them. However, many believers, just as Israel, have not relinquished the desires that the world's system imparted to them as unbelievers. For this reason they can be easily enticed by those things.

We must bring our desires under submission of the Cross: "Those who are Christ's have crucified the flesh with its passions and desires" (Gal. 5:24 NKJV). It is not something God does for us; it is something we must do. We can't do it without His grace, yet we must do it! We can be enticed by any wrong desires that we have not put under the Cross. If we have not put away our desire for the world's ways, then we can easily slip back to the world, as Israel did. For this reason Paul confesses, "The world has been crucified to me, and I to the world" (Gal. 6:14 NKJV).

After I preached a message of repentance in a church in California, the pastor took me out to eat and shared a personal testimony. When he was saved, he gave up many former sins that bound him. However, he could not shake his habit of smoking two packs of cigarettes a day. He said, "John, I did everything scriptural that I knew to do to get rid of that addiction. I prayed, fasted, confessed the Word, and asked others for prayer. In fact, I responded to the invitations to come for prayer of every visiting minister to our church. I confessed my addiction and asked them to pray for my deliverance. I did that for two years." . . .

Over that two-year span the pastor told himself and others how he wanted to be free, yet it was not his true desire, only his intention. That is why he was so easily drawn to what he said he did not want. Then God exposed his true desire. Once he repented of that desire, placing it under the power of the Cross, the grace of God was there to free him. His deliverance was a cooperation between God and him.

Today we soften the message of the Cross for those who have come out of Hollywood, professional sports, public life, or some other walk of life greatly entangled with the world's system. We make concessions for them and excuse their worldly mannerisms or ways. We do this to their harm, not their good. When we preach a softer gospel to them, we block their way to the mountain of the Lord. They start out with excitement, yet gradually gravitate back to the world. If they do not go all the way back, they form a "Jesus" who is nothing like the

One sitting on the right hand of God. They may confess salvation and a desire to know the Lord, but they are out of touch with their true desires. Their true desires are in the world's system. They are professing believers who are conformed to the world.[14]

—*John Bevere*

HOW CAN I PRAY HONESTLY?

When you pray for your marriage or the marriage of a child or loved one, how do you pray? Do you feel compelled not just to go into detail but also to tell God how to fix what's wrong? Do you think you have to use your holy imagination to come up with a plan so you can pray specifically? Perhaps you have that unconscious attitude that "God helps those who help themselves." If so, do you frantically try to add sparkle to your marriage with movies or trips or parties or money or clothes or music? Yet try as creatively as you might, pray as imaginatively as you can, have you found that you just can't re-create the "wine"? It's gone.

Could you do what Mary did? She clearly and simply stated the problem: "They have no more wine." Perhaps in your case your prayer would be simply: "The love has run out," or, "There's no zest or joy or real life in the family anymore."

Jesus responded tenderly to Mary: "Dear woman, why do you involve me? . . . My time has not yet come" (John 2:4). Although kind and respectful, His response also sounds a little aloof, almost indifferent and uncaring. And it gives the impression that He doesn't intend to do anything about the problem.

If you have prayed for your marriage or that of a child or friend, has Jesus' answer seemed confusing? Do you feel that nothing will ever change? Has He appeared indifferent or unwilling to get involved? Sometimes His answer addresses not just the specific need we have brought to His attention but also something deeper.

In Mary's case, Jesus was not just her son but God's Son as well. And as God's Son, He knew what was in her heart. Apparently, she wanted to solve the problem for the young couple, to save their marriage, but she also had a hidden agenda and it was the hidden agenda that He addressed. Let's listen closely as we read between the lines of their conversation:

"Son, I know Who You are. I conceived You when I was a virgin. And I've watched You for thirty years. I've heard Your wisdom, I've witnessed Your patience, I've experienced Your love, I've seen Your joy, I've benefited from Your strength. In the last six weeks, I've heard the town talk about Your baptism by Your cousin John and how he identified You as the Lamb of God Who would take away the sin of the world. And there are many witnesses to Your Father's voice reverberating from heaven in approval.

"You've gathered some terrific, tough, thoughtful young men around You. With a mother's intuition, I know You are getting ready to make Your move. After all these years, You are finally going to reveal Yourself and declare Who You are. You are not Joseph's son; You are God's Son. You are Israel's long-awaited Messiah. And Jesus, I think this wedding celebration, in the presence of so many friends, would be a wonderful place to begin letting people know Who You are. Son, do something about the wine."

PRAYER REFLECTION

Through prayer, God establishes a trust relationship with you and me. Our faith is enlarged when God's activity becomes evident in our lives. Therefore, prayer is an act of obeying God.

—*Ronnie W. Floyd*

"Ma'am, search your heart. What is your real reason for asking Me to help this young couple? Are you trying to manipulate Me into performing a miracle so that your friends will know what you already know, that I am not only your son, but also God's Son? The timing and agenda for My public ministry have been set by God. I can't run ahead of Him or allow Myself to be pushed ahead of Him, even by My own mother."

Are there hidden agendas in your prayers? Are you praying for God to save your marriage to avoid being humiliated or rendered financially devastated by divorce, instead of striving to glorify Him?

Is there a hidden agenda in your prayer for the marriage of your child? Are you praying for that marriage because you're afraid that if your child fails, your own carefully cultivated reputation might be tarnished? Or because you don't want the responsibility of raising your grandchildren?

"Why do you involve Me?" is Jesus' challenge to us to search our hearts for hidden motives in our intercession for ourselves or for others. Why are we really asking for help?

Are you asking for physical healing because you're tired of feeling bad? Are you asking for financial relief because you're tired of budgeting? Are you asking for a better job because you want more prestige?

So many of our requests, when we listen to ourselves closely, are rooted in selfishness and pride. While Jesus understands the feelings of our infirmities—He knows how hard it is to feel sick all the time, He knows the constant struggle of trying to make ends meet, He knows our need to feel worthwhile—glorifying God should be our bottom-line agenda.

Regardless of her hidden agenda, Mary's faith was evident in that she went to Jesus for help. She may not have understood the larger picture of God's timing for His life, but she did understand the potential destruction to the marriage of the young couple if it became public knowledge that the wine had run out. She knew Jesus would do something, even if it wasn't what she expected. How did she know? Because she knew Him well enough to know He cares about the smallest details of our lives as well as the largest details in the world. She knew Him well enough to know He cares about, not just spiritual things like salvation, justification, sanctification, and glorification, but also about everyday, practical things like wine and a wedding party. Intense emotional things. Intimate personal things.

Mary may not have known and understood everything, but she knew Jesus cared. And she knew that in order for Him to have the freedom to make a difference, she would have to place total control of the situation in His hands.[15]

—*Anne Graham Lotz*

HOW DOES SIN AFFECT MY PRAYER LIFE?

Jesus promised in John 15:7, "If you remain in me and my words remain in you, ask whatever you wish, and it will be given you." But he mentions two conditions: if we are not abiding and if we are not obeying, we will not have that power.

Sin prevents us from having power in prayer. "The eyes of the Lord are on the righteous and his ears are attentive to their prayer, but the face of the Lord is against those who do evil" (1 Peter 3:12). There are two kinds of sin. The first is global sin. It is referred to in the singular—sin, not sins. Since Adam and Eve, everyone born on this planet is born in a state of sin.

In John 16:5–11 Jesus tells the disciples he will not stay with them, but he will send the Holy Spirit who will convict the world of sin. And earlier he said, "Whoever does not believe stands condemned already because he has not believed in the name of God's one and only Son" (John 3:18). That is global sin, and we are all born into it. We leave that state of sin the moment we accept Jesus Christ. Then we are justified and we become new creations in Jesus Christ. God sees us as if we had never sinned (1 John 1:9), and we are not condemned (Romans 8:1).

The second class of sin has to do with specific offenses. It is referred to in the plural—sins—and is mentioned in the Lord's Prayer: "Forgive us our debts [or sins], as we also have forgiven our debtors [those who sin against us]" (Matthew 6:12). These are the sins we commit after we become Christians.

In our prayer seminars, I spend the first hour telling the participants about the power of prayer and the answers to prayer that are possible. Then I read a list of twenty-three Bible verses about sin. This opens our minds to our sin—not our shortcomings or our personality traits, but our sin. After that, we meet in groups of four and everyone confesses out loud a sin or sins. This is the first time the participants are asked to pray aloud, and it is a powerful time.

> **PRAYER REFLECTION**
>
> *Lord, help me to let go of my past so that I can move into all You have for me. I know that You make all things new. Renew my mind and soul so that I don't allow past experiences to color my life today. Show me who I need to forgive, and help me forgive them completely. Heal me of all the painful memories in my life so that I can become all You created me to be.*
>
> —Stormie Omartian

After this I say, "I want to give you a chance to pray one more prayer. If by some chance you are not absolutely sure you know Jesus Christ as Savior and Lord, I want you, having now confessed your sin, to pray."

I quote Mark 1:15, "Repent and believe the good news!" It isn't believe and repent, it's repent and believe. They have already repented and confessed their sin; now all that is left is to believe and to ask Jesus Christ to become Savior and Lord.

Once we have asked forgiveness for our sin and our sins, we are ready to experience God's power in prayer.[16]

—*Evelyn Christenson*

HOW DO MY EMOTIONS AFFECT MY PRAYER LIFE?

Emotions are the feelings that fuel our reactions to life's challenges. They can make us soar to the heights of happiness or plunge us into the depths of despair. Sometimes our emotions burst out abruptly and surprise us—like when we cry at a wedding, laugh at a funeral, or get angry over a hairbrush.

> **PRAYER REFLECTION**
>
> *You don't pray to change God's will; you pray to become part of it.*
> —Randy Southern

Emotions can make a person say or do things he or she will regret for a lifetime. They can dent a friendship, damage a relationship, or destroy a marriage. Out of control, emotions can become the most destructive force in the world. Yet, properly guarded, emotions can be a powerful force for good.

We can't always control the initial outbursts of emotion, but we can learn to deal with them. If we don't, our emotions may destroy our relationships with family and friends. Ultimately they will destroy us, too, if we let them. . . .

Emotion is our primary motivating force. It propels our personalities, decisions, choices, and values. More and more, psychologists are coming to realize that emotions are often the cause of our behavior as well as the result of our behavior. Only when we realize that our emotions are related to our hunger for God and what He can provide can we begin to understand our own wrestling match with God. Allender observes that our emotions express our frustration with God and yet invite us to surrender to God. "We are to struggle with God until our heart surrenders to his goodness," he writes. "The proper focus of emotion is God. Once we see that struggling with God is not a sign of spiritual deficiency, but spiritual depth and hunger that drive us to taste the goodness of God . . ."

Christian psychologist Larry Crabb describes spirituality as "that profound engagement with God that establishes identity, ignites love, and releases uniqueness." He points out that counselors sometimes bypass true spirituality in their hurry to solve the very problems God may be using to drive people closer to Himself. It is here in the depth of the human heart that we meet God personally.

We see this illustrated over and over again in the terrorist attacks on New York City. Countless people stand at "Ground Zero" staring at the ruins of the World Trade Center. They are looking for answers to their deepest hurts. Searching for hope, they often turn to God.

One of the most unusual experiences of our time has been the spiritual awakening that has come to America in the days following the terrorist attacks. People have spontaneously turned to God while the secular culture has remained silent because it has no answers for the human heart. . . .

The heart is the emotional center of our lives. It is neurologically connected to every organ of your body. If the emotional center is disturbed, you will be upset and bothered by virtually everything. But if the emotional center of our beings is controlled by the Holy Spirit, we can experience His fruit of love, joy, peace, and patience. Everything our hearts desire for personal fulfillment can be provided by God. He alone can fill the vacuum of the empty human heart and fill it with the power and presence of God.

Spiritual growth is the result of the Spirit's work in our lives. Without Him, we can only attempt to develop a heart for God by the best self-effort we can muster. Otherwise, spiritual growth results from seeking God with all our hearts. . . .

The key to handling our emotions is learning to trust what God tells us to do about them. Too many people want to make their own decisions and then ask God to "bless" what they have already decided. Instead, we need to figure out what God wants us to do and do it with the confidence that He will bless it. Our obedience to His commands places us in a position to receive His blessings in our lives.

Our willingness to trust God in every circumstance of life depends on our confidence in His love. All uncertainty on our parts is an expression of distrust in His love. It is a basic rejection of God's character and nature. When we fail to trust Him with our problems, we are really distrusting His sincerity and integrity. Because He truly is an all-loving God with our best interests in mind, we must learn to trust His love for us in spite of our circumstances. . . .

Prayers of the heart open the deepest core issues of our lives to the grace of God. They are the constant expressions of our hearts toward God. The apostle Paul referred to this when he told us to "pray without ceasing" (1 Thessalonians 5:17). The psalmist expresses this idea when he says, "My soul waits for the Lord more than those who watch for the morning" (Psalm 130:6). In Psalm 42:1–2, the psalmist cries, "As the deer pants for the water brooks, so pants my soul for You, O God. My soul thirsts for God, for the living God. When shall I come and appear before God?"[17]

—*Tim LaHaye and Ed Hindson*

I'M TOO BUSY TO PRAY.

Prayer is measured, not by time, but by intensity. Earnest souls . . . hear of others who sometimes remain on their knees before God all day or all night, refusing food and scorning sleep, whilst they pray and pray and pray. They naturally wonder, "Are we to do the same?

Must all of us follow their examples?" We must remember that those men of prayer did not pray by time. They continued so long in prayer because they could not stop praying.

. . . Some have ventured to think that . . . we must all follow in their train. Child of God, do not let any such thought—such fear?—distress you. Just be willing to do what He will have you do—what He leads you to do. Think about it; pray about it. We are bidden by the Lord Jesus to pray to our loving Heavenly Father. We sometimes sing, "Oh, how He loves!" And nothing can fathom that love.

. . . Prayer is not given us as a burden to be borne, or an irksome duty to fulfill, but to be a joy and power to which there is no limit. It is given us that we "may find grace to help us in time of need" (Hebrews 4:16). And every time is a "time of need." "Pray ye" is an invitation to be accepted rather than a command to be obeyed. Is it a burden for a child to come to his father to ask for some boon? How a father loves his child, and seeks its highest good! How he shields that little one from any sorrow or pain or suffering! Our heavenly Father loves us infinitely more than any earthly father. The Lord Jesus loves us infinitely more than any earthly friend. . . . Our dear, loving Father knows all about us. He sees. He knows how little leisure some of us have for prolonged periods of prayer.

. . . A little pile of letters lies before me as I write. . . . Those letters tell of many who cannot get away from others for times of secret prayer; of those who share even bedrooms; of busy mothers, and maids, and mistresses who scarcely know how to get through the endless washing and cooking, mending and cleaning, shopping and visiting; of tired workers who are too weary to pray when the day's work is done.

. . . Child of God, our heavenly Father knows all about it. He is not a taskmaster. He is our Father. If you have no time for prayer, or no chance of secret prayer, why, just tell Him all about it—and you will discover that you are praying!

. . . To those who seem unable to get any solitude at all, or even the opportunity of stealing into a quiet church for a few moments, may we point to the wonderful prayer-life of St. Paul? Did it occur to you that he was in prison when he wrote most of those marvelous prayers of his which we possess? Picture him. He was chained to a Roman soldier day and night, and was never alone for a moment. Epaphras was there part of the time, and caught something of his master's passion for prayer. St. Luke may have been there. What prayer-meetings! No opportunity for secret prayer. No! but how much we owe to the uplifting of those chained hands! You and I may be never, or rarely ever, alone, but at least our hands are not fettered with chains, and our hearts are not fettered, nor our lips

. . . Now, the inspired command is clear enough: "Pray without ceasing" (1 Thess. 5:17). . . . This, of course, cannot mean that we are to be always on our knees. I am convinced that God does not wish us to neglect rightful work in order to pray. But it is equally certain that we might work better and do more work if we gave less time to work and more to prayer. . . . Are there not endless opportunities during every day of "lifting up holy hands"—or at least holy hearts—in prayer to our Father? Do we seize the opportunity, as we open our eyes upon each new day, of praising and blessing our Redeemer? Every day is an Easter day to the Christian. We can pray as we dress. Without a reminder we shall often forget. Stick a piece of stamp-paper in the corner of your looking-glass, bearing the words,—"Pray without ceasing." Try it. We can pray as we go from one duty to another. We can often pray at our work. The washing and the writing, the mending and the minding, the cooking and the cleaning will be done all the better for it.

. . . Do not children, both young and old, work better and play better when some loved one is watching? Will it not help us ever to remember that the Lord Jesus is always with us, watching? Aye, and helping. The very consciousness of His eye upon us will be the consciousness of His power within us.[18]

—*Anonymous*

I'M BROKEN AND HURTING. DOES GOD CARE?

I've learned that if you want to attract His presence, brokenness is His favorite perfume and tears are His favorite anointing. When something happens in the course of life that breaks your heart or bruises your soul, pull the pain to you and offer it to the Lord. There have been times when I felt that I couldn't hurt anymore and live, but suddenly I sensed Him there.

It dawned on me that when that brokenness occurs in my life, He shows up and says, "Oh, I see you've put on My favorite fragrance again." He doesn't revel in our pain or loss, but He does respond to the brokenness and need in our lives.

God doesn't come to you simply because problems come along; He comes because you are *tender.* If you can learn to stay at that tender stage of brokenness *without* the necessity of contrary circumstances, then you will be "falling *on* the Rock" as opposed to having "the Rock fall on *you.* " Both create the same fragrance of brokenness, but one is self-induced and the other one is circumstantially induced. . . .

Can you hear the footsteps of Jesus coming as He says, "I smell My favorite fragrance"? He is near to them who are of a broken heart; He can't turn His face away from brokenness. . . .

Often the presence of God hangs heavy in our prayer rooms and churches, but ten minutes after we leave them, the presence has lifted from us. Are you frustrated with that process?

The secret may be that the fragrance that drew His presence didn't come from you. Were you enjoying the fragrance of someone else's brokenness? Perhaps that is why you have nothing to carry home with you once you leave a service.

> **PRAYER REFLECTION**
> *Prayer is an act of worship by which you confess your reverence and dependence on God.*
> —*Charles Stanley*

If you're just enjoying the fragrance of others, you may never know whose brokenness brings fragrance in the room. I can tell you this: God's manifest presence will go home only with the one whose brokenness summoned Him. . . .

Remember, a baby's cry of weakness can access the strength of the Father faster than the speed of light. If you *never* chase Him, you can *never* catch Him. Besides, your weakness will qualify you for a miracle if you put your hunger and desperation on open display. Put a voice to your frustration and cry out to Him.

Zacchaeus is about to climb the tree of destiny. He has no idea that his earthly wealth will be reduced by the end of the evening meal, nor does he know that his spiritual wealth will reach cosmic proportions once he sheds his pride and climbs a sycamore tree to meet his Master.

It's time for all of us to drop our pride of position and climb the tree of destiny. We can't be late for our divine dinner appointment with the God of our dreams.

Are you desperate for God? It's time to abandon everything that would keep you blind and downtrodden in the dust of your spiritual poverty. Throw off the cloak of man's judgments and religious opinions. Follow the path of blind Bartimaeus. Stand up and let the stench of a life spent begging for the support and approval of man fall away forever.

Earthly brokenness creates heavenly openness. When the fountains of the great deep are broken up, the windows of heaven are opened up: "On that day all the fountains of the great deep were broken up, and the windows of heaven were opened." It's as if I can hear the creaking of the heavenly windows beginning to open. It's time to release the cry God can't deny:

"Daddy, I want *You!* "[20]

—*Tommy Tenney*

HOW CAN PRAYER HELP MY CHRISTIAN WALK?

"There is a budding morrow in midnight." And every juncture, every relation, and every pressure of life has in it a germ of possibility and promise for our growth in God and grace; which germ to rear is the work of constant and progressive prayer. (For as a soul has a history, prayer has its progress.) This germ we do not always see, nor can we tend it as if we did. It is often hidden up under the earthly relations, and may there be lost. . . . But also it may from there be saved . . . its growth is often visible only to the Saviour whom we keep near by prayer, whose search we invoke, and for whose action we make room in prayer. Our certainty of Him is girt round with much uncertainty, about His working, about the steps of His process. But in prayer we become more and more sure that He is sure, and knows all things to His end. All along Christ is being darkly formed within us as we pray; and our converse with God goes on rising to become an element of the intercourse of the Father and the Son, whom we overhear, as it were, at converse in us. Yet this does not insulate us from our kind; for other people are then no more alien to us, but near in a Lord who is to them what He is to us. Private prayer may thus become more really common prayer that public prayer is.

And so also with the universe itself as we rise in Christ to prayer. Joined with its Redeemer . . . we are made members of its vast whole. We are not detained and cramped in a sectional world. We are not planted in the presence of an outside, alien universe, nor in the midst of a distraught, unreconciled universe, which speaks like a crowd, in many fragments and many voices. . . . This world is not now a desert haunted by demons. And it is more than a vestibule to another; it is its prelude in the drama of all things. . . . The faith that energizes in Christian prayer sets us at the centre of that whole of which Nature is the overture part. The steps of thought and its processes of law fade away. They do not cease to act, but they retire from notice. We grasp the mobile organization of things deep at its constant and trusty heart. We receive the earnest of our salvation—Christ in us.

> There, where one centre reconciles all things,
> The world's profound heart beats.

We are planted there. . . . We are already all that we are to be. We possess our souls in the prayer which is real communion with God. We enter by faith upon that which to sight and history is but a far future reversion. When He comes to our prayer He brings with Him all that He purposes to make us. We are already the "brave creature" He means us to be. More than our desire is fulfilled—our soul is. In such hour or visitation we realize our soul or person at no one stage of it, but in its fullness, and in the context of its whole and final place in history, the world, and eternity. A phase which has no meaning in itself, yet carries, like the humble mother of a great genius, an eternal meaning in it. And we can seize that meaning in prayer; we can pierce to what we are at our true course and true destiny, i.e. what we are to God's grace. Laws and injunctions such as "Love your neighbour," even "Love your enemy," then become life principles, and they are law pressures no more. The yoke is easy. Where all is forgiven to seventy times seven there is no friction and no grief any more. We taste love and joy. All the pressure of life then goes to form the crystals of faith. It is God making up His jewels.[21]

—*P. T. Forsyth*

WHAT IF I DON'T PRAY?

The worst sin is prayerlessness. Overt sin, or crime, or the glaring inconsistencies which often surprise us in Christian people are the effect of this, or its punishment. We are left by God for lack of seeking Him. The history of the saints shows often that their lapses were the fruit and nemesis of slackness or neglect in prayer. Their life, at seasons, also tended to become inhuman by their spiritual solitude. They left men, and were left by men, because they did not in their contemplation find God; they found but the thought or the atmosphere of God. Only living prayer keeps loneliness humane. It is the great producer of sympathy. Trusting the God of Christ, and transacting with Him, we come into tune with men. Our egoism retires before the coming of God, and into the clearance there comes with our Father our brother. We realize man as he is in God and for God, his Lover. When God fills our heart He makes more room for man than the humanist heart can find. Prayer is an act, indeed *the* act, of fellowship. We cannot truly pray even for ourselves without passing beyond ourselves and our individual experience. If we should begin with these the nature of prayer carries us beyond them, both to God and to man.

. . . Not to want to pray, then, is the sin behind sin. And it ends in not being able to pray. That is its punishment—spiritual dumbness . . . and starvation. We do not take our spiritual food, and so we falter, dwindle, and die. "In the sweat of your brow ye shall eat your bread." That has been said to be true both of physical and spiritual labour. It is true both of the life of bread and of the bread of life.

> ### PRAYER REFLECTION
> *Your prayers are more effective when you fill your mind with the Word of God. Letting it penetrate your heart will increase your knowledge of the truth that can liberate you.*
> —*Stormie Omartian*

Prayer brings with it, as food does, a new sense of power and health. We are driven to it by hunger, and, having eaten, we are refreshed and strengthened for the battle which even our physical life involves. For heart and flesh cry out for the living God. God's gift is free; it is, therefore, a gift to our freedom, i.e. renewal to our moral strength, to what makes men of us. Without this gift always renewed, our very freedom can enslave us. . . . Prayer is the assimilation of a holy God's moral strength.

We must work for this living. To feed the soul we must toil at prayer. And what a labour it is! "He prayed in an agony." We must pray even to tears if need be. Our cooperation with God is our receptivity; but it is an active, a laborious receptivity, an importunity that drains our strength away if it does not tap the sources of the Strength Eternal. We work, we slave, at receiving. To him that hath this laborious expectancy it shall be given. Prayer is the powerful appropriation of power, of divine power. It is therefore creative.

Prayer is not mere wishing. It is asking—with a will. Our will goes into it. It is energy. *Orare est laborare*. We turn to an active Giver; therefore we go into action. For we could not pray without knowing and meeting Him in kind. If God has a controversy with Israel, Israel must wrestle with God. Moreover, He is the Giver not only of the answer, but first of the prayer itself. His gift provokes ours. He beseeches us, which makes us beseech Him. And what we ask for chiefly is the power to ask more and to ask better. We pray for more prayer. The true "gift of prayer" is God's grace before it is our facility.[22]

—*P. T. Forsyth*

WILL MY PRAYER LIFE AFFECT MY SPIRITUAL GROWTH?

Have you ever noticed the way married couples and even good friends become more and more alike the longer they're together? It's a natural process. If you spend enough time with someone, that person's mannerisms, habits, sense of humor, and ways of thinking are bound to rub off on you eventually.

The same thing happens in prayer. If you spend enough time in conversation with God, eventually His way of thinking, His priorities, and His love are going to have an effect on you and the way you live. The more extreme your prayer life is, the more extreme the effect will be.

If you want to put a name on it, you could call these changes spiritual growth. It doesn't happen overnight. In fact, you may not even notice it for weeks, months, or even years after you start your quest for an intense prayer life. There's a good chance that other people will pick up on it before you do. You may notice subtle changes in the way people—especially other Christians—look at you.

You'll probably find yourself being offered more opportunities to be involved in different ministries. Depending on the circumstances, some people may even look to you to assume a leadership role. At that point, things tend to snowball. The more people recognize your spiritual development, the more they will seek you out when needs arise.

Look, your pastor isn't going to turn over Sunday morning services to you or

> ### PRAYER REFLECTION
> **A Prayer for Guidance**
> *O Lord, our God, teach us, we pray, to ask rightly for the right blessings. Steer the vessel of our soul toward your heart, the tranquil Haven of all storm-tossed souls. Show us the way we should go. Renew a willing spirit within us. Let your Spirit curb our wayward senses, and guide us to that which is our true good, to keep your laws, and in all our works to rejoice in your glorious and gladdening presence. For yours is the glory and praise from all saints forever and ever.*
> *Amen.*
> —*St. Basil*

anything like that. But as your spiritual life changes as a result of spending consistent quality time with God in prayer, your role in the family of God will change as well.

That's what passionate prayer can do. The only thing that competes with prayer for the effect it has on your spiritual life is spending time in God's Word.

So that raises an obvious question: What would happen if you incorporated Bible study into your prayer life? The answer? Prepare to have your spiritual life rocked.

We can find everything God wants us to know about Him and our relationship with Him in His Word. The Bible reveals God's heart, what He wants for us—and from us. When you use the Bible as part of your prayer life, you form an immediate bond with God. Using Scripture in your prayers gives you a clearer understanding of where God is coming from. What's more, you're much less likely to find yourself on a different page from God if you allow His Word to guide your words.

The psalmists knew how important God's Word was to their prayers. Psalm 119, the longest chapter in the entire Bible, is practically a textbook example of how to use Scripture in communicating with God.

Check out these highlights:

> Teach me, O LORD, the way of Your statutes,
> And I shall keep it to the end.
> Give me understanding, and I shall keep Your law;
> Indeed, I shall observe it with my whole heart.
> Make me walk in the path of Your commandments,
> For I delight in it.
> Incline my heart to Your testimonies,
> And not to covetousness.
> Turn away my eyes from looking at worthless things,
> And revive me in Your way.
> Establish Your word to Your servant,
> Who is devoted to fearing You.
> Turn away my reproach which I dread,
> For Your judgments are good.
> Behold, I long for Your precepts;
> Revive me in Your righteousness . . .

Oh, how I love Your law!

It is my meditation all the day.

You, through Your commandments,

make me wiser than my enemies;

For they are ever with me.

I have more understanding than all my teachers,

For Your testimonies are my meditation.

I understand more than the ancients,

Because I keep Your precepts.

I have restrained my feet from every evil way,

That I may keep Your word.

I have not departed from Your judgments,

For You Yourself have taught me.

How sweet are Your words to my taste,

Sweeter than honey to my mouth!

Through Your precepts I get understanding;

Therefore I hate every false way.[23]

—*Randy Southern*

HOW CAN I TRUST GOD TO ANSWER ME?

"Pray without ceasing," the Bible says (1 Thess. 5:17). That means praying constantly, making prayer a way of life. To pray without ceasing means that we draw near to God in everything we do—our work, relationships, hobbies, entertainment, travel, and the mundane activities of daily living. It means praying about everything so that we don't leave our lives to chance.

Jesus said, "Ask, and it will be given to you; seek, and you will find; knock, and it will be opened to you" (Matt. 7:7). The problem is that we neglect to ask. We don't take time to seek. And we forget to knock. We get busy trying to live our complex lives on our own terms. There is so much vying for our attention, so many decisions to be made, so many issues to deplete our strength, distort our thinking, and steal our peace. Perhaps our greatest sin is thinking we can handle any part of our lives without talking to God about it.

We need to ask God, and we need to be specific. We should keep knocking until the door opens to everything He has for us. But He doesn't want us to just ask for anything and everything, hoping He will get us out of the mess we're in or give us whatever we want. The Bible says, "You ask and do not receive, because you ask amiss that you may spend it on your pleasures" (James 4:3). When we merely ask for things without first drawing close to God, we can miss how we're supposed to pray.

Prayer should not be reduced to a mere formula, but there are important elements that are good to include if our prayers are to be as powerful as we want them to be. In prayer, we should try to:

- Tell God how much we love Him.
- Praise Him for who He is.
- Thank Him for all He has done.
- Declare our dependence on Him.
- Confess any sin in our lives.
- Share everything that is in our hearts.
- Tell Him our requests.
- Wait on Him to speak to our souls.
- Thank Him for hearing our prayers.

We will find that the more we pray, the more we will find to pray about. But we mustn't be discouraged if the answers to our prayers don't seem to come right away. Sometimes it takes a while. And often we don't even recognize the answers to our own prayers because they are not answered in the way or time we thought they would be. We can't limit God to our timetable. Our job is to pray; God's job is to answer. We can trust that God always hears our prayers; something is happening whether we can see it or not.

Jesus said, "If you ask anything in My name, I will do it" (John 14:14). That is his promise to us. So say to Him, "Lord, touch me with Your healing love and power. Meet my every need and open up my understanding to all You have for me where I am right now. Reveal Yourself to me in every situation I face. Show me what I need to see and tell me what I need to know.

> ### PRAYER REFLECTION
>
> *Holy Father, I am in awe at how much higher Your thoughts are than mine. Forgive me for expecting You to answer my prayers only to the extent I'm able to ask. Father, I never would plan to go to restricted places, to have courage to go where humanly it is too dangerous, could never plan to break down barriers humans have erected, or physically make it with my ordinary human body.*
>
> —*Evelyn Christenson*

81

Enable me to do what I have to do. For I know that without You, I can do nothing."[24]

—*Stormie Omartian*

THE POWER OF PRAYER

[focus on the power we have through prayer]

HOW DO MY PRAYERS HAVE POWER?

For many today, prayer is the weakest link in their chain of Christian experience. Their prayers are not very meaningful, and there is a lack of satisfaction in their prayer lives. But may I say to you, our Lord never intended for it to be that way. He said:

> And whatever you ask in My name, that I will do, that the
> Father may be glorified in the Son. If you ask anything in
> My name, I will do it. (John 14:13–14 NKJV)

What potential and possibility are contained in those verses! You see, our Lord meant for prayer to be vital, real, and powerful.

In his epistle to the Ephesians, Paul presented the armor that the believer is to put on in order to meet the enemy, Satan. Every bit of that armory is for defense, with the exception of two weapons of offense, both of which are to be wielded in the power of the Holy Spirit. One of those is the sword of the Spirit, or the Word of God. But will you notice the second:

> Praying always with all prayer and supplication in the
> Spirit, being watchful to this end with all perseverance and
> supplication for all the saints (Ephesians 6:18 NKJV).

Prayer, through the Holy Spirit, is a weapon of offense against Satan. You can't get much more powerful than that. Then Jude, who gave one of the most picturesque accounts of the apostasy that you'll find in Scripture, told the children of God:

> But you, beloved, building yourselves up on your most
> holy faith, praying in the Holy Spirit (Jude 20 NKJV).

Praying in the Holy Spirit is what gives us the power to live the Christian life . . .

The Holy Spirit brings power to our prayers, my beloved. Notice what Paul said to the Ephesians:

> Now to Him who is able to do exceedingly abundantly
> above all that we ask or think, according to the *power* that
> works in us (Ephesians 3:20 NKJV, emphasis mine).

For centuries, the tremendous power of the lowly atom lay dormant because no one knew anything about it or how to release it. Have you ever stopped to think that there may be other sources of power at our fingertips that we are absolutely ignorant of today? Well, I know of one: prayer. Prayer is a great, vast, and unexplored territory that we know practically nothing about. There is a reservoir of power there that has never been tapped. . . .

The principle for power, the formula, is *yielding!* Too many believers go through life today never learning to yield to the will of God in their prayer lives. But God says that if we will be filled with the Holy Spirit and yield to His will in prayer, we will have power with Him and with men. How we need that power today![1]

—J. Vernon McGee

HOW DOES PRAYER HELP WITH MY PROBLEMS?

Our first course of action when facing a problem should be to take our burden to God in prayer and praise Him for the answer. Believers in Jesus Christ can avail ourselves of the wisdom, power, and counsel of God Himself through the supernatural gift of prayer. Unbelievers have no such resource. They must deal with crises in their limited strength and wisdom.

As a follower of Christ, you have the immeasurable, fathomless power of prayer at your disposal. When you were saved by faith in Christ through the riches of His grace, you were given access to God: "Therefore, brethren, having boldness to enter the Holiest by the blood of Jesus . . . draw near with a true heart in full assurance of faith" (Heb. 10:19, 22). You are reconciled to Christ forever.[2]

—Charles Stanley

DOES GOD REALLY INVITE ME INTO HIS PRESENCE IN PRAYER?

God wants you to move in out of the cold and live . . . with him. Under his roof there is space available. At his table a plate is set. In his living room a wingback chair is reserved just for you. And he'd like you to take up residence in his house. Why would he want you to share his home?

Simple, he's your Father.

> **PRAYER REFLECTION**
>
> *To seek aid in time of distress from a supernatural Being is an instinct of human nature. I believe in the truthfulness of this instinct, and that man prays because there is something in prayer. As when the Creator gives His creature the power of thirst, it is because water exists to meet its thirst; and as when He creates hunger there is food to correspond to the appetite; so when He inclines men to pray it is because prayer has a corresponding blessing with it.*
>
> —C. H. Spurgeon

You were intended to live in your Father's house. Any place less than his is insufficient. Any place far from his is dangerous. Only the home built for your heart can protect your heart. And your Father wants you to dwell in him.

No, you didn't misread the sentence and I didn't miswrite it. Your Father doesn't just ask you to live *with* him, he asks you to live *in* him. As Paul wrote, "For in him we live and move and have our being" (Acts 17:28 NIV).

Don't think you are separated from God, he at the top end of a great ladder, you at the other. Dismiss any thought that God is on Venus while you are on earth. Since God is Spirit (John 4:23), he is next to you: God himself is our roof. God himself is our wall. And God himself is our foundation.

Moses knew this. "Lord," he prayed, "you have been our home since the beginning" (Ps. 90:1). What a powerful thought: God as your home. Your home is the place where you can kick off your shoes and eat pickles and crackers and not worry about what people think when they see you in your bathrobe.

Your home is familiar to you. No one has to tell you how to locate your bedroom; you don't need directions to the kitchen. After a hard day scrambling to find your way around in the world, it's assuring to come home to a place you know. God can be equally familiar to you. With time you can learn where to go for nourishment, where to hide for protection, where to turn for guidance. Just as your earthly house is a place of refuge, so God's house is a place of peace. God's house has never been plundered, his walls have never been breached.

God can be your dwelling place.

God *wants* to be your dwelling place. He has no interest in being a weekend getaway or a Sunday bungalow or a summer cottage. Don't consider using God as a vacation cabin or an eventual retirement home. He wants you under his roof now and always. He wants to be your mailing address, your point of reference; he wants to be your home. Listen to the promise of his Son, "If my people love me they will obey my teaching. My father will love them and we will come to them and make our home with them" (John 14:23).

For many this is a new thought. We think of God as a deity to discuss, not a place to dwell. We think of God as a mysterious miracle worker, not a house to live in. We think of God as a creator to call on, not a home to reside in. But our Father wants to be much more. He wants to be the one in whom "we live and move and have our being" (Acts 17:28 NIV).[3]

—*Max Lucado*

I WORRY ABOUT EVERYTHING. WILL PRAYER HELP?

God has promised us His peace. Not "just" peace, but an extraordinary, unexplainable, inexpressible peace. Jesus described it as an uncommon kind of peace. "Peace I leave with you; my peace I give you. I do not give to you as the world gives. Do not let your hearts be troubled and do not be afraid" (John 14:27).

What does that kind of peace have to do with prayer? Everything!

We can experience His divine peace as we commit our needs and concerns to Him in prayer. In Paul's epistle to the Philippians, he wrote, "Do not be anxious about anything, but in everything, by prayer and petition, with thanksgiving, present your requests to God. And the peace of God, which transcends all understanding, will guard your hearts and your minds in Christ Jesus" (Phil. 4:6–7).

Years ago I memorized this passage from *The Living Bible.* I have turned to it again and again. I have found it to be a wonderful prescription for escaping from anxiety and worry and for basking in the sunshine of God's peace. I have turned to it frequently in my own life and have often quoted it from the pulpit when I have been preaching. It is a wonderful paraphrase of Paul's message on prayer: "Don't worry about anything; instead, pray about everything; tell God your needs, and don't forget to thank him for his answers. If you do this, you will experience God's peace, which is far more wonderful than the human mind can understand. His peace will keep your thoughts and your hearts quiet and at rest as you trust in Christ Jesus."

> PRAYER REFLECTION
>
> *When it is hardest to pray,*
> *pray harder.*
> —*Martin Luther*

We need not worry. We need not walk through life burdened with anxiety. Instead, we can enjoy peace, God's peace.

Still, worrying is so natural for us. In fact, most areas of worry have little to do with reality. The concerns of worry are often the "what if" questions: "What if this or that happened?" "What if he doesn't show up?" "What if I get sick?" "What if I don't have enough money?"

Most people, even Christians, spend a lot of time worrying. The "Don't worry about anything" statement of Paul is rather radical. If we did not worry, what would we do with all our spare time? What would we substitute for worry? Paul's concise and practical answer is, "Instead, *pray* about everything," *Prayer helps replace worry.*

The practical results of this insight are impressive. No longer do we need to be uptight and irritable. No longer do we need to toss and turn with sleepless nights. No longer do we need to complain or fear. Instead, we can experience God's peace, which is "far more wonderful than the human mind can understand."

Worry can be dangerous to our health. It can bring ulcers, insomnia, or even heart attacks. In contrast, prayer can bring peace, the very peace of God.

Charles Swindoll has written about this great passage in his wonderful book, *Laugh Again.*

> Paul writes of God's peace which "shall guard your hearts and your minds." When he mentions peace as a "guard," he uses a military term for "marching sentry duty" around something valuable and/or strategic. As we rest our case, we transfer our troubles to God. "Corporal Peace" is appointed the duty of marching as a silent sentry around our minds and our emotions, calming us within. How obvious will it be to others? Go back and check—it will

"surpass all comprehension." People simply will not be able to comprehend the restful peace we will model. In place of anxiety—that thief of joy—we pray. We push the worrisome, clawing monster of pressure off our shoulders and hand it over to God in prayer. I am not exaggerating; I must do that hundreds of times every year. And I cannot recall a time when it didn't provide relief. In its place, always, comes a quietness of spirit, a calming of the mind. With a relieved mind, rest returns.

Prayer opens the doors of our hearts to this remarkable peace. As Paul wrote, "Let the peace of Christ rule in your hearts, since as members of one body you were called to peace. And be thankful" (Col. 3:15). God's peace can be so authentic and present in our lives in times of turmoil and trouble that others are amazed and can't understand it. At the same time, such situations give us a wonderful opportunity for Christian witness. When people inquire about our peace, we can share with them sensitively and lovingly that the source of that incredible peace is our Lord Jesus Christ. . . .

Our Lord's peace is available to each of His children all of the time. We simply need to avail ourselves of this priceless treasure by offering to our Lord prayers of faith.[4]

—*Paul Cedar*

WILL THE TIME I SPEND PRAYING REALLY MAKE A DIFFERENCE IN MY LIFE?

Just to pray without ceasing for one hour seemed like a monumental achievement in mastering a difficult spiritual discipline, but my deeper walk with Christ has truly been most meaningful to me. Yes, amazing answers to prayer elicit whoops and hollers and persevering prayer teaches endurance, but spending time with Jesus—perhaps as His disciples did, laughing, crying, complaining, proposing, deliberating, submitting, confessing, and praising—has been the joyful part of our walk together.

Had people told me ten, even five years ago that I would be a prayer motivator, I would not have believed them, nor would my closest friends. I am often prejudged as never serious, perhaps even flighty, until I open my mouth. And of all the suitable topics someone of my personality profile could begin to expound upon, prayer would—without exception—be the last one picked by others as the love of my life.

Perhaps that paradox is the greatest argument I have in my defense when others offer their reasons (or excuses) for not praying. My experience in prayer proves the point that it is not race, sex, denomination, vocation, or education that singles out a person to be an effective prayer. It is simply one's decision to spend time with the Lord. How one arrives at that decision, whether it is out of crisis, great need, humiliation, or persuasion, seems immaterial. It is a matter of one's time—priorities, personality, and profession all set aside and boiled down to one question: Will I make time for God?

When answered with a resounding, "Yes, no matter what the cost," then the inevitable results of a deeper walk with God occur *because of prayer.*

Prayer allows God's presence into all areas and aspects of one's life, beginning with simple, daily decisions and culminating with one's life's purpose. The combination of prayer and the Word takes conjecture out of life and replaces it with certainties. And in the *practice* of prayer one is escorted farther and deeper into knowing and loving God.

Therefore, imagine one's surprise in stopping after five years of a long journey to look back over the mountains and valleys, to assess progress and be in awe of the unexpected benefits of prayer. The results of diligent prayer appear as illustrious jewels of immeasurable wealth, and just to read a list of them is appealing, but to experience them as personal possessions is life-changing!

On that journey of daily prayer and Bible reading I have experienced *and* benefited in six areas of personal, spiritual growth, not because I am a woman in ministry, but because I am a person intent on spending time alone daily with God.

I discovered that

- ◆ Prayer fuels faith to dream and hope and risk.
- ◆ Prayer "woos" us to the Word by our *need* to hear God's response to our requests.
- ◆ Prayer teaches trust in God through waiting upon *His* timing.
- ◆ Prayer reveals God's plan and our purpose in opening up to us detailed directions for both the present and the future.
- ◆ Prayer releases God's power to live and walk in the supernatural realm of the Holy Spirit.
- ◆ Prayer unleashes love for God—emotional, real, and all-consuming.

Who, then, having thought through the benefits of prayer would consciously decide to eliminate, forget, or neglect time with God?[5]

—Becky Tirabassi

DO MY PRAYERS REALLY MAKE A DIFFERENCE IN WHAT HAPPENS?

We often hear the motto, "Prayer changes things" But does it? In one sense no, and in another sense yes. As already stated, our persistence in prayer is not for the purpose of manipulating God or getting Him to do something He is reluctant to do or that is contrary to His will. So in one sense prayer does not change God or what He has sovereignly decreed will take place. However, the Bible does occasionally refer to God's changing what He had in mind to do in certain situations. When God threatened to destroy Israel because of their idolatry (Exod.

> PRAYER REFLECTION
>
> *Nothing lies outside the reach of prayer except that which lies outside the will of God.*
>
> *—Andrew Murray*

32:9–10), Moses prayed on their behalf and God an-swered his prayer by not carrying through on His threat (32:11–14). Later Moses prayed that God would not bring His threatened plague on Israel because of their unbelief, and God answered that prayer, too (Num. 14:12, 20).

True, God is immutable; He does not change His essential character (Ps. 102:24–27; Isa. 46:9–10; Mal. 3:6; James 1:17). But sometimes in answer to prayer, He does alter His attitude or intention toward specific situations or individuals. Thomas Constable explains it this way:

> There are many instances in Scripture where God altered His attitude or intended action in response to certain conditions (Gen. 6:6–7; Ex. 32:14; Num. 14:20; Deut. 32:36; Judg. 2:18; 1 Sam. 15:11; 2 Sam. 24:16; 1 Chron. 21:15; Pss. 90:13; 135:14; Jer. 18:8; 26:3, 13, 19; 42:10; Hos. 11:8; Joel 2:13–14; Amos 7:3, 6; Jonah 3:9–10; 4:2; Rev. 2:15–22).
>
> But what about the verses that say God does not change His mind? There are several of these in the Bible (cf. Num.

23:19; 1 Sam. 15:29; Ps. 110:4 [also quoted in Heb. 9:21]; Rom. 11:29). The point of these statements is that God does not change His mind as man changes his. God is not fickle or capricious, nor will His ultimate purposes change. God will not change His mind with respect to the major aspects of His decree. He has, however, changed His mind with regard to minor negotiable matters.

The parent-child analogy is . . . helpful. There are some things about which a good father who is in control of his family will not change his mind no matter how hard his child may try to convince him. "No, you may not play on the highway. You may as well stop asking me because there is nothing you can say that will convince me to let you do that." But there are other things about which he is open to influence. "Yes, you may have a chocolate ice cream cone rather than strawberry, if you prefer." Or, "Since you have done what I asked you to do, I am going to take you to the baseball game this weekend."

In other words, some of God's actions are dependent on other conditions. "If the Israelites would obey Him, He would bless them; but if they disobeyed, He would discipline them (Deut. 27–28; Josh. 8:30–35). If Christians walk in loving obedience to the Lord, He will cause them to increase and abound in their spiritual benefits (Eph. 3:14–19; Col. 2:6–7)."

On the other hand, no amount of praying will alter certain purposes of the Lord. This is seen, for example, in His promise to bless Abraham and His descendants (Gen. 12:1–3; 15:7–21) and in His promise never again to destroy the world with a flood (8:21–22). And if a person dies without receiving Christ as his or her Savior, that individual will not have eternal life (Matt. 25:46; John 3:18, 36). Joshua's praying did not alter God's intention to punish Achan for his sin (Josh. 7:6–13). Nor did prayer keep the Lord from sending the people of Judah into captivity as a result of their continued rebellion (Jer. 14:11–12).

> **PRAYER REFLECTION**
>
> *If you love God, you cannot be at a loss for something to say to Him.*
> —*Matthew Henry*

Prayer, however, is one of the means by which God accomplishes certain plans. He has designed that we pray for the salvation of the lost (e.g., Rom. 10:1), for the sending of more missionaries (Matt. 9:38), and for the spiritual growth of believers (Col. 1:9–12). He has chosen to do certain things in response to prayer. He delivered Lot and his family in response to Abraham's prayers (Gen. 18), and the Lord spared the Israelites when they were under attack by the Philistines in response to Samuel's intercessory praying (1 Sam. 7:5–9).

Sometimes, then, prayer does change certain things—God's actions, people's responses, circumstances. In another sense some things will never be changed. But another aspect of change that can come about through prayer is our own attitudes. Prayer can change us. We benefit ourselves by praying. We mature spiritually as we depend on God in prayer; we experience spiritual blessings as we fellowship with the Lord in prayer; we are encouraged as we pray.[6]

—*Paul Cedar*

WHY SHOULD I PRAY IF GOD ALREADY KNOWS EVERYTHING?

Omnipresent, omnipotent, omniscient—three words that certainly sound awesome enough to apply to a god. And they are true of our wonderful God! The fact that he is omnipresent—everywhere at once—gives us security or reminds us that our sins cannot be hidden. His omnipotence—the fact that he has all power—assures us that there is nothing too hard for God. Sometimes we wonder why he does not use that power to immediately right some of the injustices of this world, but we are usually able to believe (if not fully understand) that he has chosen to limit his power on earth for this era of time.

But even those of us who love the Lord sometimes have trouble with the idea that a God who is omniscient—who knows everything—needs to be asked for things in prayer. Especially with our business-minded American efficiency, it seems like some immense waste of time to bother God with every little thing that he already knows. But strange as it seems, God has also chosen to limit this feature of his ability, so that it becomes necessary, in most cases, for people to ask for blessings and help in order for them to receive it.

Probably the best reason for us to pray, even though God knows what we need, is because Jesus did it. He is always our supreme example (Hebrews 12:2).

When Jesus prayed for Lazarus to be raised from the dead, he made an interesting statement. "Jesus looked up and said, 'Father, I thank you that you have heard me. I knew that you always hear me, but I said this for the benefit of the people standing here, that they may believe that you sent me'" (John 11:41, 42). Notice what Jesus did not say. He did not say, "Father I know you know this already, but I'm asking you just for these people to hear it." There did not seem to be any question in his mind about the idea that he needed to ask. Rather, he made the prayer an example in order to prove that the Father had heard his request. The Father always hears us, but we are responsible for the asking. Jesus himself followed this rule.

> **PRAYER REFLECTION**
>
> *Our estimation of prayer is shown by how much time we give to it.*
> —E. M. Bounds

Jesus still lives in heaven to pray for us. Hebrews 7:25 says he "always lives to intercede." Prayer is somehow an integral part of the very being of God: God the Son asks things of God the Father, and they are done! Hebrews 4:13–16 addresses the very question we are asking: "[God] knows about everyone, everywhere. Everything about us is bare and wide open to [him]. . . . Jesus the Son . . . has gone to heaven itself to help us. . . . So let us come boldly to the very throne of God . . . to receive his mercy and to find grace to help us in our times of need" (TLB).

In a very real way, this is a continuation of the idea that God chooses to work through us. Mankind was created in God's image, and was given dominion over the earth. Men and women were given the power to control the destiny of this world. God's original and continuing purpose for earth was that people would fulfill his will. Adam and Eve talked with God in the garden. Because this seems so remote, and sinless creation so different from what we now know, we don't seem to think of this as prayer. But it was. God and Adam communicated about the destiny of this world. God himself brought the animals to Adam to be named. . . .

The best advice on the topic that I've ever read comes from a flying horse named Fledge. In *The Magician's Nephew* by C. S. Lewis, two children are sent by Aslan on a mission that will influence the destiny of Narnia for many years. They ride on Fledge's back for a whole day, and when they come down to rest for the night, Fledge begins a dinner of fresh green grass. The children realize that they have nothing to eat (much to the surprise of the horse, who didn't know they couldn't eat grass). Tempers begin to flare and the boy, Digory, says, "Well, I do think someone might have arranged about our meals."

"I'm sure Aslan would have, if you'd asked him," said Fledge.

"Wouldn't he know without being asked?" said Polly.

"I've no doubt he would," said the Horse (still with his mouth full). "But I've a sort of idea he likes to be asked."[7]

—Joan H. Young

IF GOD KNOWS MY NEEDS BEFORE I ASK HIM, WHY SHOULD I ASK?

"But when ye pray," says He, "do not speak much, as the heathen do; for they think that they shall be heard for their much speaking." As it is characteristic of the hypocrites to exhibit themselves to be gazed at when praying, and their fruit is to please men, so it is characteristic of the heathen, i.e of the Gentiles, to think they are heard for their much speaking. And in reality, every kind of much speaking comes from the Gentiles, who make it their endeavour to exercise the tongue rather than to cleanse the heart. . . ."Be not ye, therefore, like unto them," says the only true Master. "For your Father knoweth what things are necessary for you, before ye ask Him." For if many words are made use of with the intent that one who is ignorant may be instructed and taught, what need is there of them for Him who knows all things, to whom all things which exist, by the very fact of their existence, speak, and show themselves as having been brought into existence; and those things which are future do not remain concealed from His knowledge and wisdom, in which both those things which are past, and those things which will yet come to pass, are all present and cannot pass away?

But again, it may be asked (whether we are to pray in ideas or in words) what need there is for prayer itself, if God already knows what is necessary for us; unless it be that the very effort involved in prayer calms and purifies our heart, and makes it more capacious for receiving the divine gifts, which are poured into us spiritually. For it is not on account of the urgency of our prayers that God hears us, who is always ready to give us His light, not of a material kind, but that which is intellectual and spiritual: but we are not always ready to receive, since we are inclined towards other things, and are involved in darkness through our desire for temporal things. Hence there is brought about in prayer a turning of the heart to Him, who is ever ready to give, if we will but take what He has given; and in the very act of turning there is effected a purging of the inner eye, inasmuch as those things of a temporal kind which were desired are excluded, so that the vision of the pure heart may be able to bear the pure light, divinely shining, without any setting or change: and not only to bear it, but also to remain in it; not merely without annoyance, but also with ineffable joy, in which a life truly and sincerely blessed is perfected.[8]

—*Augustine*

WHAT DOES IT MEAN TO PRAY FOR GOD'S WILL?

When we decide to follow Jesus, we must first "deny" ourselves and move from our own agenda to His. We need to turn from our own desires and preferences to follow Him in all we do. The apostle Paul stated this truth in forthright terms: "For Christ's love compels us, because we are convinced that one died for all, and therefore all died. And he died for all, that those who live should no longer live for themselves, but for him who died for them and was raised again" (2 Cor. 5:14–15). . . .

Prayer is not merely asking Jesus for what we think we want for ourselves or others. Even if our motives are sincere and our desires are noble, our prayers need to be more than that. We need to pray for God's will to be done. We need to ask for things that will strengthen our faith in Christ and will advance His work. . . .

We must surrender our will to God; we must surrender all we are and have, even our loved ones.

Many professing Christians, even leaders, seem to violate this basic principle of prayer. Often they pray for their own will to be done rather than God's, and then they wonder why their prayers are not answered. As a result, many become frustrated, angry, and even bitter because they contend that God has not answered their prayers. They simply do not seem to understand that the Lord has not forsaken them. He loves us deeply and wants to supply all we need.

In truth, the Lord has answered their prayers. He has said no to their request. In essence He has said, "My child, I love you, and I want what is best for you. I cannot grant your request because it would be harmful to you or to others or to the advancement of My work."

James 4:3 prompts us to think about the why of our praying. For example, why does a pastor pray for increased attendance in his church? Is it so he will have a reputation for being "successful" or is it so more people will be reached with the gospel and ministered to by the Word? Why do church elders pray for increased giving by believers in the congregation? Is it so they can have funds to build a facility larger than other churches in the community, or is it so people will learn the joy of giving and of being wise stewards of God's resources? Why does a Sunday school teacher pray that her lesson will "go over" well? Is it so she will have the reputation of being the best teacher in that Sunday school, or is it so her students will learn and apply the Word? The basic concern in our praying should always be for God's glory and not ours (John 14:13).

PRAYER REFLECTION

When we are praying, the thought will often cross our minds that (if only we knew it) the event is already decided one way or the other. I believe this to be no good reason for ceasing our prayers. The event certainly has been decided—in a sense it was decided "before all worlds." But one of the things that really cause it to happen may be this very prayer that we are now offering.

—C. S. Lewis

If we are to be effective in prayer and Christian discipleship, we ... must come to the place of surrender to our Lord. The goal of our lives must no longer be to live for our pleasures or even to live in a "comfort zone."

Dwight L. Moody expressed that truth with this practical advice about how we should pray: "Spread out your petition before God, and then say, 'Thy will, not mine, be done.' The sweetest lesson I have learned in God's school is to let the Lord choose for me."

That is where God wants us to be. That is where He meets us. He will always respond to that kind of praying.[9]

—Paul Cedar

DOES IT REALLY MATTER IF I DON'T PRAY?

Just as the Public Safety Department of the Automobile Club of Southern California has developed a survey indicating possible problem drinkers—answer one yes and consider it a warning to your problem, two yes answers and you just might be, and three yes answers mean you most likely are a problem drinker—so O. Hallesby has developed a list of the dangerous results of prayerlessness:

♦ We have more "world" in our thoughts.

- We feel farther away from God.
- We have less "God " talk in our conversations with others.
- Slowly an unwilling or rebellious spirit creeps into our personality.
- Sin doesn't sting as much, because it is less honestly confessed.
- We deal with sin as the world does, by hiding it!

Isn't it *almost* humorous how those with the disease are the least likely to pick up a book or be involved in a setting where they would ever hear a convicting message? But like some reading this book even now, if I had read a list of the results of neglected prayer, such as the one above, perhaps I would have been caught long before I had reached a serious, spiritual drought.

It's too bad that the word *prayer* on the cover of a book or in the title of a workshop can keep us from what has the potential to radically release a supernatural power to change our lives while here on earth. So what is left? Not much! But that's where it seems that the victory over prayerlessness begins . . . with helplessness.

> **PRAYER REFLECTION**
>
> *If you want God to hear you when you pray, you must hear Him when He speaks.*
>
> —*Thomas Brooks*

Andrew Murray in his classic, *The Prayer Life,* devotes numerous chapters to the issue of prayerlessness in a believer's life. A sincere study of his findings, consolations, rebukings, and encouragement offers great hope to someone discouraged by self-effort and continuous lack of victory in the pursuit of a *true* prayer life.

He says,

> My advice to you is: Give over your restlessness and effort; *fall helpless* at the feet of the Lord Jesus; He will speak the word, and your soul will "live." If you have done this, then, second, comes the message: "This is but the beginning of everything. *It will require deep earnestness,* and the exercise of all your power, and a watchfulness of the entire heart— eager to detect the least backsliding. Above all, it will require a *surrender* to a life of self-sacrifice that God really desires to see in us and which He will work out for us."

Bottom line, he powerfully suggests,

If we recognize, in the first place, that a right relationship to the Lord Jesus, above all else, *includes prayer;* with both the desire and power to pray according to God's will, then we have something which gives us the right to rejoice in Him and to rest in Him (emphasis added).

Once again, like alcoholics faced with the truth of the problem, we as believers are forced to examine our own prayer lives in the privacy of our hearts. It is only then, with complete dependency upon the Holy Spirit and *His* renewing, revealing power, that we can allow God to speak to us, perhaps as we have never before experienced Him, regarding our relationship with Him and our prayer lives.

Perhaps it is time for you to

- Let God convince you that prayerlessness in a believer's life is sin.
- Admit your helplessness.
- Confess your sin and accept God's forgiveness.
- Be encouraged that you are not alone in the world, but you may be a trailblazer for prayer in your home, youth group, church, organization, city, synod, or state.

Then as C. S. Lewis put it, be challenged to change with "a fellow-patient in the same hospital who, having been admitted a little earlier, could give some advice."[10]

—*Becky Tirabassi*

WHAT ABOUT PRAYING WITH OTHER PEOPLE?

Agreeing prayer

I say to you that if two of you agree on earth concerning anything that they ask, it will be done for them by My Father in heaven. For where two or three are gathered together in My name, I am there in the midst of them (Matthew 18:19–20 NKJV).

I have a prayer partner who lives 2,500 miles away from me. When we first became prayer partners, we lived only about 45 miles apart. In reality, both distances were far enough to cause us to pray over the telephone for the past eleven years.

Early in my prayer discovery, God used our friendship and prayer partnership to teach about the principle of agreeing prayer. But prior to my discovery of prayer in February of 1984, I always felt that prayer partners and prayer rooms were for older people or for prayer warriors. None of those titles appealed to me, so I avoided them. . . .

We came together as prayer partners naturally. Immediately following my decision to pray for one hour a day, Kinney was the first friend I challenged to join me in my prayer hour. Our friendship was relatively new at that time because her husband was recently named to the board of directors of Cleveland Youth For Christ and my husband was the executive director of Cleveland Youth For Christ. We were about the same age (thirty years old), and both had been Christians for only eight years.

Not coincidentally as my enthusiasm and commitment bubbled over afresh about prayer, her enthusiasm for prayer grew. As I barraged her with my exciting discoveries about prayer and as the determination to write my prayers became a discipline in my life, she was the first to hear about them. She also was the local friend who kept me accountable to my hour prayer commitment.

The answers to prayer that we witnessed seemed so awesome, even miraculous, that we found ourselves agreeing more and more often in prayer. We would even meet in parking lots, halfway between our homes, to pray! . . .

If Kinney and I had been close friends one year earlier, we probably wouldn't have felt that strongly about the power of prayer. But for the previous eight months, we had been on a wild jungle safari, uncovering new truths about prayer as two young thirty-year-olds finally getting serious about the serious things of God. Not having other options or answers, we impulsively decided to visit the prayer room.

As we walked into the empty room, I mused that it was a first-ever visit to a prayer room in my entire life. Compelled to kneel by two chairs, we prayed for almost forty-five minutes over the situation at hand: the inability to have children (though every conceivable test and operation had been tried), a terribly disappointing, incomplete adoption, and now, perhaps even worse, a loss of hope. We prayed. We cried and tremblingly asked God for a baby, allowing Matthew 18:19 to serve as a reminder "that if two of you agree on earth concerning anything that they ask, it will be done for them by My Father in heaven" (NKJV).

That night, during a concert, a woman neither of us knew tapped Kinney on the shoulder and said, "I understand you are looking for a baby." We slowly looked at each other in awe and amazement! The incredible account of the next six weeks included an interview, more prayer, lots of applications, renewed hope, and a beautiful baby girl named Ginny! The story of Kinney's Ginny is perhaps the most dramatic account of agreeing prayer that has occurred in my life, but on a weekly basis it has become a practice to sit with family, friends, and staff members at spontaneous and planned moments and lift great and small needs up to God, agreeing with them in Jesus' name and leaving the incredible results up to Him. . . .

Prayer triplets

What is a prayer triplet? It is a way to win other people to Christ. You link up with two Christians and pray together regularly for the salvation of nine friends or relatives who do not know Jesus personally and a country where Jesus is not known. Then rejoice as you see Matthew 18:19–20 fulfilled.

Here are the instructions:

Choose two Christian friends or relatives to make your triplet.

Each of you choose the names of three people who do not know Jesus as their personal Savior and Lord. Choose a country where Jesus' name is not now known or is rare.

Agree on a time to meet once a week to pray together for your nine. Just fifteen minutes in your home, at work, or at school, before or after a meeting, is all it takes.

Pray together for the nine people by name to accept Christ as their personal Savior and Lord, including their personal needs and frailties. Also pray for your country.

As much as possible, as God leads, involve yourself with your three in a friendly way. Pray for each other as you seek to do this.

When your friends become Christians, continue to pray for them, even if your triplet takes on other names to pray for.

If possible, incorporate them into your church, Bible study and/or fellowship after they accept Jesus. . . .

E. M. Bounds's famous exhortation, "Much prayer, much power. Little prayer, little power. No prayer, no power," has often prompted me to enlist others in a prayer request. Often a person will share a need or a situation that is currently unfolding and will request my prayer. I have tried to make it my habit to stop *right then and there* to agree with the person in prayer, believing that the more prayer offered for a situation, the more power is released!

From small to large agreeing prayers, God continually shows us that He is listening and is faithful. No matter the size or significance of the prayer request, I believe our prayers are important to Him. From the lost wallet to the potential job opening, from the mending of a relationship to prayer for financial rescue, agreeing prayer becomes a faith-building experience for those who are involved in it.

Praying with others for God's intervention creates excitement and motivation to keep on agreeing in prayer! I encourage you not only at prayer meetings but with your friends, during recreation times, at planning meetings, or on family vacations to make time for agreeing prayer."

—*Becky Tirabassi*

HOW IS NEW TESTAMENT PRAYING DIFFERENT FROM OLD TESTAMENT PRAYING?

What changed so dramatically about prayer at Christ's Resurrection? When God the Father gave His Son a human body, Jesus became the only pre-existent person ever to be born on this earth. He was the fulfillment of all of B.C.'s waiting, and He would birth a whole new system of people's relationships with the Father and the Holy Spirit.

After finding in my Bible the following staggering list of differences in B.C. and A.D. praying, I cried out to God, "Oh Lord, I am so grateful you let me live on this side of Jesus. How many of the wonderful things of prayer I would have missed!"

Praying and pondering over each one's affect on our praying, little by little God unfolded it to me. Here are some of the awesome differences Jesus' death and Resurrection made in our praying as Christians:

Direct access to the holy of holies. One of the awesome blessings of living in A.D. time is that there is no veil in our churches allowing only our leaders access to the holy of holies. We all now have direct access to the Father's holy presence in prayer.

Even when Jesus' birth was imminent and God was about to announce Jesus' forerunner, John the Baptist, only his father, Zacharias, was chosen by lot to enter the temple of the Lord and burn incense while the whole multitude of people were in prayer outside (see Luke 1:8–10).

Before Jesus was born, only the high priest of Israel had access to the holy of holies, the inner chamber of the temple in which God's presence literally dwelled. One day each year, the Day of Atonement, the high priest would go through the veil into the holy of holies to offer a sacrifice to pay for the sins of the people. All the people had to stay on the outside. Hebrews 9:7 describes this limited access to God:

> Into the [holy of holies] only the high priest enters, once
> a year, not without taking blood, which he offers for him-
> self and for the sins of the people committed in ignorance.

However, when Jesus died on the cross, the veil was supernaturally torn in two from top to bottom, and suddenly there was access directly to God's throne room for every believer! (see Matt. 27:51). I wrote in the margin of my Bible beside Luke 1:10 with a big exclamation mark and large capital letters, "Jesus' birth and death gave us the right to come directly to God in prayer. We are inside now! Only a priest was permitted inside before Jesus died."

The last time I was in Jerusalem, my guide was an archaeology professor. He told me that archaeologists now think they know the exact place the veil of the temple stood—on what is now an outcropping of solid granite. I knelt, laid my hands on that rock, and wept as my whole being was enwrapped in groaning prayer as I poured out my heart in deep gratitude to my Jesus! Gratitude for suffering and dying and splitting the veil that kept me on the outside—and opening up heaven's throne room personally to me.

Confidence through Jesus' blood. However, more than a split veil, it is by the *blood of Jesus* that we Christians have confidence to enter the holy place of God.

As Hebrews 10:18–20 explains:

> Now where there is forgiveness of these things, there is no longer any offering for sin. Since therefore, brethren, *we have confidence to enter the holy place by the blood of Jesus,* by a new and living way which He inaugurated for us through the veil, that is, His flesh (emphasis added).

Why did the Cross change prayer for us in A.D.? It was because forgiveness of sins has always been necessary for sinful humans to come into the presence of a holy God. "And whatever we ask we receive from Him, because we keep His commandments and do the things that are pleasing in His sight" (1 John 3:22).

But the good news about sin separating us from God is in Revelation 1:5: "Jesus Christ . . . the ruler of the kings of the earth. To Him who loves us, and *released us from our sins by His blood"* (emphasis added).

There no longer needs to be offering for sin by humans. Jesus' cry, "It is finished!" on the cross closed the door on B.C. sacrifices as He became the A.D. propitiation for our sins (see 1 John 2:2). . . .

PRAYER REFLECTION
The man who kneels to God can stand up to anything.
—*Lewis H. Evans*

Praying with A.D. Doctrine. How differently the first believers were able to pray with A.D. doctrine after Jesus continuously explained the whole Old Testament to them and then wrapped it all up in Luke 24:44–47 in the light of His death and Resurrection! How thrilled they must have been that the mysteries of the Old Testament were revealed first to them! How they must have prayed for understanding as the awesomeness of it all unfolded before their eyes!

They evidently embraced this fulfilled doctrine immediately, for Acts 2:42 tells us that from that time on they continued steadfastly in four things: the apostles' teaching, fellowship, breaking of bread, and prayer. And these prayers progressed as they sought to apply all the things Jesus had taught them and demonstrated for them. It instructed them how to pray effectively to obey their new marching orders from Jesus.

The apostles' doctrine contained what they were to pray for and about—brought up to A.D. by Jesus' teaching. The truths they clung to when imprisoned, scattered, hiding in caves, and martyred were all covered by Jesus—ready to sustain them no matter what. But it also encouraged more and deeper praying as they saw that victory after victory came from their new A.D. prayers.[12]

—*Evelyn Christenson*

IT SEEMS SELFISH TO PRAY FOR MYSELF.

From the time we were children, we have learned to ask others for what we feel we need. Unfortunately many Christians tend to share their needs or problems with everyone around them but are often uncertain about going to God in prayer and asking Him to meet their needs.

Thomas Constable speaks to this point. "Some sincere Christians believe that it is selfish and not very trusting to ask God to give us anything. Some Christians believe that praying for personal needs is more a mark of unbelief than of trust in God. After all, since God loves us perfectly, will he not do what is best for us?

"Such an attitude may superficially sound spiritual. However, it contradicts Jesus' clear teaching that God's children should ask him for their needs (Matt. 6:9–13; Luke 11:1–4). . . . God not only encourages us to ask him for what we need, but also commands us to do so. He does so to teach us to look to him for our needs because he is our provider."

The Book of James describes the natural way human beings attempt to secure what they want. James asked a couple of very important questions: "What causes fights and quarrels among you? Don't they come from your desires that battle within you? You want something but don't get it. You kill and covet, but you cannot have what you want. You quarrel and fight" (James 4:1–2).

This is a dilemma all of us have faced either knowingly or unknowingly. We have wanted something and were unable to get it, so we followed our natural tendency to covet, quarrel, or fight to try to secure what we wanted. But often our activity has failed to secure what we wanted to gain or achieve. Many people learn subtle and even polite ways to fulfill their wants, such as scheming, deceiving, or manipulating. Yet they often do not get what they want, so they fret and strive, but to no avail. The solution to this common dilemma is quite simple. James wrote, "You do not have, because you do not ask God" (4:2).

Interestingly Martin Luther presented the simple solution to this problem in the second stanza of his great hymn, "A Mighty Fortress Is Our God."

105

Did we in our own strength confide,

Our striving would be losing,

Were not the right man on our side,

The man of God's own choosing.

Dost ask who that may be?

Christ Jesus, it is He—

Lord Sabaoth His name,

From age to age the same—

And He must win the battle.

We often lose the battle because of our own striving. We try to fight the battle ourselves. We rely on our own strength instead of asking the Lord for His help. By depending on ourselves and not asking the Lord, we deprive ourselves of good things our gracious Lord would gladly provide for us—if we would just ask Him.

Jesus shared this basic truth repeatedly. Some of His statements may seem rather radical or even unbelievable when we first consider them. For example, He said, "I will do whatever you ask in my name, so that the Son may bring glory to the Father" (John 14:13). Then He repeated that point to make it perfectly clear to those who may have been astonished by His teaching. He said, "You may ask me for anything in my name, and I will do it" (14:14). The principle seems clear. If we ask "in His name," He will give us anything and everything we ask for.

Yet it sounds too good to be true. Most of us have tried doing this. We have gone to God in prayer and simply asked Him for something we wanted. Sometimes it has worked. And many of us have been astonished at how simple and practical that kind of prayer can be. Admittedly, however, it does not always work. Virtually every Christian has been disappointed with that kind of praying at one time or another. We asked God for something in the name of Jesus, and we did not get it. We tried to be as sincere as we could. We asked with as much faith as we could muster. But regardless of what we did or how many times we prayed or how many different approaches we attempted, we did not receive what we asked for. As a result, many Christians conclude that prayer simply does not work and that God does not always keep His promise to give when we ask. There are times when we ask but do not receive, when we seek but do not find, and when we knock but no doors seem to open.[13]

—*Paul Cedar*

WHAT CAN I DO TO MAKE MY PRAYERS MORE EFFECTIVE?

We all know that when friends don't see each other and communicate frequently, they can become emotionally separated. Well, it's the same with you and God. If you don't keep in touch with Him, you begin to feel distant from Him even when you're not. This is why you must pray daily. Also, when you spend time with someone you respect, the character of that person rubs off on you. When you are in the presence of God, His character is formed in you.

> ⁓
>
> **PRAYER REFLECTION**
>
> *Prayer will make a man cease from sin, or sin will entice a man to cease from prayer.*
>
> —*John Bunyan*

Many of us are especially vulnerable to the enemy's attack on our self-worth: It doesn't take much to discourage us, and feeling distant from God will do it. That's why it's important to start the day with some kind of prayer. We have to establish ourselves and our lives as being connected to Him.

We can't receive God's best for our lives, and we can't push back the things that were never God's will for us, except through prayer. We have to learn that we can't leave our lives to chance. We have to pray over anything that concerns us, no matter how big— "With God nothing will be impossible" (Luke 1:37)—or how small—"The very hairs of your head are all numbered" (Matt. 10:30).

If you have any doubt about the importance of prayer or if you are still praying on an on-again/off-again basis, go through the fifteen reasons to pray below. I find that reading the Scripture passages that support them is very motivational too.

Fifteen reasons to pray

1. To seek the face of the Lord and know Him better (Ps. 27:8)
2. To get your eyes off your problems and onto the Lord (Ps. 121:1)
3. To speak to God (1 Peter 3:12)
4. To unburden your heart (Ps. 142:1–2)
5. To make your requests known to God (Matt. 21:22)
6. To hear God (Prov. 8:34)
7. To be free of suffering (James 5:13)
8. To resist temptation (Matt 26:41)

9. To be rescued from distress (Ps. 107:19)
10. To receive God's reward (Matt 6:6)
11. To withstand evil (Eph. 6:13)
12. To have joy (John 16:24)
13. To get close to God (Isa. 64:7)
14. To be healed emotionally (James 5:13)
15. To have peace (Phil. 4:6–7)

Do whatever you have to do to secure a place and time to pray. When I was single and during the first few years of marriage, that was not a problem. However, after our first child was born it was much more difficult. When our second child arrived, the only way I could spend time with the Lord was to get up at 5:30 a.m. The only place I could go at that hour and not disturb anyone was a small walk-in closet off the master bath. What a contrast to my early years of being locked in the closet for punishment! Now I went there to commune with God. This went well for a while until I was discovered. First I was visited regularly by my eighteen-month-old daughter, who learned to climb out of her crib and come looking for me. Soon she was followed by her six-year-old brother.

One morning, when both of them, plus my husband, two dogs, and several hamsters, ended up in the closet, I knew it was time to either get up earlier or find a new location. Sometimes we have to revise our plans, but securing a time and place to be alone with God is worth any effort.

Without reducing prayer to a formula, I found that it is good to include certain key points in each prayer time:

- Tell the Lord how much you love Him.
- Thank Him for all He has done for you.
- State how dependent you are upon Him.
- Tell Him everything that's in your heart.
- Confess anything that needs to be confessed.
- Give Him all your requests.
- Wait for Him to speak to your heart.
- Praise Him for working powerfully in your life.

Don't ever feel inhibited because you think you can't pray. If you can talk, you can pray. And don't be concerned about prayer talk, church talk, or Christianese talk. The Bible tells us the only qualifications we need: "He who comes to God must believe that He is, and that He is a rewarder of those who diligent-ly seek Him" (Heb. 11:6). We just have to believe that He is a good God.

The more you pray, the more you will find to pray about, and the more you'll be led to pray for others: family members (as in my books *The Power of a Praying Wife* and *The Power of a Praying Parent), friends, enemies, and all those in authority in any area of your life (pas-tor, teacher, boss, governor, president). You'll pray for them not only because they influence your emotional health and because part of the peace you experience will result directly from that type of praying, but because Jesus asked you to do it.[14]

—*Stormie Omartian*

IS ANY REQUEST TOO BIG OR TOO SMALL FOR GOD?

> Be anxious for nothing, but in everything by prayer and supplication, with thanksgiving, let your requests be made known to God (Philippians 4:6 NKJV).

What Paul did was make a contrast between two indefinite pronouns: nothing and every-thing. Let me give you my translation, which I call the McGee-icus Ad Absurdum translation. It goes like this: *Worry* about nothing; *pray* about everything. This is a direct commandment. In other words, Paul said that it is wrong and sinful for a Christian to worry. Most of us would have to confess that we've sinned in this area, because we do worry. But we are not to worry. Instead, we are to pray about everything.

Now these two little indefinite pronouns have tremendous significance. The first one, *nothing,* is probably the most exclusive word there is in the English language—it excludes everything. We are not to worry about a single thing. And the reason we are to worry about nothing is because we are to pray about everything. And just as *nothing* excludes all, *everything* includes all. That means we are to talk to the Lord about everything in our lives.

Years ago, a widow went to Dr. G. Campbell Morgan and asked him, "Dr. Morgan, do you think we ought to pray about the little things in our lives?" And Dr. Morgan, in his characteristic British manner, replied, "Madam, can you mention anything in your life that is big to God?" May I say, when we begin to divide the things in our lives as big or little, we are making a false division. All areas of your life and my life just happen to be very small as far as God is concerned. But even what we call little, He wants us to bring to Him. As believers, we need to get in the habit of bringing *everything* to Him in prayer—excluding *nothing*. So these two little pronouns are exact opposites. Nothing means *nothing,* and everything means *everything.*

When Paul said that a Christian is not to worry, he was not advancing a foolish philosophy of shutting our eyes to reality and denying that disease and sickness and death and trouble and pain are realities. Paul was not saying that we are to pray as if those things don't exist. He never indulged in that kind of foolish philosophy at all. He said that the reason we are to worry about nothing is because everything is to be removed from the realm of worry and moved over to the area of prayer.

I'd like to illustrate this with a little joke I heard years ago about a man who couldn't sleep one night. He rolled and tossed, and his wife finally said to him, "What is the matter? Why can't you sleep?" He said, "I owe the tax man six thousand dollars, the note is coming due, and I can't pay it." "Well," his wife said, "you get up, dress, and go over and tell the tax man that you can't pay him. Then come back and go to sleep and let *him* stay awake." May I say to you, my friends, that is exactly what Paul the apostle was really saying here. Paul was saying that when we tell God everything, it becomes *His* problem. We have the right as His children to go to Him in prayer and say, "This is something for *You* to handle" and then turn everything over to Him. Worry about nothing; pray about everything.

> **PRAYER REFLECTION**
>
> *The chief purpose of prayer is that God may be glorified in the answer.*
>
> —R. A. Torrey

I personally do not think there is anything in the Christian's life that should not be made a matter of prayer to God. It doesn't make any difference what it is. He is our heavenly Father, and we can talk to Him very frankly. We can open and unburden our hearts to Him as we can to no one else. [15]

—*J. Vernon McGee*

We have to remind ourselves continually that God has a perfect plan for us. Every action we take and every choice we make becomes a part of that plan—no matter how small and insignificant it seems to us.

Years ago one of my colleagues made a scoffing reference to people who pray for a parking spot. "God answers our prayers, of course, but he doesn't want us to bother him with trivial things like that," the person said.

I responded, "Hey, wait a minute. Let the scoffers scoff! I'm going to keep on trusting for a parking place and remembering that if God is God at all, he is God of all!"

It's true that where I park my car is usually unimportant. And yet in some circumstances, parking spaces can be very important. If I park in a no-parking zone, for instance, parking can even become a moral question!

I remember the time a missionary who was escorting me in a foreign country came late to pick me up. I kept looking at my watch, realizing that a number of high government officials were waiting for me and that the success of my presentation depended a great deal on my being there to give it. As it turned out, the missionary had been driving around the block over and over again because he hadn't wanted to put a nickel in the parking meter. That parking problem almost cost my organization some valuable contacts in a needy country.

I pray every day of my life, asking God to guide every inch of my movement and every second of my time. That means big things, and it also means little things. It includes moral choices, and it includes choices that do not have moral implications. As I look back over the years, I think the most significant way God has led in my life has been through the synchronization of his purposes. Miracles of timing have repeatedly occurred, and little things that would not otherwise have significance suddenly became important.

For example, I once missed a flight leaving Africa. This "misfortune" led to a chance meeting with an ambassador from another African country whom I had missed when I was in his country. En route to Paris, I had no idea how I could track this man down. But because I missed my flight, I ended up on the bus with the very ambassador I needed to see. Out of that meeting came a program of help that took hundreds of thousands of pounds of desperately needed food into his country. God had watched over that day and timed things for his own purposes.

Another time, I explained to the non-Christian friend with whom I was traveling that he was going to witness God's timing. He would see God put things together. At our first stop, with a four-hour wait between planes, we decided to go to the U.S. embassy so my friend could have some needed adjustments made to his passport.

At the embassy we learned that U.S. officials and the Belgian air force had joined forces to put together a food airdrop. The ambassador, however, had never before performed an airdrop and was not sure how to proceed. I had just spent a year in Bangladesh engineering similar airdrops, so I passed on information about things we had done right and things we had done wrong.

> PRAYER REFLECTION
>
> *Finally at the center we are filled by the power and strength of God as Holy Spirit. There is a resurgence of confidence and expectancy. We receive insight and wisdom; faith that removes mountains is generated, and our love for others, even for the unlovable, begins to grow.*
>
> *—Becky Tirabassi*

Even though we were there for only four hours, I could fly on that important first airdrop effort and coach the inexperienced crew.

We had trusted God with our whole day, right down to the tiniest details, and therefore the day's activities became a mosaic where every part fit together beautifully. God put it all together and enabled us to make a significant contribution.

We can trust God to superintend every aspect of life because he is God of all. We can pray about everything that in any way affects us, because he is willing to gather up the details and make them part of his plan.

I have a prayer I often say. I ask God to guide me through each new day, because I have never lived it before and will never live it again. I ask for his grace and direction in everything, because I know his greatness extends to every aspect of life—every choice, every decision, every move. I depend on him for every breath and every step, and each breath and each step is part of his perfect plan for me.[16]

—Larry Ward

WHAT IS THE POWER OF PRAYER AGAINST SATAN?

You are to have God's power in your life as you pray against Satan. You are to operate at a high spiritual level by being empowered by the Holy Spirit rather than by yourself. If you are in Christ, your authority is great. You have the name of Jesus as your banner, the blood of Jesus as your covering, and the Word of God as your sword. You are prepared to pray against Satan when you are being controlled by the Spirit. . . .

One of the best ways to prepare for combat is to know everything you can know about your enemy. You need to study your enemy thoroughly, along with his tactics and strategies. You can never assume you know these things. If you do, defeat is inevitable.

What you need to know about your enemy

There are four critical facts about Satan that you need to know. These four facts are . . .

You Are in a Spiritual War with Satan

Let me reaffirm to you that you are not in a war with people. Stop seeing people as the source of your problems and conflicts. You are in a spiritual war with Satan. If you don't wake up and go into combat, you will be continually defeated.

Satan Is Your Only Enemy

You need to understand that Satan is your only enemy. It is critical that you stop viewing persons, institutions, systems, and circumstances as your enemies. Yes, Satan can operate through each one of these, but the essence of your problem lies with the spiritual force of darkness, Satan himself. Put on your spiritual glasses and begin to see what God sees. Satan is your only enemy.

Satan Wants to Destroy You, Your Family, Your Church, and the Work of Jesus Christ across the World

Satan is never interested in building you up. He does not desire for you to experience victory or success. He wants to destroy every person in this world so they will experience an eternity of destruction with him in hell.

He wants to destroy your marriage. Your spouse is not where the combat really is; your war is against Satan. Satan is ending as many marriages as he can. Satan will do anything to take out the man of God called your pastor. He hates men of God. This is why so many pastors are falling to the lure of gold, glory, and girls.

Satan wants to destroy the church. This is why so many churches are in never-ending battles over insignificant things. The church is to be a unified body of Christ, but this is rarely the case due to the level of division going on in the body of Christ.

Satan wants to do anything he can to put a stop to the work of Jesus Christ around the world. He does not want the Good News told, so he will get the church involved in many good things in order to keep them away from the main thing of taking the gospel to the world.

Yes, Satan is out to destroy all he can. You are his target! If you are questioning whether this is reality, you are right in the middle of his deceitful plan. Satan has deceived you, and you have bought his lies. Remember this about Satan: He always plays for keeps. His wins are not just short-term wins. Many times his wins are eternal.

Even Though Satan Is Alive and Well Today, His Doom Is Certain

Satan is tearing up and wrecking lives all across the world today. It is very obvious how destructive he is when you witness the dysfunctional relationships in every segment of society. Our enemy is wreaking havoc upon our culture. We read daily about the torment and adversity that he is bringing into the lives of people. He appears to have the upper hand in the lives of people everywhere. Yes, Satan is alive and well.

However, Satan's doom is certain! One day, the evil one will be thrown into hell once and for all. When Satan points you to your past, which may be filled with defeat and despair, you should point him to his future, which will be finalized with certain defeat. As a believer in Jesus Christ, you will win in eternity and Satan will lose.

This is why your praying can be warfare praying. Periodically, you need to pray something like the following:

> Lord, I stand against the power of Satan in my life today. I
> declare him powerless over me because I am a child of the
> King. I am born again by Your Spirit. I am forgiven because
> I am covered with Jesus' blood. So Satan, I stand against you
> in Jesus' name. You have no authority over me, my family,
> or my church. You are a defeated foe. You have no author-
> ity in my life. In Jesus' name, I stand my ground. Amen.

This warfare praying calls upon God for strength. It reminds Satan that you are not to be his prey because of what Jesus has done for you. This kind of praying equips you not to give up any ground at all to Satan in your life. This kind of praying will lead you to experience true spiritual victory.

As you perform warfare praying, it is important to be covered daily with the armor of God. . . . One of the spiritual practices I follow daily is to place God's armor upon the members of my family. Since I am up most days before the rest of them, I dress them spiritually for the day even before they get out of bed. As the spiritual leader of the home, I have the responsibility to put the armor of God upon my family. . . .

This kind of praying brings rest upon your heart, knowing that you have placed the members of your family under the armor of God. They are now truly dressed for spiritual success. They are ready to face the day and even the devil. The armor is now on, and they can stand firm against their enemy.[17]

—*Ronnie W. Floyd*

HOW CAN I PRAY WHEN I'M TEMPTED?

Because we do not obey God without a continual warfare, without sharp and arduous contests, we here pray that he would furnish us with armour, and defend us by his protection, that we may be able to obtain the victory. By this we are reminded that we not only have need of the gift of the Spirit inwardly to soften our hearts, and turn and direct them to the obedience of God, but also of his assistance, to render us invincible by all the wiles and violent assaults of Satan. The forms of temptation are many and various. The depraved conceptions of our minds provoking us to transgress the law—conceptions which our concupiscence suggests or the devil excites, are temptations; and things which in their own nature are not evil, become temptations by the wiles of the devil, when they are presented to our eyes in such a way that the view of them makes us withdraw or decline from God. These temptations are both on the right hand and on the left. On the right, when riches, power, and honours, which by their glare, and the semblance of good which they present, generally dazzle the eyes of men . . . that, caught by their snares, and intoxicated by their sweetness, they forget their God: on the left, when offended by the hardship and bitterness of poverty, disgrace, contempt, afflictions, and other things of that description, they despond, cast away their confidence and hope, and are at length totally estranged from God. In regard to both kinds of temptation. . . we pray God the Father not to allow us to be overcome, but rather to raise and support us by his hand . . . Here, however, we do not ask to be altogether exempted from temptation, which is very necessary to excite, stimulate, and urge us on, that we may not become too lethargic. . . .But the temptations of God and Satan are very different: Satan tempts, that he may destroy, condemn, confound, throw headlong; God, that by proving his people he may make trial of their sincerity, and by exercising their strength confirm it; may mortify, tame, and cauterize their flesh, which, if not curbed in this manner, would wanton and exult above measure. . . .

Our petition, therefore, is, that we may not be overcome or overwhelmed with temptation, but in the strength of the Lord may stand firm against all the powers by which we are assailed; in other words, may not fall under temptation: that being thus taken under his charge and protection, we may remain invincible by sin, death, the gates of hell, and the whole power of the devil; in other words, be delivered from evil. . . .We have no strength to contend with such a combatant as the devil, or to sustain the violence of his assault. Were it otherwise, it would be mockery of God to ask of him what we already possess in ourselves. Assuredly those who in self-confidence prepare for such a fight, do not understand how bold and well-equipped the enemy is with whom they have to do. Now we ask to be delivered from his power, as from the mouth of some furious raging lion, who would instantly tear us with his teeth and claws, and swallow us up, did not the Lord rescue us from the midst of death; at the same time knowing that if the Lord is present and will fight for us while we stand by . . . For if the Spirit of God is our strength in waging the contest with Satan, we cannot gain the victory un-less we are filled with him, and thereby freed from all infirmity of the flesh. Therefore, when we pray to be delivered from sin and Satan, we at the same time desire to be enriched with new supplies of divine grace, until completely replenished with them, we triumph over every evil.[18]

—*John Calvin*

> ### PRAYER REFLECTION
>
> *Lord, I pray that You would deliver my feet from the snares of the enemy, and my soul from the torment and death he has prepared for me. Hide me in the shadow of Your wings. Be my fortress, shield, and strength. Give me discernment. Open my eyes to the truth. May I be quick to recognize the errors of my own thoughts. I submit my life to You. Lead me in the way You would have me go.*
>
> —*Stormie Omartian*

WHY SHOULD I FAST? WILL IT REALLY HELP MY PRAYER LIFE?

A discussion on prayer would not be complete without including a subject that is an important companion to prayer in the Bible: fasting.

Combining fasting with prayer can result in a spiritual atomic bomb that pulls down spiritual strongholds and releases the power of God in your life and the life of your church, its pastor, its leaders, and its members.

Down through the centuries, godly people who have done mighty things for the Lord have testified to the necessity of prayer with fasting. John Wesley, who shook the world for God during the Great Awakening, which gave rise to the Methodist Church toward the end of the eighteenth century, is representative of such great spiritual leaders.

John Wesley and his brother Charles with their friend George Whitefield and other fellow believers regularly fasted and prayed with students at Oxford University in 1732. These Christian "commoners" studied and worshiped in the midst of mocking young aristocrats who nicknamed them the "Holy Club." Having experienced the spiritual power of fasting and prayer, they carried this discipline into their historic ministries.

John Wesley so believed in this power that he urged early Methodists to fast and pray every Wednesday and Friday. He felt so strongly about fasting those two days a week that he refused to ordain anyone in Methodism who wouldn't agree to do it.

The roll call of other great Christian leaders who determined to make prayer with fasting a part of their lives reads like a hall of fame: Martin Luther, John Calvin, John Knox, Jonathan Edwards, Matthew Henry, Charles Finney, Andrew Murray, D. Martyn Lloyd-Jones, and many more.[19]

—Bill Bright

HOW SHOULD I FAST? WHAT SHOULD I DO?

Set aside ample time to be alone with the Lord during your fast. The more time you spend with Him in fellowship, worship, and adoration and the more you read and meditate on His Word during your fast, the greater your effectiveness will be in prayer and the more meaningful your fast will be.

Seek God in prayer and as you meditate on His Word each morning before you leave home or go about your daily routine. Return to prayer at lunch, and come before Him again in the evening for unhurried times of seeking His face. Of course, you should practice His presence and continue to have fellowship with Him constantly as you pray without ceasing throughout the day.

There is no set formula for how to pray when you fast. You may wish to pray aloud or silently, asking the Lord to grant specific requests. I suggest you make a list and add to it daily as needs come to mind. Pray earnestly for your family, your pastor, your church, your community, and our nation. Pray for revival in our land and a great worldwide spiritual harvest. Pray for the fulfillment of the Great Commission.

You may wait before God in quiet meditation as you invite the Holy Spirit to minister to you and bring to mind those things He wants you to pray about.

You should go about your daily activities mindful that you are still fasting and seeking the Lord. Some of my deepest spiritual insights have come as I continued my ministry responsibilities while seeking His face and practicing His presence.

If you do not know what to pray for, or you feel "prayed out," wait quietly before Him. Turn to the psalms or other favorite passages of Scripture and pray the Word of God back to Him. For example, pray each verse of Psalm 23 aloud, thanking Him for performing each of those promises in your life. Worship and praise the Lord. Tell God how much you love Him and want to serve Him. Invite His presence into your life in a fresh way.

You may wish to approach God with the Lord's Prayer recorded in Matthew 6:9–13. Generally, this prayer covers everything we could possibly ask or say to God. As an introduction to this prayer, Jesus reminded His disciples that "your Father knows the things you have need of before you ask Him" (Matt. 6:8 NKJV).[20]

—*Bill Bright*

IS IT OK TO PRAY ABOUT MONEY?

As believers, we've known from our Sunday school days that God hears and answers prayer. But somehow this situation is different. When you realized the financial crisis you were in, your first response might have been a despairing cry to God for help. But you may have wondered, even as you prayed, *Is it OK to pray about money?* . . .

The crisis you're facing is probably intruding into every aspect of your life and overwhelming you. God wants you to turn to him every time the crisis threatens to tear you down. Pray when the worry causes a knot in your stomach; send up a prayer as you open the mail or answer the phone; ask God to help you see the blessings that surround you, and thank him for them; ask for guidance and wisdom; ask for perspective; ask for peace. He wants to help you with your needs. In your quiet times of prayer, talk to God as your best friend and pour out your questions, your fears, your worries, your needs. . . .

While it seems right that we would pray for a friend's salvation or for the safety of missionaries or for God's guidance of national issues, it somehow seems wrong or selfish to bother God about our financial problems. It's even worse if we know we brought the problem on ourselves: How can we ask God to get us out of a jam that we put ourselves into? And money seems so . . . well, *worldly*. It doesn't have anything to do with salvation or heaven, so is it right to ask God for needed funds?

But if you go to the root of that question, you'll get something like this: Are some prayers insignificant to God? And the answer clearly is no. No request is insignificant; God does not ignore his children any more than a loving parent ignores a child. Whether the request is for a certain kind of cereal or for guidance in setting goals for the future, a parent responds to a child. Whether we are praying about the nation's financial state or praying over our own checkbook, God hears and responds.

God may answer your prayer for money with a resounding yes and allow the money to arrive on schedule. . . .

God may answer your prayer with a no. But a no doesn't mean he doesn't care. If your toddler asks if he can play in the street, you of course say no. And you say no because you care, not because you don't. The same goes for our heavenly Father. He has a reason for his answer. He knows the outcome; he knows what he wants you to learn. What you asked for might be as dangerous as playing in the street, so God wisely declines the request. Or what you asked for may be wrong—perhaps your motivation or attitude was wrong. Then you need to clear that up with God before you come back to your financial needs. . . .

God may answer your prayer with a 'Wait." God has a perfect plan and timing for events in our lives, and we must be patient. That's difficult when the days turn into months that turn into bills that get more and more past due. But we must never doubt God. He will respond when the time is right. . . .

The key is to pray for God's will. "This is the confidence we have in approaching God: that if we ask anything according to his will, he hears us. And if we know that he hears us—whatever we ask—we know that we have what we asked of him" (1 John 5:14–15). While prayer is communication with God, it is important to remember that we are asking according to *God's* will, not *our will*. In reality, we want him to do what is best for us—and what we want at this moment may not be best for us in the long run.

God's ultimate goal for us is to make us more like his Son: "For from the very beginning God decided that those who came to him—and all along he knew who *would—should become like his Son,* so that his Son would be the First, with many brothers" (Romans 8:29, TLB, italics mine). God wants us to be holy as he is holy. He wants us to have an intimate relationship with him; his Spirit within guides us through each step of daily life—and daily life involves major and minor decisions. While God gives us brains that we ought to use, he is never upset by our requests for guidance or help.[21]

—*Linda K. Taylor*

HOW CAN I PRAY ON BEHALF OF OTHERS?

As the Vine is Supported by the Elm, So is the Rich Man Helped by the Prayer of the Poor.

As I was walking in the field, and observing an elm and vine . . . the Shepherd appears to me, and says, "What is it that you are thinking about the elm and vine?"

"I am considering," I reply, "that they become each other exceedingly well."

"These two trees," he continues, "are intended as an example for the servants of God."

"I would like to know," said I, "the example which these trees you say, are intended to teach."

"Do you see," he says, "the elm and the vine?"

"I see them sir," I replied.

"This vine," he continued, "produces fruit, and the elm is an unfruitful tree; but unless the vine be trained upon the elm, it cannot bear much fruit when extended at length upon the ground; and the fruit which it does bear is rotten, because the plant is not suspended upon the elm. When, therefore, the vine is cast upon the elm, it yields fruit both, from itself and from the elm. You see, moreover, that the elm also produces much fruit, not less than the vine, but even more; because," he continued, "the vine, when suspended upon the elm, yields much fruit, and good; but when thrown upon the ground, what it produces is small and rotten. This similitude, therefore, is for the servants of God-for the poor man and for the rich."

"How so, sir?" said I; "explain the matter to me."

"Listen," he said: "The rich man has much wealth, but is poor in matters relating to the Lord, because he is distracted about his riches; and he offers very few confessions and intercessions to the Lord, and those which he does offer are small and weak, and have no power above. But when the rich man refreshes the poor, and assists him in his necessities, believing that what he does to the poor man will be able to find its reward with God— because the poor man is rich in intercession and confession, and his intercession has great power with God-then the rich man helps the poor in all things without hesitation; and the poor man, being helped by the rich, intercedes for him, giving thanks to God for him who bestows gifts upon him. And he still continues to interest himself zealously for the poor man, that his wants may be constantly supplied. For he knows that the intercession of the poor man is acceptable and influential with God. Both, accordingly, accomplish their work. The poor man makes intercession; a work in which he is rich, which he received from the Lord, and with which he recompenses the master who helps him. And the rich man, in like manner, unhesitatingly bestows upon the poor man the riches which he received from the Lord. And this is a great work, and acceptable before God, because he understands the object of his wealth, and has given to the poor of the gifts of the Lord, and rightly discharged his service to Him. Among men, however, the elm appears not to produce fruit, and they do not know nor understand that if a drought come, the elm, which contains water, nourishes the vine l and the vine, having an unfailing supply of water, yields double fruit both for itself and for the elm. So also poor men interceding with the Lord on behalf of the rich, increase their riches; and the rich, again, aiding the poor in their necessities, satisfy their souls. Both, therefore, are partners in the

> PRAYER REFLECTION
>
> *When a husband sees his wife praying on his behalf, he sees Christ's love.*
>
> —*Scott Alexander*

righteous work. He who does these things shall not be deserted by God, but shall be enrolled in the books of the living. Blessed are they who have riches, and who understand that they are from the Lord. [For they who are of that mind will be able to do some good]."[22]

—*Anonymous*

WHAT DOES IT MEAN TO "INTERCEDE" FOR OTHERS IN PRAYER?

Intercessory prayer is a phrase that turns off a lot of people. For one thing, they don't know what it means; for another, they don't know how to do it. Yet intercessory prayer is neither hard to understand nor complicated to practice. It simply means to bring the needs of other people before God.

Intercessory prayer can be a beautiful, enriching part of our Christian lives. Paul tells us in Romans 8:26 that "the Spirit himself intercedes for us with groans that words cannot express." In Hebrews 7:25 we read that Jesus "always lives to intercede for [those who come to God through him]." Ever since I was a child, that thought has fascinated me—the Spirit himself is praying for me with such anguished love that the groans cannot be uttered.

PRAYER REFLECTION

Pray with joy and watch your requests ascend straight to God's chamber.

—*Rebbe Nachman*

Our popular view of God is that he is active in the American vein of getting things done. We don't think of God sitting around praying. Intercessory prayer seems to be a proper endeavor for little old ladies, but not for us.

As a child I remember hearing about "prayer warriors" who sat praying with their knitting in their laps. Because they were frail, the only thing they could do was pray. We young, physically able people, by contrast, went out and evangelized or witnessed or did what we thought were important things. But that shows a distorted view of what is important—for the Holy Spirit himself even spends time praying for us.

Most Christians carry an enormous load of guilt. We feel we are not doing what we ought. We feel enormous pressures to get involved in many activities, from political action to church involvement to being great family people, and in the rush we give prayer only a small space in our lives. Yet, realistically, it is totally impossible for any human being to do everything he or she feels required to do. Paradoxically, I've found that when I give prayer more time—especially when I intercede for others—other parts of my life become unblocked, and I see progress in many areas of my daily routines.

I think the busiest among us would see tremendous changes if we would take the time to intercede for each other. Men and women who have the Spirit of Christ gain a sense of peace, love, and joy by becoming involved in intercessory prayer.

Intercessory prayer is a joyous expression of our faith and a beautiful opportunity to commit fellow human beings to God's care. It's an opportunity to think about a person, perhaps a spouse or a child, and ask for God's blessing or healing to come to him or her.

One form of intercessory prayer is to think of someone and then picture clear water or the light of Christ pouring over that person. Another form is to ask God verbally to bless or bring peace to that person. The satisfaction that comes from doing this for someone is incredible.

Intercessory prayer gives us a deep sense of joy. We feel solidarity with other Christians. After praying for other people, we think, "I have brought them before the throne of God. My time has been well spent. They are now in the hands of our loving, healing Lord." As Christians, what better blessing can we offer our fellow human beings?[23]

—*Harold Myra*

HOW CAN I PRAY FOR PEOPLE'S NEEDS?

What is intercessory prayer?

The term "intercessory prayer" may not mean a great deal to you, but it is vital to your Christian life. I believe one of the highest callings in the Christian life is the call to intercession—to pray for others. This call comes to every Christian who is growing in their faith.

When you intercede for others, you plead or offer petition on behalf of another person who is in trouble or in difficulty. You get before God in a very serious mode of prayer. When you are before God in this manner, you are praying for others who may really need your prayers.

Therefore, intercession is when you offer a prayer on behalf of another person or a group of persons. An intercessory prayer asks God to meet with them and to provide for their need. Intercessory prayer is not focused on yourself but on others. It is a call from God to stand in the gap between a holy God and a person in need. Intercessory prayer is one of the highest callings in the Christian life.

Due to the "me-driven" cultural Christianity that is rampant in churches in the world today, Christians do not hear a great deal about intercessory prayer. In fact, in most churches the term and the practice have been placed on the shelf. What we want is to have others pray for us, meet our needs, teach us, help us, fill us, and have God touch us. The focus is always on ourselves and our interests. This self-centered Christianity is a far cry from what God teaches in His Word.

What is an intercessor?

An intercessor is a Christian who prays for another person. When the Holy Spirit places a person upon your heart to pray for and you are obedient to pray for that person, you become an intercessor. When you pray for your church, you become an intercessor. Every growing Christian will perform the ministry of intercessory prayer. As you grow in your faith, the Holy Spirit will place certain people upon your heart so that you will pray for them.

Are you an intercessor? Do you let the Holy Spirit place persons upon your heart so that you can pray for them? If you are a parent, you should intercede for your children. If you are a grandparent, you should intercede for your children and grandchildren. If you are married, you should intercede for your spouse. As a Christian, you should intercede for your local church and for the work of Christ around the world. You should also intercede for your country. Undoubtedly, each growing Christian will become an intercessor by faithfully praying for others.[24]

—*Ronnie W. Floyd*

WHAT CAN I PRAY FOR PEOPLE?

The most powerful act anyone can perform is to pray for someone. Of course, the power is not in the praying, but in the release God gives in His perfect answer to our prayers. Paul provided an example of one of the most effective prayers we could utter. He prayed for the Colossian church:

- to be filled with the knowledge of God's will. What a wonderful gesture to ask God to make clear for family members or friends the precise, exact decisions He wishes them to make in every circumstance.

- to walk in a manner worthy of the Lord. This means asking that someone's life will have weight—will count eternally and not temporally.

- to bear fruit in every good work. We should pray for loved ones to remain so Christ-centered that He through them determines their conversation, conduct, and character.

- to increase in the knowledge of God. Can there be a more precious request than that of wanting someone to grow ever closer to our heavenly Father?

- to be strengthened and sustained with the power of God. Within an evil world system, we need the supernatural power of God to help us bear up under the strain.

- to give thanks for having qualified as saints of God. There is nothing for which we should be more appreciative.

Father, today I pray for those I love—that they will be filled with the knowledge of Your will and walk in a manner worthy of You. Let them bear fruit in every good work and be strengthened and sustained by Your power. [25]

—*Charles Stanley*

WHAT PART DOES PRAYER HAVE IN SHARING MY FAITH?

Several years ago I was invited by Ed Silvoso to speak at a conference in Argentina. One of the assigned subjects was "Praying for the Unconverted." As I was preparing for that plenary session, I drafted an outline of my presentation that was to be distributed to the participants gathering from all over the world.

The title I recommended for the session was simply "Prayer *As* Evangelism." However, when I arrived in Argentina and received my copy of the reproduced outline, the middle word had been misprinted. It read "Prayer *Is* Evangelism."

> **PRAYER REFLECTION**
> *The fruit of prayer is the deepening of love, the deepening of faith.*
> —*Mother Teresa*

As I reflected on that typographical error, I concluded that the revised title was better than the one I had proposed. The truth is that prayer is an effective and powerful approach to the ministry of evangelism. Prayer and evangelism are not synonymous, but prayer is an essential ingredient in any vital ministry of evangelistic outreach.

> **PRAYER REFLECTION**
>
> *As your family grows closer to God in prayer, it will grow closer together.*
> —*Bruce and Stan*

The apostle Paul prayed that all of Israel would be saved (Rom. 10:1). And he encouraged Timothy to be involved in praying for others, even kings and others in authority (1 Tim. 2:1–2). The apostle concluded, "This is good, and pleases God our Savior, who wants all men to be saved and to come to a knowledge of the truth" (2:1–4).

Prayer is not the only thing we do in evangelism, but it is the most important. As I mentioned earlier, Billy Graham's evangelistic ministry has depended primarily on God's people, who are mobilized first to pray for loved ones and friends, and then to invite them to a crusade service where the gospel is preached clearly and powerfully and an invitation is extended to receive Christ.

Some Christians debate whether praying for the lost violates the sovereignty of God or the free will of non-Christians. I do not believe either is true. Instead, I have found that praying for lost people by name somehow unleashes the special ministry of the Holy Spirit to woo, draw, and convict them of sin and of their need of the Savior (John 16:5–11). . . .

For years I have kept in my prayer notebook a list of names of friends and family members who, so far as I know, have never come to personal faith in Jesus Christ. As I have prayed and others have prayed for those individuals, we have seen literally scores of them come to Christ.

When I was a pastor I was often asked to pray for a church member's non-Christian husband, child, or friend. Jeannie and I took those requests seriously. Frequently we would covenant with that Christian to pray daily for the person who needed to come to Christ.

I remember one young wife who came to see me for a counseling session. Her husband was a non-Christian and militantly so. He was reluctant even to allow her to go to church. Jeannie and I began to pray daily for that man, whom we had never met.

Several months later, I greeted the young lady one day with the words "I'm still praying for your husband every day." Her response was one of astonishment and appreciation.

She replied, "Oh, I have some wonderful news for you. My husband came to Christ a few weeks ago. There has been a radical change in his life. In fact, he is involved in a small-group Bible study and has been attending church with me every Sunday. It's wonderful!"

Over the years, I have had similar experiences frequently. As the apostle Paul wrote, "I planted the seed, Apollos watered it, but God made it grow" (1 Cor. 3:6).

That is what evangelism praying is about. Prayer is an important part of the planting and watering process. God uses it to prepare the hearts of the lost to receive the good news of the gospel—and it prepares our hearts to share the love and grace of Jesus Christ with them. Jesus spoke of this dynamic when He said, "No one can come to me unless the Father who sent me draws him" (John 6:44). I believe that praying for the salvation of lost people is a ministry in which every one of us should be strategically involved.

Ed Silvoso has shared another important dimension of praying for the lost:

> In order to pray effectively for the unsaved, we must become aware of the difference between the most important need a person has and what that person feels is his most important need—what is known as the "felt need." Usually these two are not one and the same in the mind of the unsaved. Man's most important need has already been determined by God: the salvation of his soul. However, the felt needs of the lost are defined by the lost themselves; it is what *they feel* is most important to them.
>
> The lost are unable to clearly see their most important need because "the god of this world has blinded the minds of the unbelieving" to the gospel (2 Cor. 4:4). When we pray for their felt needs and God answers, their eyes are opened to the reality and the power of God, and this in turn leads them to recognize their need for salvation. This is what Paul may have had in mind when he said that the Lord sent him "to open their eyes so that they may turn from darkness to light and from the dominion of Satan to God" (Acts 26:18).

Very likely someone or a number of people were praying for you before you became a follower of Jesus Christ. And by God's grace He can use your prayers in bringing others to Christ.[26]

—*Paul Cedar*

WHAT IS THE RELATIONSHIP BETWEEN MY OBEDIENCE AND ANSWERS TO MY PRAYERS?

"When will I ever get to the point where I no longer hurt inside?" I asked God in prayer one day a few months after my counseling session with Mary Anne. Even though I had been set free from depression and my life was far more stable than it had ever been, I still lived on an emotional roller coaster. My questions to God during that time went on and on:

"When will I stop feeling like a failure?"

"When will I not be devastated by what other people say to me?"

"When will I not view every hint of misfortune as the end of the world?"

"When will I be able to go through the normal occurrences of life without being traumatized by them?"

There were no answers from God at that moment, but as I read the Bible the next morning, my eyes fell on the words, "Why do you call me 'Lord, Lord,' and not do the things which I say?" (Luke 6:46). The passage went on to explain that anyone who hears the words of the Lord and does not put them into practice is building a house with no foundation. When the storm comes, it will collapse and be completely destroyed.

> **PRAYER REFLECTION**
>
> *What God gives is precisely what we should have desired to ask.*
>
> —*Francois Fenelon*

Could it be that I'm getting blown over and destroyed by every wind of circumstance that comes my way because I'm not doing what the Lord says to do in some area? I wondered. I knew I had laid a strong foundation by giving my life to the Lord, but it appeared that this foundation could only be stabilized and protected through my obedience.

I searched the Bible for more information, and every place I turned I read more about the rewards of obeying God, passages like "Blessed are those who hear the word of God and keep it!" (Luke 11:28).

And the more I read, the more I saw the link between *obedience* and the *presence of*

God. "If anyone loves Me he will keep My word; and My Father will love him, and We will come to him and make Our home with him" (John 14:23). By this time I was convinced that I could only find wholeness and restoration in His presence, so the promise that my obedience would open the door to God's dwelling with me was particularly impressive.

I also saw a definite connection between *obedience* and the *love of God.* "If anyone obeys His Word, God's love is truly made complete in him" (1 John 2:5 NIV). According to the Bible, God doesn't stop loving us if we *don't* obey. Even if He doesn't love the way we live, He still loves *us.* But we are unable to feel or enjoy that love fully if we're not living as God intended us to live.

The more I read about obedience, the more I realized that my disobedience of God's directives could explain why nothing happened when I prayed the same prayers over and over. The Bible says, "One who turns away his ear from hearing the law; even his prayer is an abomination" (Prov. 28:9).

If I'm not obeying God in some way, then I shouldn't expect to get my prayers answered, I thought.

For anyone who has been emotionally wounded in any way, a certain amount of deliverance and healing will happen in your life just because you are obedient to God. The Bible says, "He who obeys instructions guards his life" (Prov. 19:16 NIV). The more obedient you are, the more bondage will be stripped away from your life. There is also a certain healthy confidence that comes from knowing you've obeyed God. This confidence builds self-worth and nourishes a broken personality. You start the process by being willing to say:

God, I don't want to be someone who collapses every time something shakes me. I don't want anything to separate me from Your presence and love. And I really do have a heart that wants to obey. Please show me where I am not living in obedience, and help me to do what I need to do.[27]

—*Stormie Omartian*

HOW CAN I PRAY FOR MY CHURCH?

Prayer is the very heart, blood, and heartbeat of the church. In fact, the church was born in a prayer meeting! We read:

> When the Day of Pentecost had fully come, they were all
> with one accord in one place. (Acts 2:1 NKJV)

"With one accord" means that they were together in prayer, my beloved, when the Holy Spirit came upon them, marking the beginning of the church.

The prayers of the early church were potent and powerful—they shook walls and loosened prison doors! Unfortunately, prayer in the church today is impotent, anemic, and sickly. Someone could argue that the church of today is not the same as the church of the first century. I heartily agree. The church of the first century was the apostolic church; the church of today is the apostate church. Then it was the persecuted church; today it's the petulant and petted church. Then the church was united; today it is divided. Then the church was warm and spiritual; today it is cold and materialistic. Then it was young and virile; today it is old and decrepit. The early church was committed to Christ; the church today is comfortable in the world. The church at the beginning was a church of conviction; the church today is marked by confusion. The church then had confession; today it has compromise. Then it was a church marked by consistency; today it is a church of contradiction. I'll say there's a difference between the church of the first century and the church today!

But may I say to you, the early church is still a lesson and an incentive to us in the present day, especially when it comes to the matter of prayer. If you want to get acquainted with the members of the early church, read their prayers. You will find out what kind of men and women they were by looking at the prayers that they uttered to God. Their prayers thrill my heart, and they hold valuable lessons for us today.[28]

—*J. Vernon McGee*

WILL MY PRAYERS FOR MY CHURCH HAVE ANY POWER?

Jim Cymbala became a believer in prayer. In fact, before very long he declared to the little congregation, "From this day on, the prayer meeting will be the barometer of our church. What happens on Tuesday night will be the gauge by which we will judge success or failure, because that will be the measure by which God blesses us." He concluded, "This [prayer] will be the engine that will drive the church."

Jim had discovered what Charles Haddon Spurgeon, the great British pulpiteer, declared long ago. "The condition of the church may be very accurately gauged by its prayer meetings. So is the prayer meeting a graceometer, and from it we may judge the amount of divine working among a people. If God be near a church, it must pray. And if he be not there, one of the first tokens of his absence will be a slothfulness in prayer."

Many pastors and other Christian leaders have learned that principle. So have Christian parents, other adults, young people, and even children. Great churches, families, and spiritual lives are built on the foundation of prayer.

Prayer has awesome potential—not only for pastors and churches but also for Christians in every realm of life.[29]

—*Paul Cedar*

HOW CAN PRAYER MAKE A DIFFERENCE IN MY MINISTRY?

It may be put down as a spiritual axiom that in every truly successful ministry prayer is an evident and controlling force—evident and controlling in the life of the preacher, evident and controlling in the deep spirituality of his work. A ministry may be a very thoughtful ministry without prayer; the preacher may secure fame and popularity without prayer; the whole machinery of the preacher's life and work may be run without the oil of prayer or with scarcely enough to grease one cog; but no ministry can be a spiritual one, securing holiness in the preacher and in his people, without prayer being made an evident and controlling force.

The preacher that prays indeed puts God into the work. God does not come into the preacher's work as a matter of course or on general principles, but he comes by prayer and special urgency. That God will be found of us in the day that we seek him with the whole heart is as true of the preacher as of the penitent. A prayerful ministry is the only ministry that brings the preacher into sympathy with the people. Prayer as essentially unites to the human as it does to the divine. A prayerful ministry is the only ministry qualified for the high offices and responsibilities of the preacher. Colleges, learning, books, theology, preaching cannot make a preacher, but praying does. The apostles' commission to preach was a blank till filled up by the Pentecost which praying brought. A prayerful minister has passed beyond the regions of the popular, beyond the man of mere affairs, of secularities, of pulpit attractiveness; passed beyond the ecclesiastical organizer or general into a sublimer and mightier region, the region of the spiritual. Holiness is the product of his work; transfigured hearts and lives emblazon the reality of his work, its trueness and substantial nature. God is with him. His ministry is not projected on worldly or surface principles. He is deeply stored with and deeply schooled in the things of God. His long, deep communings with God about his people and the agony of his wrestling spirit have crowned him as a prince in the things of God. The iciness of the mere professional has long since melted under the intensity of his praying.

> PRAYER REFLECTION
>
> *There is no special formula to use in prayer, but the key is for you to pray about His desire for your life.*
> —*Ronnie W. Floyd*

The superficial results of many a ministry, the deadness of others, are to be found in the lack of praying. No ministry can succeed without much praying, and this praying must be fundamental, ever-abiding, ever-increasing. The text, the sermon, should be the result of prayer. The study should be bathed in prayer, all its duties so impregnated with prayer, its whole spirit the spirit of prayer. "I am sorry that I have prayed so little," was the deathbed regret of one of God's chosen ones, a sad and remorseful regret for a preacher. "I want a life of greater, deeper, truer prayer," said the late Archbishop Tait. So may we all say, and this may we all secure.

God's true preachers have been distinguished by one great feature: they were men of prayer. Differing often in many things, they have always had a common center. They may have started from different points, and traveled by different roads, but they converged to one point: they were one in prayer. God to them was the center of attraction, and prayer was the path that led to God. These men prayed not occasionally, not a little at regular or at odd times; but they so prayed that their prayers entered into and shaped their characters; they so prayed as to affect their own lives and the lives of others; they so prayed as to make the history of the Church and influence the current of the times. They spent much time in prayer, not because they marked the shadow on the dial or the hands on the clock, but because it was to them so momentous and engaging a business that they could scarcely give over.

Prayer was to them what it was to Paul, a striving with earnest effort of soul; what it was to Jacob, a wrestling and prevailing; what it was to Christ, "strong crying and tears." They "prayed always with all prayer and supplication in the Spirit, and watching thereunto with all perseverance." "The effectual, fervent prayer" has been the mightiest weapon of God's mightiest soldiers. The statement in regard to Elijah—that he "was a man subject to like passions as we are, and he prayed earnestly that it might not rain: and it rained not on the earth by the space of three years and six months. And he prayed again, and the heaven gave rain, and the earth brought forth her fruit"—comprehends all prophets and preachers who have moved their generation for God, and shows the instrument by which they worked their wonders.[30]

—E. M. Bounds

HOW SHOULD I PRAY FOR WISDOM? WILL GOD REALLY GIVE IT?

If we need wisdom in order to make decisions about the things that come up each day, just what are we to do when we are unsure of God's will concerning our lives? James gave us a very practical answer: we're to ask God. He said:

> If any of you lacks wisdom, let him ask of God, who gives
> to all liberally and without reproach, and it will be given
> to him. (James 1:5 NKJV)

You see, it's the everyday decisions in life that take many of us out of the will of God. Many of us probably start out in the morning in the will of God, but before we come to high noon we've moved out of the will of God. The reason is because we were confronted with decisions to be made, and we thought they didn't need to be taken to God in prayer. But may I say to you, to know God's will we should be constantly in touch with Him, asking Him for His will concerning these matters.

Decisions face us constantly, and these decisions are disturbing to many folk. . . .

There are many times in our lives when we are faced with a decision and we don't have the wisdom to know which way we should turn. Imagine a Christian who sincerely wants to do God's will. But what is God's will for his life? He moves out into today and tomorrow and next week, saying, "I want to do God's will." But he comes to the crossroads of life and two ways open up to him, one to the right hand and one to the left hand. Which way shall he go? God has not put up a marker at the crossroads. He hasn't put up a signal light there that turns green for *Go* and red for *Stop*. He hasn't sent an audible voice out of heaven that says to us, "This is the way, walk ye in it." Which way are we to go, my beloved, when we come to places like that in our lives? We do not know which way to turn, and the others are blowing their horns and saying to us, "Move on!" And, friends, in life we've got to move on. But what decision shall we make?

> **PRAYER REFLECTION**
>
> *When you pray for others, pray for them to be strengthened with God's power. Pray for them to experience the power of God in their lives.*
>
> —Ronnie W. Floyd

James said, "If any man lacks wisdom, let him ask God." God is not stingy in this department—He is generous! If we look to Him for wisdom in these matters, He gives to everyone liberally. I can speak only for myself, but the highway I've come on hasn't been marked very well. I've come to many crossroads without knowing which way to turn. But I believe, my beloved, that God moves us to these crossroads purposely. If He gave us a clear road map, we'd forever be looking at that road map and not be looking to Him. So He doesn't always make it clear. That keeps us close to Him, you see. But if you and I will look to Him for wisdom, He'll let us move out.

My beloved, you and I need wisdom. And if we are willing to commit matters in our lives to Him, God will lead and guide us. That doesn't mean that all in life will go smoothly. Many have difficulty. And somebody is sure to say, "But I might make a mistake and choose the wrong path." Maybe you will. . . .

God doesn't flash green lights for us. So we need wisdom to make these decisions that confront us in life. God didn't put steering wheels on any of us for a reason—He wants to steer us! So when we come to the crossroads, we have a right to look to Him and ask for wisdom if we mean to do His will. And if we do take the wrong fork, that will be made clear. This is very practical. This is putting your prayers into shoe leather.[31]

—J. Vernon McGee

God's Word reveals a surprising reason that we need to pray before we try to shine Jesus' light to [unbelievers]: "And even if our gospel is veiled, it is veiled to those who are perishing, in whose case the god of this world [Satan] has blinded the minds of the unbelieving, that they might not see the light of the gospel of the glory of Christ, who is the image of God" (2 Cor. 4:3–4).

It is possible for Christians to be shining Jesus and showing His love by wonderful deeds of kindness—and even sharing Jesus verbally in multiple ways—but, because Satan has blinders on the lost, non-Christians cannot even see the Light of Jesus we are radiating—not until God removes their blinders when we pray.

What is the ultimate praying we can do to dispel this horrible darkness? It is praying for all people who are still in darkness to accept Jesus, the Light. Then they won't be in darkness anymore.

As Jesus said in John 12:46, "I have come as light into the world, that everyone who believes in Me may not remain in darkness" (emphasis added). . . .

One of the reasons our sharing Jesus so often fails is our lack of involving the supernatural God in their lives through prayer before we try to get them saved by our human efforts. And all along they could not even see the Jesus we were radiating toward them.

If we are truly sincere about wanting to bring the Light, Jesus, to Planet Earth, *we must see every family member, every neighbor, every colleague, every friend, every school chum, and every college roommate as condemned already if they are without Jesus!* In John 3:18, Jesus said:

> He who believes in Him [the Son of God, Himself] is not judged; he who does not believe has been judged already, because he has not believed in the name of the only begotten Son of God.

We also must realize where they are going eternally if we don't reach them with Jesus—to a Christless eternity in hell. "If anyone's name was not found written in the book of life, he was thrown into the lake of fire" (Rev. 20:15). Hell is that eternal place with no annihilation (see Mark 9:43–48) or reincarnation (see Heb. 9:27), that inescapable place (see Matt. 23:33), that place of fire and of weeping and gnashing of teeth (see Matt. 13:49–50), and that place of banishment from Jesus (see Matt. 7:21–23).

And we must keep praying the ultimate prayer for them—to accept Jesus. . . .

Is everybody you love ready to die or to meet Jesus if He should come back today?
Are you praying that ultimate prayer for them—faithfully, fervently?[32]

—*Evelyn Christenson*

MY HEART BREAKS FOR UNSAVED PEOPLE. HOW DOES GOD WANT ME TO PRAY FOR THEM?

I know that God willeth not the death of a sinner. So I come boldly in prayer: "O God, save my friend." Am I never to ask for his conversion again? George Muller prayed daily—and oftener—for sixty years for the conversion of a friend. But what light does the Bible throw upon "business-like" prayers? Our Lord gave two parables to teach persistence and continuance in prayer. The man who asked three loaves from his friend at midnight received as many as he needed "because of his importunity"— . . . his "shamelessness," as the word literally means (Luke 11:8). The widow who "troubled" the unjust judge with her "continual coming" at last secured redress. Our Lord adds "And shall not God avenge his elect which cry unto him day and night, and he is longsuffering over them?" (Luke 18:7, R.V.)

How delighted our Lord was with the poor Syro-Phoenician woman who would not take refusals or rebuffs for an answer! Because of her continual request He said: "O woman, great is thy faith: be it unto thee even as thou wilt" (Matt. 15:28). Our dear Lord, in His agony in Gethsemane, found it necessary to repeat even His prayer. "And he left them and went away and prayed a third time, saying again the same words" (Matt. 26:44). And we find St. Paul, the apostle of prayer, asking God time after time to remove his thorn in the flesh. "Concerning this thing," says he, "I besought the Lord thrice that it might depart from me" (II Cor. 12:8).

. . . Ah! there was earnestness, even agony in prayer. Now, what about our prayers? Are we called upon to agonize in prayer? Many of God's dear saints say "No!" They think such agonizing in us would reveal great want of faith. Yet most of the experiences which befell our Lord are to be ours. We have been crucified with Christ, and we are risen with Him. Shall there be, with us, no travailing for souls?

Come back to human experience. Can we refrain from agonizing in prayer over dearly beloved children who are living in sin? I question if any believer can have the burden of souls upon him—a passion for souls—and not agonize in prayer.

Can we help crying out, like John Knox, "O God, give me Scotland or I die"? Here again the Bible helps us. Was there no travail of soul and agonizing in prayer when Moses cried out to God, "O, this people have sinned a great sin, and have made gods of gold. Yet now, if thou wilt forgive their sin—; and if not, blot, me, I pray thee, out of thy book"? (Exod. 32:32)

Was there no agonizing in prayer when St. Paul said, "I could wish . . . that I myself were anathema from Christ for my brethren's sake"? (Rom. 9:3)

We may, at all events, be quite sure that our Lord, Who wept over Jerusalem, and Who "offered up prayers and supplications with strong crying and tears" (Heb. 5:7), will not be grieved if He sees us weeping over erring ones. Nay, will it not rather gladden His heart to see us agonizing over the sin which grieves Him? In fact, may not the paucity of conversions in so many a ministry be due to lack of agonizing in prayer?

We are told that "As soon as Zion travailed she brought forth her children" (Isa. 66:8). Was St. Paul thinking of this passage when he wrote to the Galatians, "My little children, of whom I am again in travail until Christ be formed in you"? (Gal. 4:19) And will not this be true of spiritual children? Oh, how cold our hearts often are! How little we grieve over the lost! . . . No; there is such a thing as wrestling in prayer. Not because God is unwilling to answer, but because of the opposition of the "world-rulers of this darkness" (Eph. 6:12, R.V.).[33]

—*Anonymous*

WHAT ABOUT PRAYING FOR HEALING?

God has invited us to pray about all our needs, anything that concerns us. He has given us faith to believe for answers to our prayers. He has made it abundantly clear that it is His will to heal us. And He has promised that our praying will get results. Jesus said,

"Ask, and it shall be given you; seek, and ye shall find; knock, and it shall be opened unto you: for every one that asketh receiveth; and he that seeketh findeth; and to him that knocketh it shall be opened" (Matt. 7:7–8 KJV).

So what are we waiting for? Prayer should be our first recourse, not our last resort! . . .

How do we pray for healing? Specifically instead of generally. For example, if I were sick and you were going to pray for me, I wouldn't want you to say, "Oh, God, please heal everybody who is sick today." The problem would not be that I didn't want other sick people to get well; rather, I simply need a strong, directed prayer that releases healing power to overcome my particular attack.

I need a directed, faith-filled prayer to overcome my problem and restore my body. This is what I call "speaking to the mountain of disease" when you pray.

Jesus said, "If anyone says to this mountain, 'Go, throw yourself into the sea,' and does not doubt in his heart but believes that what he says will happen, it will be done for him" (Mark 11:23 NIV). So I believe when we pray for healing, we should speak to the specific mountain of sickness and command it to be gone. We have this authority as believers.

> ### PRAYER REFLECTION
>
> *Holy, holy Jesus—please forgive me for replacing Your name with my ministry's, my church's—with my own name. Forgive me for being ashamed to say Your name when it was not politically or socially correct. Jesus, please replace my ego and my personal ambitions with You! Thanks for suffering and dying for me. Help me to love You so much that I will want to say that name, sing that name, pray that name— Your name—JESUS— always, everywhere! Yes, in Your name I pray, amen.*
>
> —Evelyn Christenson

Suppose the person we are praying for has a blocked artery. We should speak directly to that mountain and command the blockage to be absorbed and disappear. "God, I pray that the plaque formation—this scheme and device of the enemy—be reversed, that the cholesterol be reabsorbed, and that no blood platelets stick or bind to the plaque in the artery walls and obstruct the flow of blood. Your Word says that life is in the blood, and I claim Your life to be present in this body right now." . . .

So many times I have seen what medicine calls "spontaneous remission"—I call it a healing by the power of God—occur when a patient speaks to a specific mountain of disease. As we seek and follow God's pathway, we see healings that cannot be explained by medical science.

When you pray, be bold and assertive. Don't be apologetic or timid. Be as aggressive in your praying as you are in seeking medical treatment. Martin Luther, the great Protestant reformer, described how he prayed for his sick friend, Melanchthon, also a leader of the church: "I besought the Almighty with great vigor . . . quoting from Scripture all the promises I could remember, that prayers should be granted, and said that he must grant my prayer, if I was henceforth to put faith in his promises."

Remember that you are not "bothering" God with your requests when you pray. Nothing is too great or too small to bring to Him. After all, He invites you to come to Him with your needs and cast your cares upon Him. The Amplified Bible's version of 1 Peter 5:7 says, "Casting the whole of your care [all your anxieties, all your worries, all your concerns, once and for all] on Him, for He cares for you affectionately and cares about you watchfully."[34]

—*Reginald Cherry*

CAN MY PRAYERS INFLUENCE WORLD LEADERS?

Prayer can have an influence on world leaders. Pray and there will be outcomes that, apart from prayer, would never happen. It's not that our prayers change what is going to happen but that, in God's prevision of history, he includes our prayers as factors that have a bearing on the outworking of events. . . .

So we need to recognize our obligation to pray. In 1 Timothy 2:1, 2, one of the most important passages in the Scriptures regarding intercession, the apostle Paul engaged in a fervent exhortation: "I urge, then, first of all, that requests, prayers, intercession and thanksgiving be made for everyone—for kings and all those in authority, that we may live peaceful and quiet lives in all godliness and holiness." So we need to pray for our leaders because they are unconscious instruments in his hand. King Nebuchadnezzar in the book of Daniel exemplifies this fact. Chapter 4 describes how Nebuchadnezzar was smitten with a psychic disorder and, through this divine intervention, brought to an amazing confession of faith and a change of imperial policy.

Caesar Augustus was another leader who served unwittingly as God's instrument. He issued a decree for his vast domain to be taxed (Luke 2). That decree set in motion the ponderous machinery of the Roman Empire so the Messiah could be born in Bethlehem. These and other examples of God's sovereign working permit us to assume that behind the scenes people were praying just as we pray now for rulers and kings and those in authority everywhere. And God answered those prayers.

Not only do we pray for leaders because they are the unconscious instruments of God's purposes, we also pray for them because it benefits us. As Paul mentions in 1 Timothy, one reason for such praying is that we may lead quiet and peaceful lives. . . .

As we pray for our leaders and for various political issues, we will realize no doubt that other Christians are asking that God will grant the antithesis of our own plan. He sorts out these contradictory prayers in keeping with his will. Our responsibility is to pray with the utmost discernment, honesty, and humility. We should not dictate to God, but tell him honestly how we perceive an issue and then ask him to answer in keeping with his wisdom and love.

This means operating on the Gethsemane principle. We add as the controlling postscript to any prayer, "Not as I will, but as you will" (Matthew 26:39). In the Garden of Gethsemane the night before he was crucified, Jesus longed that the cup might pass from him. But in the end, he trustfully put himself in his Father's hand. This final act of faith is to trust God's wisdom and love and goodness above our own discernment or even in contradiction to our own desires.

In pleading with God, I may be mistaken even though I use my intelligence as fully as possible. People on the other side of an issue may have a keener insight into God's will. So I pray, "I trust you, Father. Even if what you bring to pass is contrary to what I'm asking, I still have the confidence that this is as it ought to be. Your will be done, not mine." . . .

We should remember Proverbs 21:1, "The king's heart is in the hand of the Lord; he directs it like a watercourse wherever he pleases." We don't know how God does that in response to our prayers, but we know we're commanded to pray. Let God work out the theoretical puzzles. It is enough for us to know that our prayers make a difference.[35]

—*Vernon Grounds*

CAN MY PRAYERS MAKE A DIFFERENCE IN MY NEIGHBORHOOD?

Another significant way for you to grow in your prayer life and to mentor others is prayer-walking. In recent years prayer-walking has become an increasingly significant ministry for many Christians. I well remember the first time I was introduced to this concept. It came from a very unexpected source.

While I was pastoring in Southern California a number of years ago, one of the couples in our church family lived just two blocks from our house. Sometimes early in the morning, I would see them walk by our house. One day I happened to mention to them that it

was good to see them out walking together. They responded by saying they enjoyed it greatly and that one of the things they had begun to do was to pray for Jeannie and me and our family every morning when they passed our house. Soon they were praying not only for us but for other neighbors as well. Without fully realizing it, they were involved in a prayer-walking ministry.

Steve Hawthorne and Graham Kendrick have written a very helpful book entitled *Prayer-Walking: Praying on Site with Insight.*

> Across the globe God is stirring ordinary believers to pray persistently while walking their cities street by street. Some use rather well-arranged plans. Others flow with Spirit-given prompts. Their prayers run the gamut from lofty appeals to pinpoint petitions, ranging beyond their own homes to their neighbors. It's hard to stop there, so most of them eventually burst into prayers for the entire campus or city or nation. No quick fix is envisioned. But expectancy seems to expand with every mile. Most of these pray-ers don't imagine themselves to be just bravely holding flickering candles toward an overwhelming darkness. Rather, long fuses are being lit for anticipated explosions of God's love. Every day believers are praying, house by house, in their neighborhoods.

Peter Wagner has shared an example of a rather sophisticated and systematic approach to prayer-walking that focuses on evangelistic outreach.

> Most prayerwalking to date has been spontaneous. Ministry and results have been good. But suppose we went

beyond doing it here and there. Suppose that once a week every single block of every single street in our city were covered by a prayerwalk. Would you believe that within a year this would be a different city? I believe it would, but it would take more effort, more leadership and more coordination.

My friend John Huffman has pioneered that kind of citywide neighborhood prayerwalking that might give us the clues about how to do it in our own city. His initial field experiments, called "Christ for the City," were done in Medellin, Colombia.

Although all synchronized neighborhood prayerwalking does not have to be done this way, John Huffman's plan is explicitly evangelistic. . . . The general idea is to mobilize as massive an amount of intercessory prayer for the neighborhood as possible for 14 days preceding an evangelistic event. The more targeted the prayer the better, so each neighborhood is mapped block by block. . . .

A suggested prayer program for the 2 weeks has been outlined by Huffman, but any variations the Lord indicates are welcome. The schedule includes, among other things, preparation of the intercessors, prayers of blessing, warfare praying, fasting and prayer for special groups.

Prayer-walking can vary, from simply praying in general for our neighbor's needs to praying for the salvation of entire city blocks.[36]

—*Paul Cedar*

CAN MY PRAYERS MAKE A DIFFERENCE IN OTHERS' SPIRITUAL LIVES AND EVEN BRING A REVIVAL?

If my people, who are called by my name, will humble themselves and pray and seek my face and turn from their wicked ways, then will I hear from heaven and will forgive

their sin and will heal their land. (2 Chronicles 7:14)

What *will* it take for God to reach every corner of this country and make it a God-fearing land again? I believe the answer is revival. . . .

Today there's a lot of talk among Christians about revival and how much it's needed; it's almost become a buzzword in some Christian circles. But what is it really, and do we really need it? I once read a definition that said: "Revival is something that nobody can explain but everyone recognizes when it gets there."

Dr. Armin Gesswein saw revival this way:

> The revival we need is simply a return to normal New Testament Christianity, where the churches are full of prayer, full of power, full of people, full of praise, full of divine happenings all the time. We want something normal, not just "special." God's normal, that is. God's normal is greater than most of our specials put together.

Revival isn't a process that people can use to manipulate God. You cannot *plan* a true revival, but you can *seek* it. I've found that God-ordained revival follows a pattern. Here's what I've observed:

1. The people pray.
2. God comes.
3. The people repent.
4. God revives the people.
5. The people begin to minister to and pour their lives into others.
6. God equips and empowers them, making up the difference.

Revival can come—but it all begins with prayer.

Any time God is going to do something wonderful, He begins with a difficulty. When He is going to do something *very* wonderful, He begins with an *impossibility*. If you look around today, I think you'll agree that our country seems to be in an impossible situation. Only God will be able to save our churches, our families, and our nation. And He will come if we begin to pray. It's time for us to get started.[37]

—*John Maxwell*

CAN I PRAY FOR SUCCESS?

How many young people have prayed a prayer similar to that of Abraham's servant—for the Lord to give them success in finding the right spouse (Gen. 24:12)! In fact, from finding a partner to finding a job, from building a business to building a life, people frequently pray for God to bless their efforts with success. Is that prayer legitimate for God's people?

In a success-driven society, people of faith often struggle with the place and pursuit of success. Some believe that material success by its nature represents a compromise of spiritual convictions. Others, however, feel that success is actually a sign that God is pleased with them. Still others say that they are not interested in success, yet their claim seems to be an excuse for poor performance in the marketplace. What does success mean for people who want to honor God in their lives?

There are no simple answers to these questions. The issue of success is complex and charged with emotion. But perhaps the following three observations will prove helpful as you devote thoughtful consideration and public discussion to the subject:

(1) Success always implies striving to meet some set of standards established by some person or group.

(2) The pursuit of success is always a personal choice. No one can make someone else pursue success.

(3) Obtaining success always exacts a cost—it takes our time, ability, and resources.

In light of these principles, ask yourself three questions as you pursue, or refrain from pursuing, success: Who is determining what success means for me? What am I choosing by my pursuit of success? What price am I paying to achieve success?[38]

—*from* The Word in Life Study Bible

THE PROCESS OF PRAYER

[focus on the process of praying]

WHAT ARE SOME DIFFERENT WAYS I CAN PRAY?

You may want to spend a few moments preparing your mind and heart for prayer. The following selections offer options—either as the opening phrase of your communication or as a separate overture.

Requesting the Lord's attention, 1 Kings 8:28—"Yet regard the prayer of Your servant and his supplication, O LORD my God, and listen to the cry and the prayer which Your servant is praying before You today."

If you are a leader, muse Nehemiah's prologue, Nehemiah 1:4–11—"So it was, when I heard these words, that I sat down and wept, and mourned for many days; I was fasting and praying before the God of heaven. And I said: 'I pray, LORD God of heaven, O great and awesome God, You who keep Your covenant and mercy with those who love You and observe Your commandments, please let Your ear be attentive and Your eyes open, that You may hear the prayer of Your servant which I pray before You now, day and night, for the children of Israel Your servants, and confess the sins of the children of Israel which we have sinned against You. Both my father's house and I have sinned. We have acted very corruptly against You, and have not kept the commandments, the statutes, nor the ordinances which You commanded Your servant Moses. Remember, I pray, the word that You commanded Your servant Moses, saying, "If you are unfaithful, I will scatter you among the nations; but if you return to Me, and keep My commandments and do them, though some of you were cast out to the farthest part of the heavens, yet I will gather them from there, and bring them to the place which I have chosen as a dwelling for My name." Now these are Your servants and Your people, whom You have redeemed by Your great power, and by Your strong hand. O LORD, I pray, please let Your ear be attentive to the prayer of Your servant, and to the prayer of Your servants who desire to fear Your name; and let Your servant prosper this day, I pray, and grant him mercy in the sight of this man.' For I was the king's cupbearer."

Good morning, Lord, Psalm 5:1–3—"Give ear to my words, O Lord, consider my meditation. Give heed to the voice of my cry, my King and my God, for to You I will pray. My voice You shall hear in the morning, O Lord; in the morning I will direct it to You, and I will look up."

Tell the Lord you love Him, Psalm 18:1–3—"I will love You, O Lord, my strength. The Lord is my rock and my fortress and my deliverer; my God, my strength, in whom I will trust; my shield and the horn of my salvation, my stronghold. I will call upon the Lord, who is worthy to be praised; so shall I be saved from my enemies."

Words and thoughts pleasing to the Lord, Psalm 19:14—"Let the words of my mouth and the meditation of my heart be acceptable in Your sight, O Lord, my strength and my Redeemer."

Humbly ask God for His attention, Psalm 27:7–8—"Hear, O Lord, when I cry with my voice! Have mercy also upon me, and answer me. When You said, 'Seek My face,' my heart said to You, 'Your face, Lord, I will seek.'"

Be still and know you are in God's presence, Psalm 46:10—"Be still, and know that I am God; I will be exalted among the nations, I will be exalted in the earth!"

Going through tough times? Here's help, Psalm 57:1–2—"Be merciful to me, O God, be merciful to me! For my soul trusts in You; and in the shadow of Your wings I will make my refuge, until these calamities have passed by. I will cry out to God Most High, to God who performs all things for me."

Exalt the Lord as you prepare to pray, Psalm 57:5—"Be exalted, O God, above the heavens; let your glory be above all the earth."

Early morning prayer, Psalm 63:1—"O God, You are my God; early will I seek You; my soul thirsts for You; my flesh longs for You."

> **PRAYER REFLECTION**
> **A Dinner Prayer**
> *Thou art blessed, O Lord, who nourishest me from my youth, who givest food to all flesh. Fill our hearts with joy and gladness, that having always what is sufficient for us, we may abound to every good work, in Christ Jesus our Lord, through whom glory, honour, and power be to Thee for ever. Amen.*
>
> —*Constitutions of the Holy Apostles*

It is God's plan to bless you, Psalm 84:11—"The LORD God is a sun and shield; the LORD will give grace and glory; no good thing will He withhold from those who walk uprightly."

Desperation prayer, Psalm 88:1–2—"O LORD, God of my salvation, I have cried out day and night before You. Let my prayer come before You; incline Your ear to my cry."

Please, God, hear my prayer, Psalm 102:1–2—"Hear my prayer, O LORD, and let my cry come to You. Do not hide Your face from me in the day of my trouble; incline Your ear to me; in the day that I call, answer me speedily."

Praising the Lord, Psalm 103:1–2—"Bless the LORD, O my soul; and all that is within me, bless His holy name! Bless the LORD, O my soul, and forget not all His benefits."

You can be sure God listens, Psalm 116:1–2—"I love the LORD, because He has heard my voice and my supplications. Because He has inclined His ear to me, therefore I will call upon Him as long as I live."

Enduring mercy, Psalm 118:28—"You are my God, and I will praise You; You are my God, I will exalt You."

Heart-searching encounter, Psalm 139:23–24—"Search me, O God, and know my heart; try me, and know my anxieties; and see if there is any wicked way in me, and lead me in the way everlasting."

Praise God for His greatness, Psalm 145:3—"Great is the LORD, and greatly to be praised; and His greatness is unsearchable."

The Lord's glory, Isaiah 42:8—"I am the LORD, that is My name; and My glory I will not give to another."

God knows those who trust Him, Nahum 1:7—"The LORD is good, a stronghold in the day of trouble; and He knows those who trust in Him."

How to approach God, Hebrews 4:14–16—"Seeing then that we have a great High Priest who has passed through the heavens, Jesus the Son of God, let us hold fast our confession. For we do not have a High Priest who cannot sympathize with our weakness, but was in all points tempted as we are, yet without sin. Let us therefore come boldly to the throne of grace, that we may obtain mercy and find grace to help in time of need."[1]

—*Ken Anderson*

WHAT ABOUT INCORPORATING SCRIPTURE INTO MY PRAYERS?

Meant to sustain, inspire, motivate, increase faith, mature, and strengthen a believer, the Word of God, when interwoven with prayer, serves as direction and guidance, conviction and comfort, a deterrent from sin, an escape, a counselor. A deeper walk with Christ is evident when our *first* response, our most compelling desire at any given time, in any situation, is to hunger for the advice found in God's Word.

Theophan, known as the Recluse, said if they were practiced simultaneously, the Word and prayer produced a certain feeling within the believer toward the Lord:

> Do you wish to enter this Paradise as quickly as possible? Here, then, is what you must do. When you pray, do not end your prayer without having aroused in your heart some feeling towards God, whether it be reverence, or devotion, or thanksgiving, or glorification, or humility and contrition, or hope and trust. Also when after prayer you begin to read, do not finish reading without having felt in your heart the truth of what you read. These two feelings—the one inspired by prayer, the other by reading—mutually warm one another; and if you pay attention to yourself, they will keep you under their influence during the whole day. Take pains to practice these two methods exactly and you will see for yourself what will happen.

What *will* happen? "God's spark, the ray of grace will fall at last into your heart. There is no way in which you, yourself, can produce it: it comes forth direct from God.". . .

Prayer draws us to the Word, and the two ignite to create a spark, even a flame, for the Lord. The Word and prayer, if *applied* to all circumstances of our lives, are *intended* to change, transform, motivate, and propel us to make certain decisions, take deliberate steps, and stretch to live and walk in the Spirit. But until Bible reading and

> **PRAYER REFLECTION**
> *Prayer is nothing more than turning our hearts toward God and receiving in turn His love.*
> —*Madame Guyon*

prayer become our *natural* reaction when faced with a dilemma or a decision, we'll not experience the warmth described by Theophan—the spark that allows God to confirm direction or grant peace amidst turmoil. If prayer is simply a last resort "call for help" and if one only haphazardly searches the Scriptures for guidance (when all other avenues have failed), one has missed God's true intent of how prayer and the Word are able to integrate moment by moment into a believer's life. . . .

A deeper walk with God emerges when the Word is constantly *blended* with prayer in a believer's life. David mentions several times in Psalm 119 that he put his hope in the Word. Because of that exhortation, it has become my practice to hope in the Word by asking God for a scriptural promise to hold on to or to "hope in" when my endurance level is waning or when I have a long wait or big decision to make. It is as if He gives a promise—His promise—to be my *visible* possession while waiting for the invisible to happen. My Bible, especially the Books of Isaiah and Psalms, is splashed with underlined verses, highlighted paragraphs, and dated ink marks next to verses that were my hope during a court case, a broken relationship waiting to be mended, timely sermon texts, encouragement when I needed a lift, guidance for purchasing a new car or in accepting an invitation. . . .

> **PRAYER REFLECTION**
>
> *God is never more than a prayer away from you. . . . We address and stamp a letter and send it on its way, confident that it will reach its destination, but we doubtfully wonder if our prayer will be heard by an ever-present God.*
>
> —William A. Ward

Daily Bible reading, *along* with prayer, encourages a two-way conversation with God, allowing the warmth of the right direction to overpower the dullness or confusion that accompanies wrong or incorrect choices.

In *The Inner Life,* Andrew Murray proposes,

> Prayer and the Word are inseparably linked together. Power in the use of either depends upon the presence of the other. The Word gives me guidance for prayer, telling me what God will do for me. It shows me the path of prayer, telling me how God would have me come. It gives me the power for prayer, the courage to accept the assurance that I will be heard. And it brings me the answer to prayer, as it

teaches what God will do for me. And so, prayer prepares
the heart for receiving the Word from God Himself, for
the teaching of the Spirit which gives spiritual understanding, and for the faith that carries out God's will.

It takes a *time commitment* and *daily practice* to walk deeper into knowing God through
the utterly available combination of the Word and prayer. When opening the Bible and
talking to God in prayer become our *first* option, our natural instinct, our immediate reaction when faced with a decision or problem, then we will have a deep assurance that we
are walking hand in hand along the pathway of our earthly lives with our Lord and
Friend.[2]

—*Becky Tirabassi*

WHAT CAN I LEARN ABOUT HOW AND WHEN TO PRAY FROM JESUS' EXAMPLE?

How long has it been since you let God have you? I mean really *have* you? How long
since you gave him a portion of undiluted, uninterrupted time listening for his voice?
Apparently Jesus did, He made a deliberate effort to spend time with God.

Spend much time reading about the listening life of Jesus and a distinct pattern
emerges. He spent regular time with God, praying and listening. Mark says, "Very early
in the morning, while it was still dark, Jesus got up, left the house and went off to a solitary place, where he prayed" (Mark 1:35 NIV). Luke tells us, "Jesus often withdrew to lonely places and prayed" (Luke 5:16 NIV).

Let me ask the obvious. If Jesus, the Son of God, the sinless Savior of humankind,
thought it worthwhile to clear his calendar to pray, wouldn't we be wise to do the same?

Not only did he spend regular time with God in prayer, he spent regular time in
God's Word. Of course we don't find Jesus pulling a leather-bound New Testament from
his satchel and reading it. We do, however, see the stunning example of Jesus, in the throes
of the wilderness temptation, using the Word of God to deal with Satan. Three times he
is tempted, and each time he repels the attack with the phrase: "It is written in the
Scriptures" (Luke 4:4, 8, 12), and then he quotes a verse. Jesus is so familiar with Scripture
that he not only knows the verse, he knows how to use it.

> **PRAYER REFLECTION**
> *Prayer can encourage the one you are praying for, but it can also encourage and change you.*
> —H. Norman Wright

And then there's the occasion when Jesus was asked to read in the synagogue. He is handed the book of Isaiah the prophet. He finds the passage, reads it, and declares, "While you heard these words just now, they were coming true!" (Luke 4:21). We are given the picture of a person who knows his way around in Scripture and can recognize its fulfillment. If Jesus thought it wise to grow familiar with the Bible, shouldn't we do the same?

If we are to be just like Jesus—if we are to have ears that hear God's voice—then we have just found two habits worth imitating: the habits of prayer and Bible reading. Consider these verses:

> Base your happiness on your hope in Christ. When trials come endure them patiently; steadfastly maintain *the habit of prayer.* (Rom. 12:12 PHILLIPS, italics mine)

> The man who looks into the perfect law, the law of liberty, and makes a habit of so doing, is not the man who hears and forgets. He puts the law into practice and he wins true happiness. (James 1:25 PHILLIPS)

If we are to be just like Jesus, we must have a regular time of talking to God and listening to his Word.[3]

—*Max Lucado*

WHAT DID JESUS PRAY ABOUT?

"He went up on a mountainside by Himself to pray."

Jesus faced an impossible task. More than five thousand people were ready to fight a battle he had not come to fight. How could he show them that he didn't come to be a king, but to be a sacrifice? How could he take their eyes off an earthly kingdom so that they would see the spiritual one? How could they see the eternal when they only had eyes for the temporal?

What Jesus dreamed of doing and what he seemed able to do were separated by an impossible gulf. So Jesus prayed.

We don't know what he prayed about. But I have my guesses:

- He prayed that eyes blinded by power could see God's truth.
- He prayed that disciples dizzied by success could endure failure.
- He prayed that leaders longing for power would follow him to a cross.
- He prayed that people desiring bread for the body would hunger for bread for the soul.

He prayed for the impossible to happen.

Or maybe I'm wrong. Maybe he didn't ask for anything. Maybe he just stood quietly in the presence of Presence and basked in the Majesty. Perhaps he placed his war-weary self before the throne and rested.

Maybe he lifted his head out of the confusion of earth long enough to hear the solution of heaven. Perhaps he was reminded that hard hearts don't faze the Father. That problem people don't perturb the Eternal One.

We don't know what he did or what he said. But we do know the result. The hill became a steppingstone; the storm became a path. And the disciples saw Jesus as they had never seen him before.

During the storm, Jesus prayed. The sky darkened. The winds howled. Yet he prayed. The people grumbled. The disciples doubted. Yet he prayed. When forced to choose between the muscles of men and the mountain of prayer, he prayed.

Jesus did not try to do it by himself. Why should you?[4]

—*Max Lucado*

HOW CAN I REALLY HAVE FAITH IN MY PRAYING?

"Lord, if it's you," Peter says, "tell me to come to you on the water."

Peter is not testing Jesus; he is pleading with Jesus. Stepping onto a stormy sea is not a move of logic; it is a move of desperation.

Peter grabs the edge of the boat. Throws out a leg . . . follows with the other. Several steps are taken. It's as if an invisible ridge of rocks runs beneath his feet. At the end of the ridge is the glowing face of a never-say-die friend.

We do the same, don't we? We come to Christ in an hour of deep need. We abandon the boat of good works. We realize, like Moses, that human strength won't save us. So we

153

look to God in desperation. We realize, like Paul, that all the good works in the world are puny when laid before the Perfect One. We realize, like Peter, that spanning the gap between us and Jesus is a feat too great for our feet. So we beg for help. Hear his voice. And step out in fear, hoping that our little faith will be enough.

Faith is not born at the negotiating table where we barter our gifts in exchange for God's goodness. Faith is not an award given to the most learned. It's not a prize given to the most disciplined. It's not a title bequeathed to the most religious.

Faith is a desperate dive out of the sinking boat of human effort and a prayer that God will be there to pull us out of the water. Paul wrote about this kind of faith in the letter to the Ephesians:

"For it is by grace you have been saved, through faith—and this not from yourselves, it is the gift of God—not by works, so that no one can boast."

Paul is clear. The supreme force in salvation is God's grace. Not our works. Not our talents. Not our feelings. Not our strength.

Salvation is God's sudden, calming presence during the stormy seas of our lives. We hear his voice; we take the step.

We, like Paul, are aware of two things: We are great sinners and we need a great Savior.

We, like Peter, are aware of two facts: We are going down and God is standing up. So we scramble out. We leave behind the *Titanic* of self-righteousness and stand on the solid path of God's grace.

And, surprisingly, we are able to walk on water. Death is disarmed. Failures are forgivable. Life has real purpose. And God is not only within sight, he is within reach.

With precious, wobbly steps, we draw closer to him. For a season of surprising strength, we stand upon his promises. It doesn't make sense that we are able to do this. We don't claim to be worthy of such an incredible gift. When people ask how in the world we can keep our balance during such stormy times, we don't boast. We don't brag. We point unabashedly to the One who makes it possible. Our eyes are on him.

"Nothing in my hand I bring; Simply to Thy cross I cling," we sing.

"Dressed in His righteousness alone, Faultless to stand before the throne," we declare.

" 'Twas grace that taught my heart to fear, And grace my fears relieved," we explain.

Some of us, unlike Peter, never look back.

Others of us, like Peter, feel the wind and are afraid.

Maybe we face the wind of pride: "I'm not such a bad sinner after all. Look at what I can do."

Perhaps we face the wind of legalism: "I know that Jesus is doing part of this, but I have to do the rest."

Most of us, though, face the wind of doubt: "I'm too bad for God to treat me this well. I don't deserve such a rescue."

And downward we plunge. Heavied by mortality's mortar, we sink. Gulping and thrashing, we fall into a dark, wet world. We open our eyes and see only blackness. We try to breathe, and no air comes. We kick and fight our way back to the surface.

With our heads barely above the water, we have to make a decision.

The prideful ask: "Do we 'save face' and drown in pride? Or do we scream for help and take God's hand?"

The legalists ask: "Do we sink under the lead-heavy weight of the Law? Or do we abandon the codes and beg for grace?"

The doubters ask: "Do we nurture doubt by mumbling, 'I've really let him down this time?' Or do we hope that the same Christ who called us out of the boat will call us out of the sea?"

We know Peter's choice.

"[As he was] beginning to sink, [he] cried out, 'Lord, save me!' "

"Immediately Jesus reached out his hand and caught him."[5]

—*Max Lucado*

I KNOW I'M SUPPOSED TO FORGIVE OTHERS BEFORE I COME TO PRAYER, BUT I'M HAVING A HARD TIME FORGIVING.

Forgiveness leads to life. Unforgiveness is a slow death. It doesn't mean you aren't saved, and it doesn't mean you won't go to heaven. But it does mean you can't have all that God has for you and you will not be free of emotional pain.

The first step to forgiving is to *receive God's forgiveness* and let its reality penetrate the deepest part of our being. When we realize how much we have been forgiven, it's easier to understand that we have no right to pass judgment on one another. Once we are forgiven and released from everything we've ever done wrong, how can we refuse to obey God when He asks us to forgive others? Easy! We focus our thoughts on the person who has wronged us rather than on the God who makes all things right.

Forgiveness is a two-way street. God forgives you, and you forgive others. God forgives you quickly and completely upon your confession of wrongdoing. You are to forgive others quickly and completely, whether they admit failure or not. Most of the time people don't feel they've done anything wrong anyway, and if they do, they certainly don't want to admit it to you.

> ~
> **PRAYER REFLECTION**
> *To pray, "Thy will be done" is to*
> *seek the heart of God.*
> —*Max Lucado*

Forgiveness is a choice that we make. We base our decision not on what we feel like doing but on what we *know is right.* I did not *feel* like forgiving my mother. Instead I *chose* to forgive her because God's Word says, "Forgive, and you will be forgiven" (Luke 6:37). That verse also says that we shouldn't judge if we don't want to be judged ourselves.

It was hard for me to understand that God loved my mother as much as He loves me. He loves *all* people as much as He loves me. He loves the murderer, the rapist, the prostitute, and the thief. And He hates their murdering, raping, whoring, and stealing as much as He hates my pride, gossiping, and unforgiveness. We may sit and compare our sins to other people's and say, "Mine aren't so bad," but God says they all stink so we shouldn't worry about whose smell the worst. The most important thing to remember about forgiveness is that *forgiveness doesn't make the other person right; it makes you free. . . .*

You can never be completely released from, or reconciled to, a person you haven't forgiven. You have to be willing to say, "Lord, I choose to forgive this person. Help me to forgive her (him) completely." When you do that, the cleansing process has begun. That's because *the law of the Lord is to let go, not get even.*

If you forgive one day and then the next day you find you are still angry, hurt, and intensely bitter toward that same person, don't be discouraged. Continue to take it to the Lord again and again. There are times we can forgive quickly, but usually forgiving a person who has caused deep wounds is an ongoing, step-by-step process. This is especially true if there has been no reconciliation. You will know the work is complete when you can honestly say you want God's best for that person.[6]

—*Stormie Omartian*

HOW DOES THE HOLY SPIRIT HELP ME AS I PRAY?

When I first heard the names Helper and Comforter in reference to the Holy Spirit, I knew immediately I wanted those attributes of God in my life. I realized that to get them, I first had to acknowledge the Holy Spirit's existence and then be open to His working in me. When I did that, I learned three important reasons to be filled with God's Holy Spirit:

- ◆ to worship God more fully
- ◆ to experience and communicate God's love more completely
- ◆ to appropriate God's power in my life more effectively

If you acknowledge Jesus as Savior and God as Father, you have to acknowledge the Holy Spirit. I've heard certain Christians speak of the Trinity as Father, Son, and H-H-L-L-S-S-P-P-S-S-H-H. They can hardly say "Holy Spirit" without choking, let alone acknowledge His working in their lives. Perhaps it's because they know too little about Him. Or maybe they were in a situation in which odd things were done in the name of the Holy Spirit. (Or perhaps they heard the term "Holy Ghost" and were afraid of ghosts!) Whatever the reason, let me assure you that the Holy Spirit is the Spirit of God sent by Jesus to give us comfort, to build us up, to guide us in all truth, to bring us spiritual gifts, to help us pray more effectively, to give us wisdom and revelation, and to help us know God's will for our lives. Are there people who can honestly say they don't ever need those things?

The Holy Spirit cannot be ignored. We can't pretend He doesn't exist or say that Jesus didn't mean it when He promised He would send the Holy Spirit to us, or suggest that God was just kidding when He said He was pouring out His Spirit on all humankind. The Holy Spirit is not a vapor or a mystical cloud; He is another part of God. . . . He is God's power and the means by which God speaks to us. If we ignore or reject Him, we will cut off this power and communication from working in our lives.

If your lips can say, "Jesus is Lord," you can be sure the Spirit of God is working in your life already. Being filled with the Spirit is mentioned in many scriptures. Since there seem to be just as many interpretations of them as there are denominations, I'm not going to confine you to mine. Simply ask the Holy Spirit what those scriptures should mean to you, and leave it in His hands to tell you.

The Bible says, "I will put My Spirit within you and cause you to walk in My statutes, and you will keep My judgments and do them" (Ezek. 36:27). The Holy Spirit works the wholeness of God into us. And there need be no fear or mystery about this, because we alone of God's creation have a special place built in us where His Spirit can reside. That place will always be empty until it is filled with Him.

We don't want to have "a form of godliness" but deny "its power" (2 Tim. 3:5); denying God's power limits what God can do in our lives and prevents us from moving into all God has for us. Nor do we want to be "always learning and never able to come to the knowledge of the truth" (2 Tim. 3:7). Unless the Holy Spirit coaches us from within, our knowledge of the truth will always be limited, and our spiritual health will be incomplete. Don't limit what God can do in you by failing to acknowledge His Holy Spirit in your life.

I have discovered over the years, however, that the infilling of the Holy Spirit is ongoing and ever deepening. We have to be willing to open up to each new level and dimension so that He can enable us to accomplish what we could never do without this full measure of His love, power, and life.

No matter how long you have known the Lord, it's good to pray the following prayer to Him frequently:

> God, help me understand all I need to know about You and the workings of Your Spirit in my life. Fill me with Your Holy Spirit in a fresh new way this day, and work powerfully in me.[7]

—Stormie Omartian

I'VE HEARD THAT I SHOULD PRAY "IN THE SPIRIT." WHAT DOES THAT MEAN?

Pray according to the leadership of the Spirit

When you pray, do you pray under the leadership of the Holy Spirit? Do you run through a prayer agenda without considering the Spirit's guidance in your time of prayer? When you pray under the Spirit's leadership, you cannot be in a hurry. If you are in a rush, you cannot pray under the Spirit's leadership. How can you begin to pray according to the leadership of the Holy Spirit?

You begin with moments of not saying anything. Meditate on the things of God. I would encourage you to begin by praying something like, "Lord, I come to You in the name of Jesus today. I do not want to have moments of vain repetition that will not please You, but I want You to show me what to pray for right now." It is important to have a plan to pray. . . . Yet, whatever your plan is, you need to have enough flexibility to let the Holy Spirit lead you in your prayer time. A plan should be used to give you a general direction, not to place you into bondage as you pray.

When you pray under the leadership of the Holy Spirit, He will lead you to pray by the Word of God. At times, I have had some people say to me, "Pastor, I am praying about getting a divorce, and I really sense the Holy Spirit is leading me to do so." The Bible is very clear about divorce: God does not like it. The Holy Spirit will always lead you to fulfill the Word of God. Therefore, the Spirit will not lead you to be divorced if Scripture does not permit it to take place. You cannot let the phrase "the Spirit is leading me" become a means to justify an action that is contrary to God's Word.

Praying under the leadership of the Spirit means that you will pray by and with the Word of God. When you pray under the leadership of the Holy Spirit, you will let God show you what you need to pray for and about in your time of prayer. God will show you what to pray for. Listen to Him. Let His Spirit talk to your spirit. At times, just be quiet and let God lead you.

Praying in the Holy Spirit also means that you . . .

Pray with assistance from the Holy Spirit

. . . The Holy Spirit pulls you toward God and to spiritual victory. Romans 8:26 says, "And in the same way the Spirit also helps our weakness; for we do not know how to pray as we should, but the Spirit Himself intercedes for us with groanings too deep for words."

There are times in the Christian life when you do not know how to pray. This passage is very clear that God is not talking about groanings with words or in a prayer language. This passage is speaking of how the Holy Spirit comes to assist you in prayer when you do not know what to pray. The Holy Spirit is praying for you to have victory. He is praying for you to fulfill God's will in your life. He is praying for you to have assistance from Him.

When you pray with assistance from the Holy Spirit, your prayer will be something like this: "Lord, I do not know how to pray about this matter. I must have Your help. I must have Your assistance. As You lead me to pray about this, may Your Spirit utter to the Father what the depths of my heart feel about this matter. Assist me, Holy Spirit, right now as I pray."

Praying in the Holy Spirit is letting the Spirit assist you in your time of prayer. Praying in the Spirit also means to . . .

Pray with power from the Spirit

In October 1997, more than one million men filled the Washington, D.C., Mall to beseech God to send revival to America. This event, called Stand in the Gap, was a great moment in the history of American Christianity. In fact, it could have been the largest gathering of Christians in the history of the world.

I was asked to speak during the program. On the evening prior to this significant event, the speakers and participants gathered together in a prayer meeting. The power of God came upon the meeting as we prayed for one another. As we laid hands on various people, the power of God was ushered into that place. We prayed with true spiritual power.

One of the reasons Stand in the Gap was so powerful in the lives of many Christians was that the power of God first fell upon the leadership. The power of God in prayer usually precedes the power of God demonstrated in a public meeting.

Prayer leads you to the power of God, both in personal times of prayer and in

> **PRAYER REFLECTION**
>
> *You can talk to God because God listens. Your voice matters in heaven. He takes you very seriously. When you enter his presence, the attendants turn to you to hear your voice. No need to fear that you will be ignored. Even if you stammer or stumble, even if what you have to say impresses no one, it impresses God—and he listens.*
>
> —*Max Lucado*

public meetings of believers. God is attracted to men and women who want to pray in the Spirit. He will bless those who will pray in the Spirit with power.

Prayerlessness means you are depending on yourself. Prayer in the Spirit means that you are depending on God. When you depend on God, you will receive His power when you pray.

When His power comes upon you, mighty things begin to happen. You begin to experience power from on high. You begin to pray for things you did not have a burden to pray for before this time. You are energized, filled, and empowered by His Spirit. You are granted the authority of Jesus Christ. You will experience boldness, courage, and faith like never before. It is a faith-building moment. A powerful moment. A true God moment! When you are praying in the Spirit, experiencing His power, you become God's tool. At times, you are simply a vessel in the hand of God as you represent His people and their needs before God. Yes, prayer leads you to the power of God.[8]

—*Ronnie W. Floyd*

IS THERE A PARTICULAR POSTURE I SHOULD TAKE WHEN I PRAY?

I have often wondered why the church in the past has not been divided on the subject of the posture of prayer. This is an issue that could divide the church, as it seems just about everything else has. The mode of baptism has certainly divided the church. There are those who believe sprinkling is the correct mode, a few believe pouring (that means getting a pitcher of water and dousing the head) is the correct mode, and others believe immersion is the correct mode. Still others believe you should be immersed not just one time, but three times. Then some say you should go down headfirst, and others say backwards. There are even some today who believe that if it's not done by running water then you haven't really been baptized. As you can see, baptism has certainly divided the church.

That's why I say it's a wonder that the posture of prayer hasn't divided the church. I'm surprised we don't have a group today known as "standers." They believe in standing up when you pray. Then it's a wonder that we don't have a group of "kneelers" who believe you should kneel down when you pray. Then there ought to be a group of "sitters." They believe you should sit when you pray. Then there's another group that believes you ought to lie down—they're the "liars." That would really be a large group! I didn't realize anyone else had considered this issue before, but then I discovered this poem called "The Prayer of Cyrus Brown."

> "The proper way for a man to pray," said Deacon Lemuel Keyes, "and the only proper attitude is down upon his knees."
>
> "No, I should say the way to pray," said Reverend Doctor Wise, "is standing straight with outstretched arms and rapt and upturned eyes."
>
> "Oh, no, no, no!" said Elder Sloe. "Such posture is too proud. A man should pray with eyes fast closed and head contritely bowed."
>
> "It seems to me his hands should be austerely clasped in front with both thumbs pointing toward the ground," said Reverend Doctor Blunt.
>
> "Last year I fell in Hodkin's well, head first," said Cyrus Brown. "With both my heels a-stickin' up, my head a-pointin' down, the prayenist prayer I ever prayed was a-standin' on my head."[9]

—*J. Vernon McGee*

I'M SO BUSY. HOW CAN I MAKE TIME TO PRAY?

With your busy schedule, how much time can you set aside for prayer? Half an hour a day? Fifteen minutes? The Bible doesn't specify a minimum amount, so we're on our own when it comes to creating a prayer schedule.

David seems to have preferred three-a-days:

> As for me, I will call upon God,
> And the LORD shall save me.
> Evening and morning and at noon
> I will pray, and cry aloud,
> And He shall hear my voice. (Ps. 55:16–17)

We don't know whether this number included just his regularly scheduled prayer times or whether it was an estimate of the number of times he talked to God, formally or informally, in the course of a day.

Either way, the fact that David prayed three times a day (or more) doesn't mean we have to. David's schedule might have allowed him to have three uninterrupted times during the day when he could chat with God. You may not have that same luxury.

Whatever your schedule allows, the important thing is that you spend as much scheduled time with God as possible. Praying whenever you think of it or whenever you feel that you "need" it just isn't good enough. Passionate pray-ers give prayer the same (or higher) priority as working, going to school, working out, or anything else on their schedules.

To become an extreme pray-er, you need to carve out time in your day in which you do nothing but pray. If your relationship with the Lord is a priority in your life, your schedule should reflect that. Obviously, the more time you set aside, the more quickly your prayer life will mature and the more positive results you'll see.

In between your scheduled prayer times, too, you can turn to God for quickie conversations or extra boosts of encouragement or peace of mind. You don't even need to make an appointment!

And if you really want to get into it, pay attention to what the apostle Paul suggested: "Pray without ceasing" (1 Thess. 5:17). That would be like installing a DSL between you and God. The link would always be open, and information would be continuously flowing back and forth at all hours of the day.

That's what you call *extreme,* extreme prayer.[10]

—Randy Southern

HOW CAN I PRAY "WITHOUT CEASING"?

Breathing is a good model for constant prayer. Breathing brings life and health to my body, likewise prayer to my spiritual life. Something is very wrong if I'm finding it difficult to breathe. My spiritual state will also be more labored and depressed without regular prayer. So for prayer to be unceasing, it's going to be a very natural, regular occurrence that I seldom notice. Like breathing, it will be something so habitual that it rarely calls my attention, except perhaps in the extremes of sorrow or joy.

If I am going to put constant prayer into practice, I will need to understand two things. I need a right understanding of what prayer is and I need to see it as a growth process, not an instantaneous gift.

God is a person, not a process. He deals with me personally. Prayer is the communicative expression of my relationship with God. It is intimate conversation and communion with my personal God that takes place, not at special times such as at meals, bedtime, or in church, but on a continual basis. The constant give and take results in my becoming more and more like him.

Jesus told us to pray that God's will be done here on earth and that we are the instruments by which he will carry out his will. We are his body, the body of Christ. Our goal is to imitate him (Ephesians 5:1), to become more and more deeply involved in his wants, purposes, and desires for this world. As we tune our lives to his wavelength, we become channels of his love. In that living, active, and loving state, our whole life becomes an unceasing prayer to God.

> PRAYER REFLECTION
>
> *How vital that we pray, armed with the knowledge that God is in heaven. Pray with any lesser conviction and your prayers are timid, shallow, and hollow. But spend time walking in the workshop of the heavens, seeing what God has done, and watch how your prayers are energized.*
>
> —Max Lucado

One doesn't try to pray without ceasing. As we encourage our relationship with God, prayer follows as the light of day follows the sun; as breath follows the new life. As breath draws oxygen, our moment-by-moment need from our environment, so prayer draws our very life from God. Breathing doesn't cause a lot of excitement; neither does prayer, our quiet intimate exchange with God. As we begin to pray it usually takes much willpower and effort. As our relationship with God becomes more natural, prayer becomes a regular give and take that fills our life with love, joy, and peace, but of which we're rarely aware.

Jesus stresses the intimacy of prayer and condemns its showy observance. There are times to draw away in lonely, intense communion but there should also be an everyday, continual communion with God to be healthy in our spiritual lives. Family counselors will tell us that the most critical element in a healthy relationship is good communication. That communication should take place in a continual interchange. We can come to God all day long with our joys, sorrows, worries, pleasures, and pains. We can ask in brief moments for guidance, help, strength, and intercession for others. I commune with God driving in my car, in a checkout line at the supermarket, visiting a friend.

Our relationship with God and the communicating prayerful part of our lives is cyclical. Our continual, everyday communication with God builds and channels his life with us, which encourages us to pray. We must desire to commune with him. Likewise, anything that separates our natural communion (e.g., our sin or false guilt) often quenches our desire to pray.

We pray unceasingly, as we breathe unceasingly, unconsciously as a natural result of a healthy life. Unceasing prayer is the by-product of a growing, deepening relationship with the personal God of our universe. It is mostly unconscious, a natural response to our daily activities and needs. It is found in the small everyday events of life. It results from God's life in us and our desire for him, not in our efforts to pray without ceasing. We pray with our lives wherever we are. We become more and more like him in the give and take of unceasing prayer.[11]

—*Dave Bastedo*

HOW CAN I HAVE THE MINDSET OF CONSTANT PRAYER?

But although . . . we ought always to raise our minds upwards towards God, and pray without ceasing, yet such is our weakness, which requires to be supported, such our torpor, which requires to be stimulated, that it is requisite for us to appoint special hours for this exercise, hours which are not to pass away without prayer, and during which the whole affections of our minds are to be completely occupied; namely, when we rise in the morning, before we commence our daily work, when we sit down to food, when by the blessing of God we have taken it, and when we retire to rest.

This, however, must not be a superstitious observance of hours, by which, as it were, performing a task to God, we think we are discharged as to other hours; it should rather be considered as a discipline by which our weakness is exercised. . . . In particular, it must be our anxious care, whenever we are ourselves pressed, or see others pressed by any strait, instantly to have recourse to him not only with quickened pace, but with quickened minds; and again, we must not . . . omit to testify our recognition of his hand by praise and thanksgiving.

Lastly, we must in all our prayers carefully avoid wishing to confine God to certain circumstances, or prescribe to him the time, place, or mode of action. In like manner, we are taught by this prayer not to fix any law or impose any condition upon him, but leave it entirely to him to adopt whatever course of procedure seems to him best, in respect of method, time, and place. For before we offer up any petition for ourselves, we ask that his will may be done, and by so doing place our will in subordination to his, just as if we had laid a curb upon it, that, instead of presuming to give law to God, it may regard him as the ruler and disposer of all its wishes.[12]

—*John Calvin*

HOW CAN I DEEPEN MY PRAYER LIFE?

As my children began to outgrow their diapers, I would try to talk them into leaving the kiddie pool and launching out into the deep. For them the kiddie pool was all there was and ever would be. That is, of course, until they experienced the deep. Once they learned how to swim in the ocean, they forever lost their appetite for shallow water.

As I led each one of my children into an experience with the vastness of the ocean, so too Jesus led his disciples out of the shallow tidepools of prayer into an ever deepening relationship with their heavenly Father.

Here are some practical guidelines for diving in.

One—Make the paradigm shift. Stop seeing prayer as merely a means of obtaining your requests. Start seeing prayer as a means of enjoying the riches of a relationship with God. . . .

Two—Confess your sins daily. Every single prayer, including the prayer of Jesus, will bounce right off the ceiling if there is unforgiveness in your heart, which is precisely why Jesus ended his public sermon on prayer with these words: "For if you forgive men when they sin against you, your heavenly Father will also forgive you. But if you do not forgive men their sins, your Father will not forgive your sins" (Matthew 6:14–15).

Three—Get into the Bible. God's will is revealed in his Word. Thus the only way you can know his will is to know his Word. The more we meditate upon God's Word, the clearer his voice will be as we daily commune with him in prayer.

Four—Discover your secret place. The secret to prayer is secret prayer. Your public presence is a direct reflection of your private prayer life. If you spend time in the secret place, you will exude peace in the midst of life's storms. If you do not, you will be a poster child for Busy-anity rather than Christianity.

Five—Make prayer a priority. Wisdom is the application of knowledge. As the Master put it, "Therefore everyone who hears these words of mine and puts them into practice [or applies them] is like a wise man who built his house on the rock" (Matthew 7:24). My experience in teaching memory for over two decades demonstrates that, if you faithfully practice a new discipline for twenty-one days, it may well stay with you for the rest of your life.[13]

—Hank Hanegraaff

I'M A PARENT. WHAT ABOUT PRAYING FOR MY CHILDREN?

Perhaps the greatest ministry parents can undertake is to pray for their children.

All too often we busy ourselves to such a great extent—even doing the Lord's business—that we fail to minister to those whom God has specifically called us to. We may be a success on the business front or the ministry front, but if we neglect to train up our children in the way they should go—in the training and admonition of the Lord (Eph. 6:4)—we have fallen miserably short. To put a twist on a familiar Scripture: "For what will it profit a man if he gains the whole world, and loses his own family?" (Mark 8:36).

Into the hands of each parent, God has placed the responsibility of raising a child not only to be a responsible, productive adult, but a *godly* man or woman as well. Our actions in the lives of our children pay dividends

> **PRAYER REFLECTION**
>
> *Personally, I am very pleased that God does not let my will determine my prayers. If He did, my life would probably be in chaos heading for destruction.*
>
> *—Ronnie W. Floyd*

throughout the rest of their lives: If we sow seeds of negativity or harm, we will ultimately reap a harvest of negativity and further harm. If not toward us, then toward others. If we sow seeds of righteousness and love, we will ultimately reap a harvest of further righteousness and love.

At the same time, releasing a child into the perils of a world that is no longer safe can leave a parent feeling powerless. What happens if someone abuses your son? What if your daughter gets a teacher who humiliates her in front of the class? What if your child starts hanging around the wrong crowd? There are so many variables that lie beyond our control. But as much as we would like, governing every area of their life is not only untenable, it's downright unhealthy. And yet there is something remotely healthy about entrusting them to God.

> **PRAYER REFLECTION**
> *When Jesus hears, thunder falls.*
> —Max Lucado

The one variable we *can* control is the decision to pray for our children. No one knows our children like we do. No one can pray as specifically (and therefore as effectively) as we do. No one cares for our children like we do. Our prayer waters the seeds of righteousness and love we sow into their lives.

Praying for our children is not enough. But prayer coupled with godly parenting gives our children a chance to see the mountains in their lives moved.[14]

—*from* Prayers to Move Your Mountains

MY CHILD IS DEALING WITH A LOT OF PEER PRESSURE. HOW CAN I PRAY FOR HIM/HER?

And do not be conformed to this world, but be transformed by the renewing of your mind, that you may prove what is that good and acceptable and perfect will of God. (Rom. 12:2 NKJV)

Lord Jesus, I see all the daily pressures my child faces: pressure from friends, classmates, coworkers, even teachers. Your Word says the devil is like a roaring lion, seeking someone to devour (1 Peter 5:8). It's only because of Your grace that anyone can avoid being devoured by sin. Jesus, please stand in the way of the devil coming near my child and enticing him to lead an unholy life, to take drugs and alcohol, to lie and cheat, to steal, to be involved in sexual perversion, or to commit violent acts.

May my child find the strength, by Your Holy Spirit, to be like the men of Judah, who "remained loyal to their king" when the rest of Israel went astray (2 Sam. 20:2 NKJV). Instill within my child the determination to desert the things of the devil rather than the things of God.

More important than being accepted by the "in" crowd is being accepted by You. Please make real to my child a love and acceptance that the world cannot duplicate. May You be the One my child seeks to please.

Please create within my child a thirst for more of You and Your Word. May Your Word be a lamp unto the feet of my child so that he can find his way through the darkness (Ps. 119:105). Bring into his path friends who are sold out for You and who will encourage him in his faith. Lord, may he become an active participant in our church.

Popular opinion isn't Your opinion, God, but it's not always easy for a young, impressionable person to see it that way. So make Your ways known to him. Give him a divine revelation of Your changeless nature (Heb. 13:8), and let him know You are with him every step of the way.[15]

—*from* Prayers to Move Your Mountains

HOW CAN I PRAY FOR MY HUSBAND (OR WIFE)?

Marriage was God's idea. He was the first to declare that it was a bad idea for man to be alone. So God said He would make the man a helper. Someone to stand beside him through the best and worst of each day. Someone to encourage him. Someone to honor him.

When we pray for our husbands we honor them. By praying for them each day we choose to value them, to show our love for the life-partners God has given us.

When we pray for our husbands the incense of our prayers rises before God's throne. He is pleased when we come to Him with the struggles, questions, and heartaches of life. He is pleased when we come in thanksgiving and praise for His goodness.

When we pray God's promises for our husbands we are affirming what God has already promised to us. We agree with His wisdom. We demonstrate our faith and honor Him as our God.

When we pray God's Word for our husbands:

> we pray God's will,
> we claim what God has promised to us,
> we deal a fatal blow to Satan's destructive designs,
> we pray what is honorable and godly,
> we pray light into darkness, joy into sorrow.

The validity of God's promises rest on His character and His resources, which are revealed to us in the Bible. It tells of His faithfulness, His resources, and His mighty works. And these encourage us to believe that this loving God will also work on behalf of our husbands. We can pray God's promises with great confidence!

We love our husbands and want God's best for them. But God loves them even more than we do. He has a perfect, optimum plan for them. A plan to accomplish His best for them, even when that must be accomplished through difficulties. Circumstances may change, but God never does. Pray faithfully and pray full of faith. . . .

Perhaps you are wondering how to pray God's promises. Here is a sample prayer based on Proverbs 3:5–6:

> Trust in the LORD with all your heart,
> And lean not on your own understanding;
> In all your ways acknowledge Him,
> And He shall direct your paths.

Prayer:

Lord, I pray that _____ would trust in You with all his might. I pray that he would not lean on his own knowledge and understanding but that he would acknowledge You and Your guidance. Then I pray, dear Father, that You will make _____ paths straight. Let Your Holy Spirit guide him on those straight paths. [16]

—*Terri Gibbs*

HOW CAN I PRAY FOR MY FAMILY?

Our families can be a source of both joy and sorrow in our lives. Job saw his children as a great blessing, and was overwhelmed with grief when they were suddenly and tragically taken away. In the midst of his despair, he cried out to God, wishing that he had never been born (Job 10:18–22).

Do you use prayer to talk to God about the tragedies and triumphs of your family life? Do you pray about long-term concerns as well? The Bible gives us numerous examples of people who prayed about their families. Their prayers tend to be honest expressions about belonging to a community where love and sin coexist. By considering their prayers, you can gain insight into how to pray constructively about your family situation. . . .

- Abraham—Prayed about his and Sarah's lack of a child, grieving that he had no heir (Gen. 15:1–6).
- Abraham's servant—Prayed for help in finding a wife for Isaac (Gen. 24:12–14).
- Isaac—Prayed about Rebekah's barrenness (Gen. 25:21).
- Jacob—Prayed in preparation for meeting his estranged brother Esau, whom he had not seen in many years (Gen. 32:9–12).
- Moses—Prayed for God's mercy on his brother Aaron after the incident with the golden calf (Deut. 9:20).
- Hannah—Prayed for a son and promised to give him back to God if He would end her barrenness (1 Sam. 1:9–20).
- David—Prayed that God would spare the life of his infant son born to Bathsheba (2 Sam. 12:15–16).
- David—Prayed for his son Solomon, that God would grant him a faithful heart to lead Israel and build the temple (1 Chr. 29:16–19).

Do you pray for your family? Do you let God hear your deepest feelings and hopes for them? He longs for you to express yourself to Him.[17]

—*from* The Word in Life Study Bible

WHAT ABOUT WHEN MY SPOUSE AND I ARE IN CONFLICT? HOW DO I PRAY THEN?

But the wisdom that is from above is first pure, then peaceable, gentle, *willing* to *yield,* full of mercy and good fruits, without partiality and without hypocrisy. Now the fruit of righteousness is sown in peace by those who make peace. (James 3:17–18 NKJV, italics added)

Lord God, Your Word proclaims that all things work together for good to those who love You (Rom. 8:28). In the midst of my marital crossfire, I trust that You are working something good.

Regardless how our conflict began, I bless my spouse (Matt. 5:44). Overwhelm me with Your love and compassion. I will not allow dissension to drive a wedge between the two of us. Therefore what You have joined together, let neither my spouse nor I separate (Matt. 19:6).

More than changing my spouse, Lord, change me. I want to be more like You. May You increase and I decrease (John 3:30). Search my heart and weed out any pride that prevents me from being part of the solution rather than the problem. I can't be so arrogant as to assume I have no liability in our disagreement. Convict me of my sin. Cultivate Your humility in me so I can openly confess my wrongdoing and be restored.

What part my spouse is responsible for in our conflict, change her (or him). No matter how hard I try, no matter how well I can argue, I am incapable of changing my spouse, so I release her (or him) to the conviction of Your Holy Spirit. I refuse to usurp Your role in my spouse's life.

I lay aside all anger, wrath, resentment, and offenses of the past. My love keeps no record of wrongs but always protects, always trusts, always hopes, always perseveres (1 Cor. 13:5b, 7 NIV). It's to my glory to overlook an offense (Prov. 19:11 NIV) so I forgive my spouse for any hurts that have been inflicted—whether accidental or intentional. I will not be ensnared by the devil through foolish and ignorant disputes (2 Tim 2:23).

I place a hedge of protection around my household (Job 1:10) that the enemy would not have a foothold in the covenant my spouse and I have established with God (Eph. 4:26–27). Show us that we are on the same side fighting one opponent.

The wisdom that comes from above is willing to yield (James 3:17). Grant me Your wisdom to discern my fleshly desires from truth. Give me a sense of which battles are worth fighting and which ones aren't.

More importantly, restore us so we can live together again in agreement. Strengthen

---

PRAYER REFLECTION

Your prayers move God to change the world. You may not understand the mystery of prayer. You don't need to. But this much is clear: Actions in heaven begin when someone prays on earth. What an amazing thought!

—*Max Lucado*

us as a result of our conflict, and draw us closer to one another. May the seeds of peace sown in our relationship yield a harvest of righteousness (James 3:18).[18]

—*from* Prayers to Move Your Mountains

IS THERE A PATTERN I CAN USE TO HELP ME REMEMBER THE DIFFERENT PARTS OF PRAYER?

If we are to nurture a strong bond with our Creator, we must continually communicate with him. And prayer is our primary way of doing just that. A memorable way of prioritizing the principles of such communication through prayer is found in the acronym F-A-C-T-S.

Faith

Faith is only as good as the object in which it is placed. Put another way, it is the object of faith that renders faith faithful. The secret is not in the phrases we utter but in coming to know ever more fully the One to whom we pray. Since God is awesomely revealed in his Word, the prayer of faith must always be rooted in Scripture. Prayer becomes truly meaningful when we enter into a relationship with God through Christ. We can then build on that foundation by saturating ourselves with Scripture. As R. A. Torrey so wonderfully expressed it:

> To pray the prayer of faith we must, first of all, study the Word of God, especially the promises of God, and find out what the will of God is. . . . We cannot believe by just trying to make ourselves believe. Such belief as that is not faith but credulity; it is "make believe." The great warrant for intelligent faith is God's Word. As Paul puts it in Romans 10:17, "Faith comes by hearing the message, and the message is heard through the word of Christ."

Jesus summed up the prayer of faith with these words: "If you remain in me and my words remain in you, ask whatever you wish, and it will be given you" (John 15:7).

Adoration

Faith in God naturally leads to adoration. Prayer without adoration is like a body without a soul. It is not only incomplete, but it just doesn't work. Through adoration we express our genuine, heartfelt love and longing for God. Adoration inevitably leads to praise and worship, as our thoughts are focused on God's surpassing greatness. The Scriptures are a vast treasury overflowing with descriptions of God's grandeur and glory. The Psalms, in particular, can be transformed into passionate prayers of adoration.

> Come, let us worship and bow down;
> Let us kneel before the Lord our Maker.
> For He is our God,
> and we are the people of His pasture,
> And the sheep of His hand.
> (Psalm 95:6–7 NASB)

Confession

Not only do the Psalms abound with illustrations of adoration, but they are replete with exclamations of confession as well. Those who are redeemed by the person and work of Jesus are positionally declared righteous before God. In practical terms, however, we are still sinners who sin every day. While unconfessed sin will not break our union with God, it will break our *communion* with God. Thus confession is a crucial aspect of daily prayer.

The concept of confession carries the acknowledgment that we stand guilty before God's bar of justice. There's no place for self-righteousness before God. We can only develop intimacy with the Lord through prayer when we confess our need for forgiveness and contritely seek his pardon. The apostle John sums it up beautifully when he writes, "If we confess our sins, he is faithful and just and will forgive us our sins and purify us from all unrighteousness" (1 John 1:9).

Thanksgiving

Nothing, and I mean nothing, is more basic to prayer than thanksgiving. Scripture teaches us to "enter his gates with thanksgiving and his courts with praise" (Psalm 100:4). Failure to do so is the stuff of pagan babblings and carnal Christianity. Pagans, says Paul, know about God, but "they neither glorified him as God *nor gave thanks to him*" (Romans 1:21, emphasis added).

Carnal Christians likewise fail to thank God regularly for his many blessings. They suffer from what might best be described as selective memories and live by their feelings rather than by faith. They are prone to forget the bless-ings of yesterday as they thanklessly barrage the throne of grace with new requests each day.

That, according to the Apostle Paul, is a far cry from how we should pray. Instead we ought to approach God "overflowing with thankfulness"(Colossians 2:7) as we devote ourselves "to prayer, being watchful and thank-ful" (4:2). Such thankfulness is an action that flows from the sure knowledge that our heavenly Father knows exactly what we need and will supply it. Thus says Paul we are to "be joyful always; pray continually; give thanks in all circumstances, for this is God's will for you in Christ Jesus" (1 Thessalonians 5:16–18; also Ephesians 5:20).

> **PRAYER REFLECTION**
>
> *Just remember this: If you do not plan to pray, you will not pray. In order to be an effective prayer warrior, you need to plan to meet with God daily.*
>
> —*Ronnie W. Floyd*

Supplication

Before we launch into a discussion of the place and priority of supplication, let's quickly review the aspects of prayer we have covered thus far. We began by noting that prayer begins with a humble faith in the love and resources of our heavenly Father. Thus prayer becomes a means through which we learn to lean more heavily upon him and less heav-ily upon ourselves. Such faith inevitably leads to adoration as we express our longing for an ever deeper and richer relationship with the One who knit us together in our moth-ers' wombs. The more we get to know him in the fullness of his majesty, the more we are inclined to confess our unworthiness and to thank him not only for his saving and sanc-tifying grace but also for his goodness in supplying all our needs.

It is in the context of such a relationship that God desires that his children bring their requests before his throne of grace with praise and thanksgiving. After all it was Jesus him-self who taught us to pray, "Give us this day our daily bread." And as we do we must ever be mindful of the fact that the purpose of supplication is not to pressure God into providing us with provisions and pleasures, but rather to conform us to his purposes. As we read in 1 John

5:14–15, "This is the confidence we have in approaching God: that if we ask anything according to his will, he hears us. And if we know that he hears us—whatever we ask—we know that we have what we have asked of him" (emphasis added).[19]

—Hank Hanegraaff

GIVE ME SOME ADVICE ON PRAYING WHEN TIMES ARE REALLY TOUGH.

In our day-to-day experience it is sometimes difficult to determine the source of our adversity. Adversity related to our personal sin is usually easy to identify. Beyond that, though, things begin to run together. We certainly do not want to rebuke the devil for something God is behind. Neither do we want to just grin and bear it if there is something we can do to put an end to our suffering.

The Bible does not give us three simple steps to aid us in determining the source of our adversity. This used to really bother me. For a long time, when I faced adversity, I would pray and pray for God to give me some indication as to why I was suffering. Then I realized why those kinds of prayers rarely seemed to be answered. There was and is a much more important issue at stake.

Far more important than the *source* of adversity is the response to adversity. Why? Because adversity, regardless of the source, is God's most effective tool for deepening your faith and commitment to Him. The areas in which you are experiencing the most adversity are the areas in which God is at work. When someone says, "God is not doing anything in my life," my response is always, "So then, you don't have any problems?" Why? Because the best way to identify God's involvement in your life is to consider your response to adversity. God uses adversity, regardless of the source. But your response to adversity determines whether or not God is able to use it to accomplish His purpose. In fact, adversity can destroy your faith. If you do not respond correctly, adversity can put you into a spiritual tailspin from which you may never recover. It all hinges on your response.

As much as we all want to know the answer to the *why* question, it is really not the most significant question. The real question each of us needs to ask is, "*How* should I respond?" To spend too much time trying to answer the *why* question is to run the risk of missing what God wants to teach us. Ironically enough, concentrating on *why* often hinders us from ever discovering why. If it is in God's sovereign will to reveal to us, this side of eternity, the answer to that question, it will be as we respond correctly.

One of the greatest struggles of my life surrounded my decision to move from Bartow, Florida, to Atlanta. Bartow is a small town in central Florida. Our home was in walking distance of three lakes. The neighborhood was safe. We knew all of our neighbors. Bartow seemed like the perfect environment in which to raise our children. To complicate things even further, we had only lived there about one year when a friend of mine approached me about moving to Atlanta to be the associate pastor at First Baptist Church. I thanked him for his vote of confidence but made it clear that I was not at all interested.

A few weeks later a pulpit committee showed up to hear me preach. Once again, I was polite, but I told them I was not interested. They asked me to pray about it. I told them I would. What else could I say? So one evening my wife, Anna, and I began praying about whether or not it was God's will for us to move to Atlanta. The strangest thing happened. The more we prayed, the more both of us became convinced we should go. When we would talk about it, it did not make any sense at all. Why would God want me to become an associate pastor when I had already been the senior pastor for three churches? Why would God move us after being in Bartow only thirteen months? Why would a good God want me to move my family to a place like Atlanta?

Two months later we moved. And about two years after that, I understood *why*. My point is this: oftentimes, the explanations we are so desperately seeking will become clear as we respond properly to adversity.

Surely the disciples stood at Calvary wondering why such a thing was allowed to take place. Humanly speaking, it made no sense at all. But in a few days all the pieces fit together. Oftentimes we stand like the disciples at Calvary. We watch our hopes and dreams shatter before our eyes. We see our loved ones suffer. We see family members die. And like the disciples, we wonder why.

We must remember that Christ's death, burial, and resurrection serve as the context of all our suffering. God, through those events, took the greatest tragedy in the history of the world and used it to accomplish His greatest triumph—the salvation of man. If the murder of the perfect Son of God can be explained, how much more can we trust that God is accomplishing His purposes through the adversity we face every day?

The source of our adversity is not to be our primary concern. Think about it. What was the source of the adversity Christ faced? Sin, Satan, or God? Actually, all three were involved. Yet Christ's response allowed our heavenly Father to take this tragedy and use it for the greatest good. That is the pattern. That is God's goal for us through all the adversities of life.

Have you been so hung up on trying to figure out *why* adversity has come your way that perhaps you have missed God? Has the adversity in your life strengthened your faith, or has it weakened your faith? Adversity is a reality that none of us can avoid. Therefore, it is in your best interest to begin responding in such a way that the negative can be used to accomplish the will of God in your life. And as you begin responding correctly, perhaps you will begin to understand *why!*[20]

—*Charles Stanley*

I'VE HEARD ABOUT PRAYER JOURNALS. HOW DO I USE ONE?

You may find that keeping a diary or journal of your personal prayer retreat times or your daily devotional prayer time can make a significant contribution to your spiritual growth. Putting things in writing can help solidify spiritual truths and lessons. I have found prayer journaling to be that kind of experience. Many others have affirmed that experience in their prayer lives as well.

Journaling can take a number of different forms. For example, I keep a simple prayer diary in which I write just a few sentences each day, reflecting some of my prayer experiences of the previous day along with some specific answers to prayer.

Interestingly, nothing seems to motivate our praying more powerfully than clear answers to prayer. I find it immensely helpful to recount those answers from the previous day every morning during my devotional time, and then to record them in my prayer diary. None of us should be like the nine lepers who were healed by Jesus but never returned to express their thanks (Luke 17:11–19).

Recognizing what God has done for us and giving Him thanks for His goodness is not merely an obligation. It is one of the great joys of our lives. It is wonderful to write those things down and to review them from time to time. How great is our Lord, and how gracious and generous He is to us. Thanksgiving can be a very important part of our prayer journaling experience.

Sometimes much of my prayer diary page for a given day is filled simply with expressions of praise to God. One of the most significant contributions of communing with God in prayer is to focus on Him and to offer Him praise. I have found it helpful at times to put some of those expressions of praise into writing.

Other times, even in the midst of our thanksgiving and praise, we may be experiencing difficult times or great challenges. Within that context, I like to write down some of my deepest concerns and most urgent prayer requests I am facing at a given time. In addition, sometimes it is exceedingly helpful to express our deep

> **PRAYER REFLECTION**
>
> *Through prayer you can accompany any missionary to remote reaches of the earth. . . . Through prayer you can contribute to the ministry of any pastor or evangelist in a church or gospel hall anywhere in the world. . . . Through prayer you can take a suffering infant in your arms. Through prayer you can touch a fevered brow in any hospital, mediating the healing love of Jesus.*
>
> —*Wesley Duewel*

concerns or pain in writing in the form of a prayer to God. Usually I write in my prayer diary a mixture of praise and thanksgiving, a review of some of the highlights of the previous day, and then some specific requests, which I write as a prayer to God.

As I have said, my prayer journaling is very simple. Others find it more meaningful to be more creative and comprehensive in their journaling. For example, some Christians enjoy writing a prayer to the Lord every day. In it they share their hearts very personally and intimately. That approach to prayer journaling is somewhat akin to a personal diary in which people record intimate details of their lives.

I would suggest you keep a place in your prayer notebook to do some type of journaling. Try some different approaches. Find out what is most helpful to you. Do not be afraid to vary your approach from day to day as you sense the Spirit of God leading and guiding you.[21]

—*Paul Cedar*

HOW CAN KEEPING A PRAYER JOURNAL HELP MY PRAYER LIFE?

I believe in the life-changing power of closing your time with God by writing a one-page letter to God. On this one page, you will be recapturing your main burdens as well as the joy of answered prayers. Journaling provides a means of concrete communication with God. It also provides a sense of relief from your burdens. As you document your walk with God in this way, your faith in the power of prayer will increase. Journaling can become one of the greatest dynamics in your prayer life.[22]

—*Ronnie W. Floyd*

WHAT SHOULD I INCLUDE ON A PRAYER LIST?

I pray for specific people and particular needs by various categories. In a prayer list I include the names of the persons and ministries for which I pray regularly.

I use the word *regularly.* I cannot pray for every person on my list daily. Of course, there are some people and ministries for which I do pray every day, including members of my family and my ministry colleagues.

Others I pray for every three or four days, and some I pray for once a week. However, one of the wonderful ministries of the Holy Spirit is to bring people to mind who need our prayers at a given time for a specific reason. Our prayer lists need not control or limit our praying; they are simply tools to help us be consistent and faithful. At the same time, I marvel at the wonderful way our Lord leads us in our praying if we are open to His guidance.

My prayer list includes the following categories of persons and ministries. . . .

a. My family. I pray daily for each family member, along with specific requests for them, including God's provision and protection, His presence and His peace, His perspective and His power, His patience and perseverance.

b. Our pastor and church family. I pray by name for our pastor and for other members of the pastoral team, our church leaders, our church family, and the ministry of our local church.

c. My ministry colleagues. For years I have prayed daily for my ministry colleagues by name. I believe it is one of the most important investments I can make on their behalf.

d. Pastors and missionaries. I pray regularly for a significant list of friends who are serving the Lord as pastors or missionaries, including national and international denominational leaders.

e. My support-group members. For years I have belonged to a small group of Christian brothers with whom I meet at least monthly and pray for regularly.

f. Ministry leaders. I pray for a long list of friends who are serving as national or international leaders in the ministry of our Lord. In addition, I pray regularly for a number of Christian leaders whom I have never had the privilege of meeting, but whom I believe God has called to strategic ministry roles.

g. Other ministry colleagues and friends. Once again, it is a privilege to pray for many brothers and sisters in Christ on a regular basis. For example, Jeannie and I have several scores of friends who are a part of our Ministry Prayer Team. As they pray for us, we enjoy praying for them.

h. Non-Christian neighbors and friends. One of the great privileges of praying for others is to pray for neighbors and friends who have never come to faith in Christ.

i. Our nation and the world. I have a systematic approach for praying regularly for the leaders of our nation, state, and community. In addition, I pray regularly for various nations of the world and for specific unreached people groups. Each day I pray for at least three key "gateway cities" to the unreached people groups.

j. Personal requests. After praying for others, I usually pray for myself. Daily I ask for the Lord's provision of wisdom, love, generosity, purity, holiness, self-control, the fear of the Lord, freedom, faith, absence of anger, a forgiving spirit, and a good name and reputation. And I pray that I may glorify my Lord both in life and in death.

k. Special and urgent requests. I usually close this segment of prayer by falling prostrate before the Lord and bringing to Him urgent requests that have been shared by others. I keep these special requests on a loose-leaf page in my prayer notebook with the date the requests have been shared with me printed to the left of the actual request. Then in the right column I

> **PRAYER REFLECTION**
>
> *Nothing is more important than your daily meeting with God, so nothing should ever interfere with it—not work or play or even a date. Nothing. Regardless of how crazy things get in your life or how jammed your schedule becomes, it's absolutely important that you keep your appointment with God everyday.*
>
> —Randy Southern

reserve space to record the date when the prayer is answered in an observable way. Most requests are answered graciously by the Lord in a matter of days. Others are in my notebook for a few weeks or even months. Some requests have been there for several years.[23]

—*Paul Cedar*

I LIKE TO TALK OUT LOUD WHEN I PRAY.

Here is one thing God honors according to His Word: Confess. Out loud!

> That if you confess with your mouth, "Jesus is Lord," and believe in your heart that God raised him from the dead, you will be saved. For it is with your heart that you believe and are justified, and it is with your mouth that you confess and are saved. (Romans 10:9–10)

Just as we must confess *with our mouths,* "Jesus is Lord," we must confess our sins (out loud) to one another during the healing process:

> Therefore confess your sins to each other and pray for each other so that you may be healed. (James 5:16)

Why out loud? If God hears our silent prayers and the intercessory interpretations of the Holy Spirit through our moans and the urging of our hearts, why do we have to go through God's healing process *out loud* with others in confession? That's so scary. Whom do I trust enough to reveal what I have so carefully kept hidden in my shame, anger, and unforgiveness?

First of all, please note that the enemy can put thoughts and desires into our minds, but he cannot read our minds! Only God is omniscient; only God knows our hearts and knows our thoughts. Yes, He hears our silent prayers. Yet, when it comes to the releasing of strongholds of the enemy, rebuking Satan, and moving in the power of the Holy Spirit, God wants Satan to know he has been put on notice. He will be immobilized, defeated, kicked out, uninvited, and banished from

---

PRAYER REFLECTION

Regardless of the prayer you pray, whether it be the Lord's Prayer or another, there is a grand omission unless it is made in the name of Christ. And it cannot be made in the name of Christ until you are in Christ, fully trusting Him, and you are in the will of God.

—*J. Vernon McGee*

his dirty little works in our lives! God wants us to speak it out loud, and speak it into being.

So we know we have to confess out loud . . . but where do we find those with whom we can feel "safe"? Is it possible to find fellowship in others who will help me uncover my areas of dodging and denial without later holding me hostage with their criticisms and opinions? How can I become that safe haven, a nonjudgmental, uplifting, nurturing sister [or brother] in Christ for others?

> My purpose is that they may be encouraged in heart and
> united in love, so that they may have the full riches of
> complete understanding, in order that they may know the
> mystery of God, namely, Christ, in whom are hidden all
> the treasures of wisdom and knowledge. (Colossians 2:2–3)[24]

—*Jennifer O'Neill*

WHY SHOULD I PRAY IN JESUS' NAME?

Jesus' name is the gateway to God

. . . A gateway is an entry point. Jesus' name is the entry point into the presence of God. It is the code of entry into God's throne room. Coming to the Father in Jesus' name gives you the assurance of being able to approach God.

You cannot approach God in your own name. You cannot approach God in your own ability. You can approach God only in the name of Jesus Christ. He is the gateway, the entry point, into the presence of God. This initial entry point takes place at your salvation experience. In John 14:6, Jesus says, "I am the way, and the truth, and the life; no one comes to the Father, but through Me."

The Bible teaches that Jesus is the only way to have a personal relationship with God. Jesus regarded Himself as the only way to God. He said He is the only truth. There is no truth apart from Him. He also understood that He is the only One who can grant spiritual life. Jesus is the gateway to God!

If you are going to do serious business with God, then you must pray in the name above all names—the name of Jesus. An example of this would be:

> Father, I do not come to You today in my own name or
> my own ability. I do not even have a right to talk to You
> except by and through the person of Jesus Christ. I
> approach You, but not in my own name or my own abili-
> ty. Father, I approach You in the strong and powerful name
> of Jesus Christ. Amen.

When you pray in Jesus' name as illustrated for you here, you have punched the code. You have used the key that will get you into God's presence.

The first reason you should pray in Jesus' name is because His name is the entry point, the gateway to God. His name gives you access into the presence of God, where you can do some serious communication with God. Another reason you should pray in Jesus' name is . . .

It reminds the Father of Jesus

. . . When you go to the Father in prayer, mention the name of His Son, Jesus. He loves that name. He is reminded of His Son and all He has done every time you mention Jesus' name. Whenever God hears Jesus' name, He is reminded of being one with Him. He is reminded of the preexistence of His Son. He is reminded of how Jesus substituted Himself to die for your sins. He is reminded of how Jesus is at His right hand right now and lives to make inter-cession for you. Therefore, anytime I pray in Jesus' name, I am reminding the Father of all of these things and more about His Son, Jesus Christ. . . .

Another reason why you should pray in Jesus' name is . . .

Jesus' name is your authority to tie your request to the Father's will

The name of Jesus is the most powerful name in heaven and on earth. Any time you take a request to God the Father in Jesus' name, you are tying it to the most authoritative name that has ever been given anywhere in the world. This means that you are taking your requests to God with authority.

Much of the time, prayer is uncertain ground for many believers. By observing the tentative nature of many Christians, you might think the ground is filled with more land mines than blessings. This is not the kind of praying I am writing about here. You should not feel as if you are walking on eggshells with God. You should sense you are walking with the authority of His Son, Jesus.

By offering your request to the Father in Jesus' name, you are tying your request with great authority. The Father loves Jesus' name. Offering your requests in Jesus' name gains the Father's attention. By tying your requests to Jesus' name, you are submitting to the will of God about each request. Remember, it is not "My kingdom come and my will be done"; it is "Thy kingdom come" and "Thy will be done, on earth as it is in heaven" (Matt. 6:10).[25]

—*Ronnie Floyd*

HOW CAN I PRAY WHEN I'M REALLY MAD ABOUT SOMETHING?

For a book of worship, the Psalms contain some rather harsh expressions of hatred and vengeance. For example, Psalm 137 seems to delight in the image of Babylonian babies being dashed against rocks (Ps. 137:8–9). Likewise, David prays down curses on his enemy, asking that no one would extend kindness to him, nor to his orphaned children after him (109:12). Similar expressions can be found in Psalms 35, 55, 58, 59, 69, 83, and 140.

> PRAYER REFLECTION
>
> *When you are willing to call out loudly to the Lord, summoning His aid into your life, God will do great and mighty things.*
>
> —*Ronnie W. Floyd*

What are we to make of these prayers? What are they doing in a collection of songs for worship? Opinions differ on the answer to that question. But one point of view is that worship means expressing to God our honest feelings, no matter how "ugly" they may seem. God is not intimidated by our pain nor unaware of the poison that lurks in our innermost being. He invites us to bare all before Him.

In fact, the Bible presents a number of accounts of people who brought their anger, disappointment, or pain to God. Their raw emotion is clearly expressed, providing encouragement to us to approach God when we are in personal agony. Some of these figures include:

- *Job,* whose cries of pain and loss were welcomed, heard, and responded to by God.
- *Solomon,* whose "diary" of reflections on life, at times bordering on depression and despair, can be found in the Book of Ecclesiastes.

185

- *Habakkuk,* whose despair over Israel's plight and complaint to God were heard (Hab. 1:1–17).
- *Jeremiah,* whose lament over the destruction of Jerusalem, including vivid and ugly descriptions of agony and pain is included in Scripture in the Book of Lamentations.
- *Paul,* whose internal conflicts over sinful patterns speak eloquently for many of us (Rom. 7:14–25).

True worship involves speaking the truth. That includes the truth about how we feel, no matter how dark our emotions may be. God will hear us. However, He also expects us to hear Him, as each of those mentioned above did.

Do you bring your innermost hatreds, hostilities, fears and frustrations to God? Where better to take them? If buried, they will only fester, sooner or later to emerge and cause great harm to us and those in our path.[26]

—*from* The Word in Life Study Bible

I'M NOT A THEOLOGIAN—MY PRAYERS ARE VERY SIMPLE. IS THAT OKAY?

Blessed are the simple of heart for they shall enjoy peace in abundance. . . . We are too occupied with our own whims and fancies, too taken up with passing things. Rarely do we completely conquer even one vice, and we are not inflamed with the desire to improve ourselves day by day; hence, we remain cold and indifferent. If we mortified our bodies perfectly and allowed no distractions to enter our minds, we could appreciate divine things and experience something of heavenly contemplation. . . . If we were to uproot only one vice each year, we should soon become perfect. The contrary, however, is often the case—we feel that we were better and purer in the first fervor of our conversion than we are after many years in the practice of our faith. Our fervor and progress ought to increase day by day; yet it is now considered noteworthy if a man can retain even a part of his first fervor.

If we did a little violence to ourselves at the start, we should afterwards be able to do all things with ease and joy. It is hard to break old habits, but harder still to go against our will.

If you do not overcome small, trifling things, how will you overcome the more difficult? Resist temptations in the beginning, and unlearn the evil habit lest perhaps, little by little, it leads to a more evil one.

A man is raised up from the earth by two wings—simplicity and purity. There must be simplicity in his intention and purity in his desires. Simplicity leads to God, purity embraces and enjoys Him.

If your heart is free from ill-ordered affection, no good deed will be difficult for you. If you aim at and seek after nothing but the pleasure of God and the welfare of your neighbor, you will enjoy freedom within.

If your heart were right, then every created thing would be a mirror of life for you and a book of holy teaching, for there is no creature so small and worthless that it does not show forth the goodness of God. If inwardly you were good and pure, you would see all things clearly and understand them rightly, for a pure heart penetrates to heaven and hell, and as a man is within, so he judges what is without. If there be joy in the world, the pure of heart certainly possess it; and if there be anguish and affliction anywhere, an evil conscience knows it too well.

> **PRAYER REFLECTION**
>
> *Holy, holy God, forgive me for not listening enough, uninterrupted, to You the eternal God of the Universe—and for perhaps not recognizing Your voice. Thank You that You are anxious to give me Your omniscient thoughts. I long for this precious relationship with You. I promise I will do my part. In Jesus' precious name, amen.*
>
> *—Evelyn Christenson*

As iron cast into fire loses its rust and becomes glowing white, so he who turns completely to God is stripped of his sluggishness and changed into a new man. When a man begins to grow lax, he fears a little toil and welcomes external comfort, but when he begins perfectly to conquer himself and to walk bravely in the ways of God, then he thinks those things less difficult which he thought so hard before.

God does well in giving the grace of consolation, but man does evil in not returning everything gratefully to God. Thus, the gifts of grace cannot flow in us when we are ungrateful to the Giver, when we do not return them to the Fountainhead. Grace is always given to him who is duly grateful, and what is wont to be given the humble will be taken away from the proud.

I do not desire consolation that robs me of contrition, nor do I care for contemplation that leads to pride, for not all that is high is holy, nor is all that is sweet good, nor every desire pure, nor all that is dear to us pleasing to God. I accept willingly the grace whereby I become more humble and contrite, more willing to renounce self.

The man who has been taught by the gift of grace, and who learns by the lash of its withdrawal, will never dare to attribute any good to himself, but will rather admit his poverty and emptiness. Give to God what is God's and ascribe to yourself what is yours. Give Him thanks, then, for His grace, but place upon yourself alone the blame and the punishment your fault deserves.

Always take the lowest place and the highest will be given you, for the highest cannot exist apart from the lowest. The saints who are greatest before God are those who consider themselves the least, and the more humble they are within themselves, so much the more glorious they are. Since they do not desire vainglory, they are full of truth and heavenly glory. Being established and strengthened in God, they can by no means be proud. They attribute to God whatever good they have received; they seek no glory from one another but only that which comes from God alone. They desire above all things that He be praised in themselves and in all His saints—this is their constant purpose.

Be grateful, therefore, for the least gift and you will be worthy to receive a greater. Consider the least gift as the greatest, the most contemptible as something special. And, if you but look to the dignity of the Giver, no gift will appear too small or worthless. Even though He give punishments and scourges, accept them, because He acts for our welfare in whatever He allows to befall us. He who desires to keep the grace of God ought to be grateful when it is given and patient when it is withdrawn. Let him pray that it return; let him be cautious and humble lest he lose it.[27]

—*Thomas à Kempis*

PRAYER REFLECTION

We bring to you, O Lord, the troubles and dangers of people and countries, the cries of prisoners and the captured, the griefs of the bereaved, the needs of strangers, the powerlessness of the weak, the sadness of the bone tired, and the declining abilities of the elderly. O Lord, draw near to each; for the sake of our Lord Jesus Christ.

—*Attributed to Anselm*
(adaptation)

HOW WILL I BE DRAWN TO PRAYER?

I am glad, sir, to see this fire of heaven, thus far kindled in your soul; but wonder that you should want to know, how you are to keep up its flame, which is like wanting to know, how you are to love and desire that, which you do love and desire. . . . Now you can have no desire or prayer for any grace, or help from God, till you in some degree as surely feel the want of them, and desire the good of them, as the sick man feels the want, and desires the good of health. But when this is your case, you want no more to be told how to pray, than the thirsty man wants to be told what he shall ask for. Have you not fully consented to this truth, that the heart only can pray, and that it prays for nothing but that, which it loves, wills, and wishes to have? But can love or desire want art, or method, to teach it to be, that which it is? . . . Ask not therefore . . . for a book of prayers; but ask your heart what is within it, what it desires? . . .

For this turning to God according to the inward feeling, want, and motion of your own heart, in love, in trust, in faith of having from him all that you want, and wish to have, this turning thus unto God, whether it be with, or without words, is the best form of prayer in the world. Now no man can be ignorant of the state of his own heart, or a stranger to those tempers, that are alive and stirring in him, and therefore no man can want a form of prayer; for what should be the form of his prayer, but that which the condition and state of his heart demands? If you know of no trouble, feel no burden, want nothing to be altered, or removed, nothing to be increased or strengthened in you, how can you pray for anything of this kind? But if your heart knows its own plague, feels its inward evil, knows what it wants to have removed, will you not let your distress form the manner of your prayer? or will you pray in a form of words, that have no more agreement with your state, than if a man walking above-ground, should beg every man he met, to pull him out of a deep pit. For prayers not formed according to the real state of your heart, are but like a prayer to be pulled out of a deep well, when you are not in it. Hence you may see, how unreasonable it is to make a mystery of prayer, or an art, that needs so much instruction; since every man is, and only can be, directed by his own inward state and condition, when, and how, and what he is to pray for, as every man's outward state shows him what he outwardly wants. And yet it should seem, as if a prayer book was highly necessary, and ought to be the performance of great learning and abilities, since only our learned men and scholars make our prayer books.

. . . If you, Academicus, were obliged to go a long journey on foot, and yet through a weakness in your legs could not set one foot before another, you would do well to get the best travelling crutches that you could.

But if, with sound and good legs, you would not stir one step, till you had gotten crutches to hop with, surely a man might show you the folly of not walking with your own legs, without being thought a declared enemy to crutches, or the makers of them.

Now a manual is not so good a help, as crutches, and yet you see crutches are only proper, when our legs cannot do their office. . . . A fine manual therefore is not to be considered as a means of praying, or as something that puts you in a state of prayer, as crutches help you to travel; but its chief use, as a book of prayers to a dead and hardened heart that has no prayer of its own, is to show it, what a state and spirit of prayer it wants, and at what a sad distance it is from feeling all that variety of humble, penitent, grateful, fervent, resigned, loving sentiments, which are described in the manual, that so, being touched with a view of its own miserable state, it may begin its own prayer to God for help.[28]

—*William Law*

SOMETIMES I JUST WANT TO SIT AND BE QUIET IN MY PRAYER TIME. CAN I DO THAT?

There are times when to speak is to violate the moment . . . when silence represents the highest respect. The word for such times is reverence. The prayer for such times is "Hallowed be thy name." . . .

If there are walls, you won't notice them. If there is a pew, you won't need it. Your eyes will be fixed on God, and your knees will be on the floor. In the center of the room is a throne, and before the throne is a bench on which to kneel. Only you and God are here, and you can surmise who occupies the throne.

Don't worry about having the right words; worry more about having the right heart. It's not eloquence he seeks, just honesty. . . .

"Be still, and know that I am God" (Ps. 46:10). This verse contains a command with a promise.

The command?

Be *still*.

Cover your mouth.

Bend your knees.

The promise? You will *know that I am God*.

The vessel of faith journeys on soft waters. Belief rides on the wings of waiting.

. . . In the midst of your daily storms, make it a point to be still and set your sights on him. Let God be God. Let him bathe you in his glory so that both your breath and your troubles are sucked from your soul. Be still. Be quiet. Be open and willing. Then you will know that God is God, and you can't help but confess, "Hallowed be thy name."[29]

—*Max Lucado*

HOW CAN I MAKE THE MOST OF THOSE TIMES OF SILENCE BEFORE GOD?

At least half of the time you spend in prayer should be devoted to silence. Now, don't assume it's the kind of silence that makes your mind wander and your eyelids droop, though. It's the kind of silence during which you block out everything else and concentrate solely on listening to God.

You could spend part of that time searching your conscience, listening for God's still small voice speaking to you about a situation in your life. You could spend part of it reading Scripture, giving God an opportunity to speak to you that way. You could spend part of it thinking about the advice of trusted Christian friends. You could spend part of it reviewing recent events in your life, trying to identify any doors that have been opened or closed.

> **PRAYER REFLECTION**
> *The harder you look for evidence of answered prayer, the better chance you'll have of seeing him at work.*
> —*Randy Southern*

However you choose to spend your quiet time, treat it just as seriously as you do the verbal part of your prayers. Extreme prayer is not possible without an extreme quiet time.[30]

—*Randy Southern*

PRAYERS OF INTERCESSION

A PRAYER IN THE FACE OF GREAT EVIL
GENESIS 18:22–33

> "Suppose there were fifty righteous within the city; would
> You also destroy the place and not spare it for the fifty
> righteous that were in it? Far be it from You to do such a
> thing as this, to slay the righteous with the wicked, so that
> the righteous should be as the wicked; far be it from You!
> Shall not the Judge of all the earth do right?"
> —*Genesis 18:24–25*

As Christians, we often feel compelled to cry out to God on behalf of those whom we know personally. Our personal involvement with others facilitates Christlike feelings of concern and compassion. Sometimes, however, we find ourselves praying for people we don't know personally but somehow feel compelled to bring before God's throne. Abraham provides a good example of this in his prayer of intercession for the city of Sodom and teaches us some valuable lessons about praying for others.

You see, in the wicked city of Sodom lived someone near and dear to Abraham—his nephew Lot. We read earlier that when King Chedorlaomer captured the cities of Sodom and Gomorrah, "They also took Lot, Abram's brother's son who dwelt in Sodom, and his goods, and departed" (Genesis 14:12). Abraham (then called Abram) gathered his servants and rescued Lot and those living in the cities that had been plundered. His love for Lot motivated him to action for Lot's neighbors in the city of Sodom, as well as those in the surrounding cities of Gomorrah, Admah, Zeboiim, and Bela.

The city of Sodom was an evil place, however. In fact, God explained to Abraham, "Because the outcry against Sodom and Gomorrah is great, and because their sin is very grave, I will go down now and see whether they have done altogether according to the outcry against it that has come to Me; and if not, I will know" (Genesis 18:20–21). It was clear that God was going to destroy the city because of its great evil. This situation brought Abraham to his knees on behalf of the city of Sodom.

Abraham must have been quite an advocate, a very good man to have as a friend. For Abraham, friendship meant praying many times for people facing trouble or hardship. Abraham was determined and persistent in his concern for others. By appealing for the preservation of the city on account of fewer and fewer righteous people, Abraham shows that he himself doubted the integrity of the city at large; yet even this did not deter his concern for all. Abraham approached God in the most humble way possible, yet his earnest concern placed him at the risk of sounding presumptuous. Even so, he pressed forward and pursued God to show mercy and glory by sparing the people from disaster.

> PRAYER REFLECTION
>
> *God, Our Father, who exhortest us to pray . . . since when we make supplication to Thee, we live better, and are better: hear me groping in these glooms, and stretch forth Thy right hand to me. Shed over me Thy light; . . . bring Thyself into me that I may likewise return into Thee. Amen*
>
> —St. Augustine

This prayer teaches us to call on the God of all justice to uphold righteousness in our society, and especially among those who are near to us. The prayer reminds us to be compassionate, eager for God to deliver and save those under judgment. Praying like this should also humble us before a righteous God who really does punish the wicked. In fact, the city was indeed destroyed, but God mercifully led Lot and his family away from the destruction.

In light of this prayer, we must ask: Will we follow the pattern of Abraham and intercede for those we know—and those we don't? Will we call upon God to show mercy to those around us? While God is not obligated to shed his mercy upon any (and praise Him that He does!), those who have received His grace are called to extend the same grace to others (Matthew 10:8). Dare to follow the example of faithful Abraham by pouring your heart out to God on behalf of someone who is in need of help. Strange as it may sound, the God of all mercy asks us to pray that His mercy extend toward hurting people. Find them; pray for them. God will be pleased.

God of all nations and all people, I ask for Your protection on those in need today. Some are facing war, terror, and fear on every side. Some are facing persecution for their faith. Some whom I know personally are in danger. I pray, Lord, that You will intervene with Your protection and saving hand.

A PRAYER FOR SINFUL PEOPLE
NUMBERS 14:11–19

"Pardon the iniquity of this people, I pray, according to the greatness of Your mercy, just as You have forgiven this people, from Egypt even until now."

—*Numbers 14:19*

It was not going well for the Israelites. They had been miraculously saved from slavery in Egypt and brought to the very border of the land God had promised them. Yet as they stood poised to enter *their* land, they got scared. After hearing the disheartening report of the ten spies, the people wanted a leader who would take them back to Egypt. Their current leaders, Moses and Aaron, sent urgent petitions to God, while their future leader, Joshua, reasoned with the people. The people had forgotten that God was in their midst showing His great love and doing mighty miracles.

> **PRAYER REFLECTION**
>
> *If you want maximum power from your prayer life, you've got to put maximum effort into it.*
>
> —*Randy Southern*

Even God was getting fed up. "How long will these people reject Me? And how long will they not believe Me, with all the signs which I have performed among them? I will strike them with the pestilence and disinherit them, and I will make of you a nation greater and mightier than they" (Numbers 14:11–12). In response, Moses pleads with God to forgive the iniquity of the Israelites and appeals to His great mercy. God had been forgiving the Israelites ever since they left Egypt—from their complaining in the wilderness to their worshiping a golden calf. "Just forgive again, Lord," Moses was pleading, "because you're a God of mercy."

God is longsuffering and abundant in mercy. This sentiment can be found throughout the Old Testament. Jonah discovered it when God spared the wicked city of Nineveh after the people repented: "I know that You are a gracious and merciful God, slow to anger and abundant in lovingkindness, One who relents from doing harm" (Jonah 4:2). David knew it too, and wrote, "The LORD is merciful and gracious, slow to anger, and abounding in mercy" (Psalm 103:8).

Do you feel like you just can't pray about a situation anymore—it's too hopeless, the person is too far gone, you've lost patience with attempting to intercede? The Bible reminds us that God is longsuffering and abundant in mercy. He is full of mercy and patience with us beyond the mercy and patience we have for ourselves or for others. Don't give up. Keep praying; keep interceding. You may not see any results, but God sees the person's heart and you can be assured that He's at work.

Take a lesson from the prophet Samuel. He later interceded on behalf of the nation of Israel that had rejected God yet again—this time in clamoring for a king to rule over them. Yet Samuel said, "Moreover, as for me, far be it from me that I should sin against the LORD in ceasing to pray for you; but I will teach you the good and the right way" (1 Samuel 12:23).

Besides, the Bible promises that our fervent prayers can have powerful results. So no matter how hopeless it seems, keep praying. You may not know what God is doing—or will do—because of your intercession.

Merciful God, here I am again, praying for this person. I have to admit that I'm getting tired of praying because he doesn't seem to get it. In fact, he seems to be going backward instead of forward. I feel like I'm wasting my time praying for him. Yet Lord, I know that You can do great things in his life. I know that You are merciful, gracious, and patient. I trust that You are at work in his life and that my prayers will have powerful results, just as You promise.

A PRAYER FOR BELIEVERS ACROSS THE WORLD
ROMANS 1:8–10

> First, I thank my God through Jesus Christ for you all, that your faith is spoken of throughout the whole world. For God is my witness, whom I serve with my spirit in the gospel of His Son, that without ceasing I make mention of you always in my prayers, making request if, by some means, now at last I may find a way in the will of God to come to you.
>
> —*Romans 1:8–10*

Ever sit in a service and pray for "the Christians all over the world" or the "believers in other countries who face persecution"? How can you generate prayers for people you don't even know? Well, we can learn from Paul, who made it a habit to pray for believers all over the world—even believers he'd never met.

The Apostle Paul had not been to Rome when he wrote this prayer, though he is passionate in his desire to visit there. The Book of Romans, cherished by many Christians, does not address a grand crisis in the church, so this allows Paul the opportunity to systematically explain the faith to this beloved church. The prayer in the first chapter reflects this purpose as well, as do other letters that open with a prayer to reflect the purpose of the book.

> PRAYER REFLECTION
>
> *We have got to understand that the only way to experience spiritual power, direction, and purpose is to have a meaningful time with God daily.*
>
> —Ronnie W. Floyd

Paul thanks God, through the Son, for the faith of the Roman church that was made up of Jews and Gentiles. Located in the center of the world, many had heard of the faith of this group of Christians. Paul is thankful for their witness and "without ceasing" prays to God on their behalf, although he had never met them. Paul's fervent prayer is that he can find a way to Rome to meet them face to face. As Paul writes, he is not privy to the end of the story. Of course, Paul will get to Rome through a strange sequence of events, which we see in the final chapters of Acts. As a prisoner under house arrest, Paul does indeed preach the gospel in Rome.

Paul teaches us two lessons: the importance of praying for our brothers and sisters in the faith whom we have never met and the power of answered prayer. Most of the Christians throughout the world we do not know, yet we can lift them up in our prayers. We share a common heritage as children of God and can edify each other without a face-to-face meeting. Yet we can look forward to such a meeting—in heaven itself!

So don't let prayers for unknown people put you off. Think of them as future, "heavenly" friends. You may not know them, but God does. And He hears and answers your prayers on their behalf.

Father, I don't know the Christians in far-off places. In some ways, I'm sure they are just like me—providing for a family, loving their children, seeking to serve You. In some ways, they are very different from me. Many face persecution for their faith; many do not own a Bible or even have one in their own language. Yet I pray for these people, Lord, asking that You bless them, guide them, give them wisdom to serve You in the place You have put them. May they grow in You just as I seek to grow in You. And I look forward to meeting them someday in our heavenly home.

> Now I pray to God that you do no evil, not that we should
> appear approved, but that you should do what is honor-
> able, though we may seem disqualified. For we can do
> nothing against the truth, but for the truth. For we are glad
> when we are weak and you are strong. And this also we
> pray, that you may be made complete.
>
> —*2 Corinthians 13:7–9*

Many parents know the mixed emotions that come with letting their children go. We know that we have raised our children for eighteen years so they can go off on their own. But when that moment finally comes, when independence has arrived, when the prover-bial "apron strings" are untied, most parents can't help but feel a lump in the throat. Will all those lessons be remembered? Is my child ready? Have we done enough?

The apostle Paul felt that way every time he planted a church. He was a busy man, called by God to spread the gospel all across the Roman empire. That meant he rarely stayed long in any one place. As he left a group of new believers, he hoped and prayed that the lessons he had taught them would be remembered, that they were ready, that he had done enough. He knew that Satan was waiting in the wings to try to bring the believers down, make them doubt their faith, mire them in sin. Fortunately, the Holy Spirit would be there to guide and protect the believers. Paul prayed that even though he had to move on, the new believers would be made complete, strong, and mature in the Lord.

Just as Paul had to let go of his churches, so we have to let go of our children. We really wouldn't have it any other way, but that doesn't make it any easier. Fortunately, we don't have to toss our children to the winds of fate and hope for the best. We are letting them go into the hands of a loving God who has a great plan for their lives. We can also continue to pray—no one's stopping us from that! We can pray that our children will "do no evil" and instead "do what is honorable." We can pray that they will "be made com-plete." We can ask that the presence of the Holy Spirit in their lives will protect them when doubts and difficulties come and when temptation and sin surround them.

Our children may have moved on in life, but they still need our prayers. Best of all, we can pray for them to become mature in their faith. The privilege of praying such a prayer brings great joy to any parent's heart. Jesus promised that when we pray according to His will, He hears and answers (John 14:13–14).

Maybe you don't have children, but there are others for whom you need to pray this prayer for spiritual growth and maturity. Pray as Paul did for your church, for your Sunday school class, for the youth group, for groups of believers in the local schools. Ask God to bring maturity to these people so that they can become all that God wants them to be.

Dear God, I pray that You will guide my children [or other fellow believers] in growing to maturity in You. I ask, along with Paul, that they will do no evil, but that they will instead do what is honorable. I pray that they will be made complete in You. I pray for Your Spirit to protect them from Satan's schemes. Give them strength to stand for You.

A PRAYER FOR WISDOM AND SPIRITUAL GROWTH
EPHESIANS 1:16–23

> [I] do not cease to give thanks for you, making mention of
> you in my prayers: that the God of our Lord Jesus Christ,
> the Father of glory, may give to you the spirit of wisdom
> and revelation in the knowledge of Him, the eyes of your
> understanding being enlightened; that you may know
> what is the hope of His calling, what are the riches of the
> glory of His inheritance in the saints, and what is the
> exceeding greatness of His power toward us who believe.
>
> —*Ephesians 1:16–19*

Have you ever wondered how to pray for your brothers and sisters in Christ? How can you pray for the friend who's in a heart-breaking relationship, or for the acquaintance who seems stuck in a spiritual rut? Thankfully, Paul gives us a model, a heartfelt prayer we can follow. At two points in this letter to the Ephesians, Paul tells the readers his prayers for them. The first is here in chapter 1.

Paul loved the believers in Ephesus. He had spent two years with them—preaching, teaching, training, and building lasting friendships. Thus, many of the believers in the church were not necessarily "new" believers, but they apparently still had some spiritual growing to do.

Don't we all?

Paul begins his prayer by thanking God for these believers and then mentions that he never stops praying for them. That's a startling concept, isn't it?

Are you ever too busy to pray? Ever feel that there just isn't enough time to intercede for others? Then close your eyes a moment and picture the great apostle Paul, world traveler and evangelist, bowing on his knees to do the one most powerful act of all—praying for the believers, and in fact, never ceasing to pray for them. Perhaps you have a full schedule, but you may need to make some adjustments in order to take the time to intercede with God on behalf of beloved friends and family who need to grow in the Lord.

What can you pray about? Bring their specific needs before the Lord. Even if you don't know specifics, you can still pray using Paul's example of intercession.

Paul wanted these believers in the busy and idolatrous city of Ephesus to have wisdom. You can never go wrong praying for wisdom on behalf of fellow believers. We can all grow in that area, and we all need new doses of wisdom for new situations. Our world is busy and filled with its own brand of idolatry. Believers need to be wise and discerning as they carry out their business in their corners of the world.

> **PRAYER REFLECTION**
>
> *There are some favors that the Almighty does not grant either the first, or the second, or the third time you ask Him, because . . . often He wills this delay to keep you in a state of humility—and to make you realize the value of His grace.*
> —Jean Eudes

Paul also prayed that the eyes of their understanding would be enlightened—that these believers would be given the insight and truth needed to grow in their personal relationship with God. To know God is not to know facts and theories about God but to enter into a deep and close communion. The enlightenment we need is deep, affecting the core of our being. The knowledge of the mind enters the understanding as we allow God's Spirit to invade our hearts. This "knowing" is an intuitive sense of presence that kindles the affections of the heart. Pray that others would grow spiritually, understanding more and more about God every day and deepening their personal walk with Him.

When we are so centered in God, that intimate relationship will give hope and power. Hope arises because God is at work healing the brokenness of the world. Pray that fellow believers will hold on to hope, even in the most difficult times, looking forward to the riches that await them in heaven with Christ.

The second result of our knowing God is to receive power—the power needed to fulfill God's purposes for us. It is not our strength on which we depend but rather the power of God which is at work in us through Christ. Pray that fellow believers will understand the "exceeding greatness" of God's power at work in them. Pray that they will lay hold of that power to overcome difficulties, step out in faith, or follow God's will for their lives so that they can do all that God calls them to do. Pray that God will use them in mighty ways to advance His kingdom!

Lord Jesus, I pray for _____. I pray that You will give them wisdom for the situations they face today. Open the eyes of their understanding so that they may know You better. Fill them with the hope that You give, remind them of their promised inheritance, and show them Your power working through them.

A PRAYER TO KNOW CHRIST'S LOVE
EPHESIANS 3:14–21

That He would grant you, according to the riches of His glory, to be strengthened with might through His Spirit in the inner man, that Christ may dwell in your hearts through faith; that you, being rooted and grounded in love, may be able to comprehend with all the saints what is the width and length and depth and height—to know the love of Christ which passes knowledge; that you may be filled with all the fullness of God.

—*Ephesians 3:16–19*

In these verses, we stumble across the second of Paul's prayers for the Ephesian believers. Again, it's an incredible model of how to come before God's throne on behalf of our friends. Here Paul prays passionately that his friends in Ephesus would know true love! And who wouldn't want a prayer like this prayed on his or her behalf? Isn't that what everyone desires? Love—not the kind of love that "makes the world go round," not what comes and goes with fleeting and fickle feelings. This is true love—solid, limitless, beyond our comprehension.

Paul prays for the believers to have inner strength. This is the work of the Holy Spirit within. This power equips us from the center of our being to stand out in an evil world as people in whom Christ dwells by faith. We have the opportunity to intercede for other believers by praying that they would draw strength from that inner reservoir of energy inspired by the Holy Spirit.

Paul prays that Christ will make His home in their hearts. The divine presence is a gift; faith is our reception of that gift. Just as a plant grows in the soil, so we are to be "rooted and grounded in love." Christ dwells deep within us, so our lives are rooted and grounded in God. With God at our center we are united with all that God is bringing together in love. As you pray for your fellow believers, pray that Christ will dwell in their hearts because of their faith in Him.

Then Paul prays that his friends in Ephesus would understand true love. Even when Christ dwells in our hearts, it can be difficult to know how much we are loved. Do any of your believing friends suffer under the weight of feeling unloved? Have they been hurt by human love gone sour? Do they need a fresh infusion of true love? Then pray that they will take root and be grounded in God's love. Pray that they will have just an ounce of comprehension of something that is incomprehensible—the width, length, depth, and height of Christ's love. Pray that they will know, feel, and be flooded by this love that is beyond understanding. That alone is enough to change the course of their entire lives.

> **PRAYER REFLECTION**
>
> *Prayer is the means by which you come to experience the loving will of God. When you pray, you confess your dependence on your sovereign, mighty God to accomplish His purposes in and through you; and His will is then done on earth as it is in heaven.*
>
> —*Charles Stanley*

Pray that your believing friends will be filled with the fullness of God. Pray that empty lives will be filled, that hopeless lives will be revived, that doubting lives will be reassured, that pain-filled lives will be infused with hope.

Paul follows his petitions with a doxology of faith that God is able to accomplish far more than we can ask or imagine. We are encouraged to trust in the power of God at work within us and in the world. Consider your wildest hopes and dreams. God's power to work in your life—and in the lives of your believing friends—is far beyond that. So don't be afraid to ask!

Strengthen my friends, _____, Lord. Dwell in their hearts by faith. Show them Your true love. I pray that they will be rooted and grounded in Your love, that they will be able to comprehend—if only a little—the width, length, depth, and height of Your love, love that is beyond our understanding. Fill them with Your fullness. I know that You can do exceedingly more than I could ever ask or even think, so I pray on behalf of these friends that they may know You and Your true love.

A PRAYER FOR ABOUNDING LOVE TOWARD OTHERS
PHILIPPIANS 1 : 8 − 11

And this I pray, that your love may abound still more and more in knowledge and all discernment, that you may approve the things that are excellent, that you may be sincere and without offense till the day of Christ.

—*Philippians 1:9–10*

How often do you pray for your Christian friends to have abounding love? That's an unusual prayer, isn't it? You can pray that others will have love with knowledge and discernment. Love that overflows. Love that approves what is excellent. Love that results in sincerity and living without offense. Bet that's a prayer you *haven't* prayed.

Paul begins his letter to the Philippian Christians by reporting to his friends exactly what he is praying for them. Paul's prayer reveals his own love for his Philippian friends and fleshes out what he has said already about their Christian lives: that Christ, who has begun a good work in them, will complete it (1:6).

As we go about our busy days, our "to-do" lists keep us running from breakfast to bedtime. But Paul prays that Christians may be able to do what is most important, or in his words, "the things that are excellent." The excellent things to be done are illuminated for us by love, Christian love (the Greek word *agape*) that is enriched by knowledge and discernment. This kind of love is best expressed in Christlike personal sacrifice for others. This is the most important and excellent thing on our to-do list, and the result is that our faith will be sincere and without offense.

PRAYER REFLECTION

In the rush and noise of life, as you have intervals, stop within yourselves and be still. Wait upon God and feel his good pleasure; this will carry you through your day's business.

—*William Penn*

204

Today, love is almost always portrayed as something to receive, not to give. But the love Paul describes is the powerful love of Jesus Christ—the love that the Cross displays to us. To love as Jesus does is to love fiercely, to never let the other person go, to never lose hope. This is the only kind of love that can make all of our busyness and effort excellent, God-praising, sincere, and innocent.

You can put this love into action today by praying for your friends as Paul did for the Philippians. Christians show love by praying for one another. We also pray so that others might experience a reorientation in attitude: from "buy more" and "get more" to "give more" and "serve more." We should pray that Christians would be more and more motivated by love for Christ, rather than love for prestige or wealth. When we pray this, we put our faith and love into tangible expression that is sincere and without offense—that God might be praised now and on the day when Christ Jesus returns.

God of love, with Paul, I pray for my fellow believers that their love will abound more and more in knowledge and discernment. I pray that they will approve the things that are excellent so that they will be sincere and without offense. I pray that Your kind of selfless love will motivate them as they seek to serve You and witness for You. I pray that others will be drawn to You because of our love for them.

A PRAYER FOR SPIRITUAL UNDERSTANDING
COLOSSIANS 1:3–14

> For this reason we also, since the day we heard it, do not cease to pray for you, and to ask that you may be filled with the knowledge of His will in all wisdom and spiritual understanding; that you may walk worthy of the Lord, fully pleasing Him, being fruitful in every good work and increasing in the knowledge of God.
>
> —*Colossians 1:9–10*

Some people are obsessed with the pursuit of knowledge. They get caught up in all the latest intellectual fads and continually find new concepts that pique their interest. Some have "spiritual insights" that help them determine which parts of the Bible are true and which aren't. They can tell you which words Jesus said and which ones He didn't. Some even dismiss the Bible as a book of myths. Whatever path they choose, they are certain to find company.

As it is today, so it was in ancient times. The New Age movement of modern Western culture is the equivalent of Colosse in Paul's day. Throughout the region, a secret, spiritualistic religion posed a real threat to Christians and made them feel like outsiders because they refused to give attention to the "secret knowledge" that everyone else treasured.

> ### PRAYER REFLECTION
>
> *Almighty God, who . . . has promised through Your well-beloved Son that when two or three are gathered together in His Name You will be in the midst of them: Fulfill now, O Lord, the . . . petitions of Your servants . . . granting us . . . a knowledge of Your truth, and life everlasting in the world to come.*
> —*St. Chrysostom*

That's why Paul writes twice in verses 9 and 10 that Christians in Colosse might be filled with the knowledge of God and God's will. The gospel of Jesus Christ is no secret; it is the message of salvation broadcast for all. It is the truth—truth that has stood the test of time. The Christians of Colosse, who rightly refused to join the pagan worship of their neighbors, were not outsiders after all. They had access to all the knowledge, wisdom, and spiritual understanding in the universe through Jesus Christ.

God wants more from us than pursuit of mere knowledge. Of course we continue to study His Word every day, but in the meantime, we step out in faith, walking "worthy of the Lord" and "being fruitful in every good work," even as we are "increasing in the knowledge of God."

By knowing God and learning God's will, Christians can live in a way that pleases God. Paul's formula for pleasing God is simple: do the good works of God and study God's Word. Paul prays that love of God would lead to an increase in knowledge of God, and that love and knowledge together would make service to God more natural and satisfying. Paul must have had the Great Commandment in the back of his mind: we are to love God with heart, soul, mind, and strength—our whole selves.

Today many philosophies compete for our attention. They offer advice on how to achieve perfection in our relationships, our looks, and our prestige. They offer us something "better" than "old-fashioned Christianity." Is Paul's prayer just another voice in the crowded market of ideas and programs? No, this prayer sets us on the certain path to God's truth and blessing.

Pray this prayer for believers who are struggling with doubts, facing the clanging of ideas and philosophies that are contrary to the Bible. In fact, don't cease to pray for them. Ask God to give them spiritual understanding and knowledge of Him. Pray that such knowledge will lead them to fruitfulness for Him.

Mighty God, I pray for those who are facing uncertainty about their faith. I ask that you will fill them with the knowledge of Your will in all wisdom and spiritual understanding. Help them to walk worthy of You, fully pleasing You, being fruitful in every good work, all the while increasing in their knowledge of You. Help them not to capitulate to feelings of unworthiness because they have faith in You and not in the latest fads. Give them the courage to stand firm on You, the Rock of their salvation.

A PRAYER FOR SPIRITUAL MATURITY
HEBREWS 13:20–21

Now may the God of peace who brought up our Lord Jesus from the dead, that great Shepherd of the sheep, through the blood of the everlasting covenant, make you complete in every good work to do His will, working in you what is well pleasing in His sight, through Jesus Christ, to whom be glory forever and ever. Amen.

—*Hebrews 13:20–21*

Teamwork makes any task so much more enjoyable. Getting up to jog every morning at five o'clock is a lot easier if a partner is banging on your door. Planning a big meeting is a lot easier when you can share the responsibilities with someone else. And when you have a dependable partner—someone who will pull his weight and always follow through on his commitments—that kind of partner is worth his weight in gold!

The author of Hebrews concludes his series of sermons with a two-verse prayer that clinches the message of the previous twelve chapters: that Christians may come to complete maturity in faith. The evidence of this maturity will be the intimate connection between their work and God's work. In fact, as believers pursue God's will in their faithful service, they will find that God is working in and through them—a true partnership. They will also discover that their Partner will stop at nothing to guarantee success in this endeavor!

Who is this God who will bring our faith journey to its goal? He is the One who "brought up our Lord Jesus from the dead," who sent Jesus Christ to be the Shepherd of our salvation, who has made an everlasting covenant with us through the blood of His Son. His promise cannot fail. The God who will "make you complete in every good work" is the God who has already done everything to make your eternal life possible. This is the God who loves us so much that Jesus Christ was sent into the world to save us.

> **PRAYER REFLECTION**
>
> *Prayer is life's greatest joy, highest privilege, and most powerful venture.*
>
> *—Paul Cedar*

The Book of Hebrews articulates how Jesus reconciles His people to God. When we pray to do God's will, we open up a dialogue between ourselves and God, but the answers will be different for each one of us. He is working in us "what is well pleasing in His sight."

Who would not want such a prayer prayed on their behalf? You can do a great service to fellow believers when you pray that they will be made "complete in every good work to do His will." Pray that God will continue working in their lives what is well pleasing in His sight. Pray that they will mature in their faith and bring great glory to God through their Savior, Jesus Christ.

And you know what? God will do it. He's the most dependable Partner anyone could ever have!

God of peace, You brought Your Son, our Lord Jesus, back from the dead. You made Him our Good Shepherd through the blood of the everlasting covenant. I pray for myself and my fellow believers that You will make us complete in every good work to do Your will. Work in us what is well pleasing in Your sight. Thank You for making us all different—with different gifts and abilities—to work as a team for You. We give you the praise and glory for ever and ever. Amen.

PRAYERS OF BLESSING

A BLESSING FOR OUR CHILDREN
GENESIS 27:28-29

"Therefore may God give you of the dew of heaven,

Of the fatness of the earth, and plenty of grain and wine.

Let peoples serve you, and nations bow down to you.

Be master over your brethren, and let your mother's sons

bow down to you.

Cursed be everyone who curses you, and blessed be those

who bless you!"

—*Genesis 27:28–29*

Isaac's prayer blessing his son Jacob was not just the prayer of a father concerned for his child's future prosperity. It was also a prayer meant to pass Abraham's spiritual inheritance on to its rightful heir (see Genesis 12). Isaac was sure this inheritance was meant to go to his eldest son, Esau; indeed, he thought this was Esau over whom he was saying this prayer. Yet throughout the story of Abraham and his descendants, God shows that this lineage is under his special care and particular choice—it includes children born under impossible odds, and usurping younger sons.

Jacob deceives his father in order to receive the blessing. In some ways, Isaac's prayer is a prayer we may hope never to pray ourselves—it is the prayer of a man who has been completely fooled. Jacob's trickery turns the blessing, intended for Esau, completely on its head. And according to the customs of the day, these words could not be taken back. A blessing given was a blessing received; nothing could change the words once they had been spoken.

But in his special purposes for Abraham's family, God uses even misguided prayers. We may hope never to be fooled as Isaac was in our petitions to God, but we can always be confident that God's will is done, even when we don't know or don't understand what we are praying for.

The impulse to pray for God's blessing on our children is very strong. One of the major reasons many people have for returning to regular Christian discipline, including prayer, is a desire for their children to flourish in a Christian home and community.

This prayer should help us focus on the most important blessing we can ask for our children. Isaac prays that God will bless his son by making him an heir of the covenant God made with Abraham. Material prosperity is a sign of this covenant, but not the center of it. Central to the covenant is the promise that Abraham and his descendants will be God's chosen people and will be redeemed from sin and death by Jesus. Our prayers for our children should not be for material wealth, but for the spiritual wealth of adoption into Abraham's family through our Savior, Jesus Christ.

> *Father in heaven, I pray Your richest blessing upon my child. I pray that You will give rich spiritual blessings all the days of his/her life. If it is Your will, I also pray for success and prosperity in whatever he/she endeavors to do for You. Give the dew of heaven, the fatness of the earth, and plenty of Your blessings so that he/she can, in turn, bless others.*

A BLESSING AS WE SAY GOOD-BYE
NUMBERS 6:24-26

The LORD bless you and keep you;

The LORD make His face shine upon you, and be gracious
   to you;

The LORD lift up His countenance upon you, and give you
   peace.

—*Numbers 6:24–26*

Have you ever had to say good-bye to a dear friend? Perhaps he or she was moving to another place and, despite promises to "stay in touch," you know that your relationship will never be the same. Distance makes for difficulty. You will no longer have daily or weekly interaction—sharing the mundane, the ups and downs, the highs and lows. There just isn't the same intensity or intimacy.

When it's time to say good-bye, perhaps these words will help. With Christian friends especially, you know that they go with God. The words of this prayer of blessing give you all the words to say at a time when words may be hard to find.

The Lord Himself gave this blessing to Moses to pass along to Aaron, the high priest of Israel. The Lord told Moses, "This is the way you shall bless the children of Israel." A blessing is a way of asking for God's divine favor on behalf of another. When you pray such a prayer for your friends, you offer great encouragement, for these words were given by God Himself.

Ask the Lord to go with your friends and "bless" them. For the ancient Israelites, "blessing" emphasized God's care through giving His people prosperity. The phrase "the LORD bless you" originally meant the granting of material well-being. In the context it meant good crops, bountiful herds, seasonable weather, and military strength. Ask that God would bless your friends with prosperity in their new endeavors. Ask that His divine favor would rest on them and that they would sense that blessing from on high.

Ask the Lord to "keep" your friends. This alludes to God's protection both from material disaster and, more especially, from evil. It is difficult to let our friends go; somehow we think that we can protect them if they stay close. However, they go in God's hands, called by Him to a new place, a new task, a new service. So put them back into God's hands, praying for His "keeping."

Pray for them to have a sense of God's grace. Change is never easy; being called by God doesn't necessarily mean it won't be painful to leave the familiar for the unfamiliar. Pray that the Lord will "make His face shine" upon them, and pray that they will see His face and sense His pleasure as they follow His will for them. As they look to God, may they see His forgiving, unconditional love inviting them to come close. May they sense His grace upon them.

The third part of this prayer emphasizes the gift of God's presence. Praying that God will "lift up His countenance" is more than the sight of a shining face. It is the impression of the divine Spirit's presence with them. It is to experience the nearness of God. It is the blessing of communion of spirit with Spirit. God's indwelling brings peace of heart and mind. Pray for them to feel God's presence and peace.

Good-byes can be a time of blessing—for everyone. For when we go with God, we're never far apart.

Father, it's hard to say good-bye. I don't want to lose the close fellowship I have with these friends. I pray that You will bless and keep them. May they find success and joy in their new endeavors. Make Your face shine upon them and be gracious to them, that they will sense Your pleasure with them as they follow Your will. Lift up Your countenance upon them and give them peace. Even though it is difficult, Father, I trust You to go with them and bless them.

A BLESSING FOR THOSE WHO NEED REFUGE
DEUTERONOMY 33:1–29

> Yes, He loves the people;
> All His saints are in Your hand;
> They sit down at Your feet;
> Everyone receives Your words. . . .
> The eternal God is your refuge.
> And underneath are the everlasting arms.
> —*Deuteronomy 33:3, 27a*

It's hard to let people learn from their own mistakes. How many parents have stepped in to keep a child from facing the consequences of wrongdoing—simply because they don't want to see the child be hurt. Yet when we are constantly bailing people out, we are not allowing God to work His lessons in their lives by using the greatest teacher of all—their own mistakes.

The people of Israel had made their share of mistakes. They had disappointed God time and time again, turning their backs on Him, moaning against Him, disobeying Him. Yet God had made a promise to a faithful man named Abraham—a promise to bless his descendants—and God would never go back on that promise. Like a father blessing his children, Moses blessed his "children"—the nation of Israel—before he died. He wanted them to remember all that God had done for them and look toward the future. Deuteronomy 33 records Moses' parting blessing on the twelve tribes of Israel as they camp on the threshold of the Promised Land. This blessing is bookended by praises to God in verses 2–5 and 26–29.

Moses' prayer of blessing upon the descendants of Abraham and their offspring focuses on each tribe's destiny before God, who will lead them. As Christians today, we are also "Abraham's seed" (Galatians 3:29) and heirs of the covenant promises of blessing to those who are faithfully obedient before the Lord.

Moses' prayer of praise provides the framework within which these blessings are pronounced. Verse 3 stands out in this regard: It is because of God's love for the "saints" that they are protected by him. We are in His hand; we sit at His feet; we receive His words. The section concludes with the tender words of verse 27: "The eternal God is your refuge, and underneath are the everlasting arms." Moses praises and blesses God because he has been the people's shelter and support in times of struggle and need. When enemies threatened, God was their defender.

Christians today can stand beside Moses and proclaim the praises of God, who is powerful and protecting. For the Israelites, the defining moment was God's deliverance of Israel from Egypt. For Christians, God's power in the New Testament is first and foremost displayed in the love of the Cross. God continues to be, through Jesus Christ, the One who defends us from our most potent enemy, Satan. Martin Luther's famous hymn, "A Mighty Fortress Is Our God," gives voice to our confidence:

And though this world, with devils filled, should threaten to undo us,
we will not fear, for God has willed His truth to triumph through us.

Pray such a blessing for other believers. Pray that they would sit at God's feet and receive His words. Pray that they will experience God as their refuge in times of trouble, supported by His everlasting arms. Pray that they will learn the lessons God can teach them through their mistakes so that they will be stronger, prepared for whatever lies ahead.

Eternal God, You are our refuge. Under us are Your everlasting arms. I pray for Your blessing on those who may feel that they have made too many mistakes for You to forgive. Perhaps they just are embarrassed to come back to You. Remind them that they can return to Your feet and receive the blessing of Your instruction. I pray that they will learn from their mistakes and move on to greater usefulness for You and Your kingdom.

A PRAYER FOR SPIRITUAL GROWTH AND HOLINESS
I THESSALONIANS 5:23–24

Now may the God of peace Himself sanctify you completely; and may your whole spirit, soul, and body be preserved blameless at the coming of our Lord Jesus Christ.
He who calls you is faithful, who also will do it.
—*1 Thessalonians 5:23–24*

Have you ever led someone to Christ? Have you ever had the privilege of watching someone suddenly grasp the gospel and step into the light of God's grace? Whether this new believer is a friend, a family member, an elderly person, or a tender child, the joy of watching a new believer discover the peace that comes with the touch of God's grace is a great privilege indeed!

The great apostle Paul must have experienced this many times. He traveled the dusty roads of the Roman empire sharing the Good News. Ahead of him went the Holy Spirit, preparing hearts to respond. When Paul moved on from a city, he always left a group of believers in his wake. Was it difficult for Paul to move on? He always burned to share the message of God's salvation with those who had not heard, but those he left behind had so much growing to do.

So Paul wrote letters, and he prayed. One such prayer is recorded here.

> **PRAYER REFLECTION**
>
> *The One who instructed us to "be still and know that I am God" must hurt when He witnesses our frantic, compulsive, agitated motions. In place of a quiet, responsive spirit we offer Him an inner washing machine-churning with anxiety, clogged with too much activity, and spilling over with resentment and impatience. Sometimes He must watch our convulsions with an inner sigh.*
>
> —*Charles Swindoll*

When Paul founded the church in Thessalonica, a leading city in Macedonia, his work met with considerable opposition. He and his team moved on after only a short time. The young church was composed mostly of converted pagans, with some Jews and devout Greeks. Paul was very concerned about these converts who had little knowledge of life in Christ. He had sent Timothy back to encourage them. When Timothy returned, Paul wrote this letter giving thanks to God for the faith, love, and endurance of the church in Thessalonica. And he records this touching prayer for the young believers.

The prayer is addressed to the God of peace. Only through God can we experience true inner peace. It is God's gift through Christ that we are at peace with God and can live in peace in our world.

Paul prays that God will "sanctify" the Thessalonian believers. Sanctification is an intimidating word that simply means "growth in holiness." It is Paul's prayer that the believers will grow spiritually, becoming more and more like Christ as God works in their hearts. He prays that they will be sanctified completely; that is, that they will be "wholly holy."

That precious new believer in your life needs your vigilant prayers. He will be besieged by doubt, fear, or the lure of an old lifestyle. Pray that the God of peace, who has touched this new believer's life with His peace, would help him to move forward in his new spiritual life. Don't expect immediate perfection from him in all areas. Allow God to convict and work in his life step by step. Your job is to support and especially to pray that he will grow in the faith and become more like Christ.

Pray that every aspect of his being is given to that purpose. Paul's prayer explicitly says "may your whole spirit, soul, and body be preserved blameless at the coming of our Lord Jesus Christ." The spirit is the inner being; soul and body make up the whole person. The prayer is that in his whole being—mentally, emotionally, and physically—he will be committed to Christ.

This prayer suggests the need for some self-examination as well. Are you ready to allow every aspect of your own spirit, soul, and body to be given completely to God? If there is a part of you that needs sanctification, then this prayer can be that you too may become wholly holy.

And you know what? Here's a prayer with a promise. Even as you pray for your new family member in Christ, you can know that spiritual growth will indeed come. For God, who has called that person into His family, is faithful. And He will do it. You can count on it.

God of peace, sanctify this new believer. I pray that You will give him Your peace and that You will help him to grow spiritually. May his whole spirit, soul, and body be preserved blameless. May he come to know You better and better; may he grow to be more and more like You. Even as he deals with doubts and difficulties, may Your presence and peace comfort him. I know You are faithful, Lord, and I claim Your promise to do this in this person's life.

A PRAYER FOR COMFORT
2 THESSALONIANS 2:13–17

Now may our Lord Jesus Christ Himself, and our God and Father, who has loved us and given us everlasting consolation and good hope by grace, comfort your hearts and establish you in every good word and work.

—*2 Thessalonians 2:16–17*

Sometimes life gets us down. We may struggle with the mundane, the frustrations, or the pain that sweeps in upon us unexpectedly. This happens to everyone—believers and unbelievers alike. Jesus told us that God "makes His sun rise on the evil and on the good, and sends rain on the just and on the unjust" (Matthew 5:45). So what good is it to be a Christian?

The answer lies in this prayer of blessing and comfort for the believers in the church in Thessalonica. They were discouraged that the promised Second Coming had not yet happened. Loved ones were dying, and they feared that those people would somehow miss out on heaven. False teachers were making trouble. It seems that being Christians had made little or no difference for them. They had pain, confusion, and uncertainty.

Does that sound like any believers you know?

Life isn't easy—in fact, God never said it would be. Pray for your fellow believers who are struggling that they would have "everlasting consolation" and "good hope." Pray that they will experience the boundlessness of God's presence and the certainty of their hope for the future. Waiting can be discouraging; pray for God's presence in the waiting.

Ask God to comfort their hearts. This is a request for inner well-being and confidence. When their hearts are right with God because they are sure of God's grace and presence, they will be comfortable with themselves. This comfort will not be easily upset even when there are disturbances in their family, church, or society. They will be able to withstand onslaughts because within them there is a reservoir of calm based in the love of God and the indwelling presence of Christ.

This prayer is a request for inner strength, that hearts may be strong for "every good word and work." Sometimes Christian service can become a drudgery. People may feel unappreciated or unsuccessful. Pray that they will sense God's pleasure in their service and see their work from His eternal perspective.

Ask God to open their hearts to His pleasure and His perspective. Life with God need never be mundane or hopeless. When we sense God's pleasure and we see from His eternal perspective, our lives are infused with new purpose. Pray that for your fellow believers who faithfully serve their Lord. And then, go tell them thank you for all that they do.

Consolation and comfort. What a wonderful God we have who would bless us so!

Thank You, Lord Jesus, for loving us. Thank You for the comfort, hope, and grace that You give. I pray for my fellow servant, Lord, who is struggling. Give her your boundless consolation so that she may sense Your presence. Revive her hope so that she will know and trust Your promises for the future. Comfort her heart as she is hurting. Reveal to her Your pleasure and Your perspective on the work that she is doing for You. May she understand that no good work done for You ever goes unnoticed or unappreciated by You.

PRAYER REFLECTION

Broken marriages, dying churches, and ineffective ministries can be transformed by the strategic ministry of united prayer.

—Paul Cedar

PRAYERS OF PRAISE

A PRAYER OF PRAISE FOR SALVATION
EXODUS 15:1–18

The LORD is my strength and song,

And He has become my salvation;

He is my God, and I will praise Him;

My father's God, and I will exalt Him.

—*Exodus 15:2*

Even the special effects masters of Hollywood could never have conceived such a scene. The Bible describes it in all of its awesome splendor:

> Then Moses stretched out his hand over the sea; and the LORD caused the sea to go back by a strong east wind all that night, and made the sea into dry land, and the waters were divided. So the children of Israel went into the midst of the sea on the dry ground, and the waters were a wall to them on their right hand and on their left (Exodus 14:21–22).

Moments before, the people had stood between the proverbial rock and a hard place—the vast sea on one side, Pharaoh's deadly soldiers on the other. The situation appeared hopeless; there was no way out.

Have you ever felt that way? Ever been crushed between a rock and a hard place? Ever faced a hopeless situation, no way to turn, no way out? Then you know what these people faced. You know their fear. You might even begin to sense Moses' panic as the mob turned on him. "Is this not the word that we told you in Egypt, saying, 'Let us alone that we may serve the Egyptians?' For it would have been better for us to serve the Egyptians than that we should die in the wilderness" (14:12).

Moses, displaying the qualities of a true leader, calmed their panic with words of unshakeable faith. And Moses said to the people, "Do not be afraid. Stand still, and see the salvation of the LORD, which He will accomplish for you today. For the Egyptians whom you see today, you shall see again no more for-ever. The Lord will fight for you, and you shall hold your peace" (14:13–14). God did not send plagues upon the Egyptians and free His people only to watch them die, trapped by the sea.

God then basically says, "Quit praying and get mov-ing!" And the people did. Right through the sea!

Safe on the other side, Moses and the people burst into a song of praise to God for saving them from their enemies and a hopeless situation. Chapter 15 begins with the words, "Then Moses and the children of Israel sang this song to the LORD." Their salvation caused unbridled joy.

This song begins with praise for God's interventions in history and ends by pro-claiming God's everlasting rule over all things (15:18). There is no one who can be com-pared with God. God was their strength, their song of joy, their salvation.

The same God revealed in the salvation of the Exodus has been revealed in the sal-vation brought to us by Jesus Christ. As believers living in Christ, we have strength: "I can do all things through Christ who strengthens me" (Philippians 4:13). We have a song of praise: "And they sang a new song, saying: 'You are worthy to take the scroll, and to open its seals; for You were slain, and have redeemed us to God by Your blood out of every tribe and tongue and people and nation" (Revelation 5:9). We have been given salvation: "For by grace you have been saved through faith, and that not of yourselves; it is the gift of God" (Ephesians 2:8).

When you don't think you can handle the difficulties of life, praise God for being your strength. When you don't think you will ever be joyful again, praise God for being your song. When you can't see the way out, praise Him for being your salvation.

Praise Him; He is your God!

You are my great and powerful God. I praise You today for being my strength when I am weak, my song when I cannot sing, my salvation when all is lost. I praise and exalt You, Lord, for You are my God.

A PRAYER OF PRAISE FOR GOD'S UNCHANGING CHARACTER
DEUTERONOMY 32:1–43

For I proclaim the name of the LORD:

Ascribe greatness to our God.

He is the Rock, His work is perfect;

For all His ways are justice,

A God of truth and without injustice;

Righteous and upright is He.

—*Deuteronomy 32:3–4*

Suppose someone were to rehearse all the ups and downs—mostly the downs—of your life before an audience? "He really wasn't very faithful to God. In fact, he was pretty foolish. God did all these things for him and yet he neglected God. In fact, I'd even say he's lazy—totally undeserving! So God saw to it that he faced all kinds of terrible situations. He really is a guy who lacks sense and is without understanding. But God will be with him in the end, even though he doesn't deserve anything."

Well, there you have this song in a nutshell. This chapter, traditionally called the Song of Moses, is in the form of a lawsuit—by the prosecuting attorney! Moses rehearses the people's history up to this point—including their deliverance from Egypt and their wanderings in the wilderness. Moses knew whereof he spoke—he had been with them every step of the way. He had gotten them safely out of Egypt and to the edge of the Promised Land and then had to turn around and wander with them for forty years through no fault of his own. He had plenty to say about the people's constant faithlessness, complaining, and rebellion.

Surprisingly, it is not judgment that is handed down upon the Israelites, but mercy. The Ultimate Judge has sentenced the other nations who have refused to worship the true God (32:28–42), while promising forgiveness and life to Israel in spite of its long history of rebellion.

The song begins by describing the character and nature of both parties involved in the contract. Thus Moses begins by praising God and declaring that the LORD is "the Rock, His work is perfect; for all His ways are justice." The God whom Israel worships is indeed a "God of truth and without injustice; righteous and upright is He." Yet in spite of God's gracious provision, His people rebelled against Him and worshiped false gods.

Moses begins his prayer by reminding Israel of the glory and majesty of God, His faithfulness, and His justice. But He also reminds them of their own penchant for rebellion. It is a form that continues to be appropriate for God's people today.

The nature of God does not change; He is still the Rock, and He is just and upright. Sadly, the people of God tend not to change either. We continue to rebel against God and to establish other gods in our hearts. Yet Moses' song does not end with God's punishment of His people. God does not forsake His people forever, and His justice is balanced with His mercy. "The LORD will judge his people and have compassion on His servants" (32:36).

For Christians today, Jesus Christ has become the Rock of our Salvation, the One whose redemptive work was perfect, the just Judge of our souls, the Word of truth, and our Righteousness. Praise Him for being "the same yesterday, today, and forever" (Hebrews 13:8).

Praise Him for being the unchanging God who keeps His promises: "Therefore know that the LORD your God, He is God, the faithful God who keeps covenant and mercy for a thousand generations with those who love Him and keep His commandments" (Deuteronomy 7:9). Praise Him for His mercy toward you.

> PRAYER REFLECTION
>
> *Father, I pray that the spirit of Bartimaeus would grip our hearts and birth desperation in our spirits right now. I pray that incredible hunger and the fire of God-ward passion would overtake and overwhelm us. We're not going to let You get this close and pass us by. We are too hungry for You; we are too desperate to hold back now. Father, we draw a line in the sand; we'll never be the same. We are hungry for you, and we cannot go back; we refuse to retreat to the closet of fear from the place of public passion.*
>
> —*Tommy Tenney*

Unchanging God, You continue to show great mercy on Your people. I know I don't deserve Your mercy and did nothing to earn my salvation. Everything I have is a gift from You. I proclaim Your Name. I ascribe greatness to You, my God. You are my Rock, Your work is perfect, all Your ways are justice. You are my God of truth without injustice; You are righteous and upright. Thank You for showing mercy toward me.

A PRAYER OF PRAISE FOR PROTECTION
JUDGES 5 : 1 – 3 1

Hear, O kings! Give ear, O princes!

I, even I, will sing to the LORD;

I will sing praise to the LORD God of Israel

Thus let all Your enemies perish, O LORD!

But let those who love Him be like the sun

When it comes out in full strength.

—*Judges 5:3, 31*

Sometimes we get ourselves into bad situations, and we see no way out. We need someone to come to our aid, to protect us from our greatest fears, to show us the way out. God, in His great mercy, often brings that protection in ways we ourselves could never have planned or even imagined.

The Book of Judges records the history of Israel from the death of Joshua to the prophet Samuel's anointing of Saul as the first king of Israel. This period is characterized by the repeated cycle of Israel's disobedience to God ("everyone did what was right in his own eyes," Judges 21:25) which is eventually followed by their repentance and God's raising up a judge who would deliver the people from the oppression of their local enemies. The Song of Deborah in Judges 5 is a poetic recitation of God's delivering Israel's enemy, specifically General Sisera, into the hands of a young woman, Jael. The prophetess and the general probably did not have that in their battle plans, but the turn of events saved the nation.

> ### PRAYER REFLECTION
> *Prayer honors God; it dishonors self. It is man's plea of weakness, ignorance, want; a plea which heaven cannot disregard. God delights to have us pray.*
> —*E.M. Bounds*

In Judges 4, God promised Israel, through the prophetess Deborah, that he would deliver the Canaanites into the hands of His people. Yet God's deliverance only came after the people had recognized their sin and "cried out to the LORD" (4:3). What is in prose form in Judges 4 is recounted in prayer and praise and poetry in Judges 5. God is praised for his incredible power that he wields on behalf of his people. When Israel called to God in repentance, the Lord responded by marching out into battle to bring victory to Israel. Even the heavens and the earth trembled before him. Deborah is called by God to rouse the people (5:12), and Barak is summoned to lead all of Israel into war against Sisera. The song comes to a climax as Sisera is violently killed by a woman, Jael, into whose tent Sisera had run for refuge. The description in 5:24–27 is horrifically beautiful Hebrew poetry. It also serves as an example that we often shy away from today. The enemies of God will ultimately fall and be destroyed. Verse 31 makes this clear with a stern warning about where one stands in relation to this God. "Let all Your enemies perish, O LORD!" Those who are against God or God's people will perish in the end. But those who are on the Lord's side will rise and "be like the sun when it comes out in full strength." This last line of the prayer resounds into the New Testament. Matthew 17:2 and Revelation 1:16 speak of Jesus (transfigured or resurrected) as radiant as the sun. As the one and only Son of the Father, Jesus rose like the sun in the full strength of the Resurrection. It is in him that we hope when enemies attack and circumstances threaten us.

Twenty-first century Christians in North America don't often face hand-to-hand battle against invading enemies. Yet, twenty-first century Christians in North America do battle enemies. "For we do not wrestle against flesh and blood, but against principalities, against powers, against the rulers of the darkness of this age, against spiritual hosts of wickedness in the heavenly places" (Ephesians 6:12). The Good News of the gospel, that Judges 5 anticipates and reminds us of, is that "having disarmed principalities and powers, He made a public spectacle of them, triumphing over them in it" (Colossians 2:15).

When the situation seems hopeless, You have a Protector. Turn to Him, for He promises to help. Then when God has delivered you, sing to God along with Deborah.

God my Protector, thank You for being with me through this battle. Thank You for protecting me from harm. I would never have survived without You. I will sing praises to You, Lord, and tell others the story of what You have done for me. I love You, Lord. Thank You for the promise that because I love You, I will be like the sun, radiant in all its strength. Make me like the sun that shines out for You.

A PRAYER OF PRAISE FOR DELIVERANCE
2 SAMUEL 22:1–51

The LORD is my rock and my fortress and my deliverer;
The God of my strength, in whom I will trust;
My shield and the horn of my salvation,

My stronghold and my refuge;

My Savior, You save me from violence.

I will call upon the LORD, who is worthy to be praised;

So shall I be saved from my enemies.

—*2 Samuel 22:2–4*

Sometimes we feel surrounded by problems, trials, enemies. They may come in different forms, but they are there. We wonder how to fight the battle, who will help, where we can turn. Will we be able to survive this latest onslaught?

The Books of Samuel trace Israel's history from the period following the Judges through the tumultuous transition into monarchy. The Second Book of Samuel begins with David's ascending to the throne and establishing order over all of Israel. In bookend fashion, this song of David (found also in Psalm 18) closes the history recorded in Samuel just as the song of Hannah (1 Samuel 2:1–10) set the stage for the history that unfolded in the books.

This Song of David is divided into three sections, which together focus praise on God who has brought peace out of threatening and treacherous times.

In 22:1–20, David thanks and praises God for the deliverance he has experienced from enemy hands. Verse 7 expresses a central theme: David called out to God in his time of distress and God heard his cry. In 22:21–28, David makes explicit the importance of obedience to God's revealed will. It was because of David's faithful obedience that God showed David His favor, and their covenant partnership stood firm.

In 22:29–51, two elements are intertwined: God's sovereign power and David's heroic deeds. It was the power of God working through David, as David was faithful and obedient to God, that brought about victory and national peace. These elements are foreshadowed at the very beginning of this prayer in 22:2–3. "The LORD is my . . . deliverer; the God of my strength, in whom I will trust." Because of this covenant partnership, David proclaims that he "will call upon the LORD, who is worthy to be praised" and so be saved from his enemies (22:4).

We all have a need for security. Whether our enemies are as literal as David's or are as complex as fear or anxiety, we need a deliverer—one who will fight on our behalf when the battle seems (or is) too much for us. David's prayer reminds us that God is always on our side when we faithfully stand in obedience to Him. It is a call to remember the God who is present (Immanuel, "God is with us") as well as a call to remember Jesus' words that if we love Him we will obey Him (John 14:23).

Christians who pray these words after David are reminded that Jesus Christ stands with us as our sure defense. We stand with the Lord in covenant partnership, wearing the armor of Christ. Before Jesus gave the Great Commission, he assured us that "all authority has been given to Me" (Matthew 28:18). And after giving our marching orders, he promised: "I am with you always" (Matthew 28:20). He's our rock, our fortress, and our deliverer.

God my deliverer, the battle is getting to be too much for me. I don't know what to do. I admit that I am afraid. I want to trust You—help me to trust You. I know that You are my rock, my fortress, my deliverer. You are the God of my strength so I can depend on You. You are like a shield around me, You are my salvation, You are my stronghold and refuge that will keep me safe. Deliver me through this situation, I pray. You are most worthy to be praised.

A PRAYER OF PRAISE FOR WHAT GOD HAS DONE
I CHRONICLES 16:8–36

Sing to the LORD, all the earth;
Proclaim the good news of His salvation from day to day.
Declare His glory among the nations,
His wonders among all peoples.
For the LORD is great and greatly to be praised;
He is also to be feared above all gods.

—*1 Chronicles 16:23–25*

What has God done for you? Have you ever taken the time to "count your blessings" as the old song used to say? If you were to sit down and begin a list of all that God has done on your behalf to guide and watch over you from the day you were born, chances are you'd discover a Lord who "is great and greatly to be praised"!

David used the occasion of bringing the ark of the covenant back to Jerusalem to call the people of God to worship. By means of a psalm, he urges the congregation of believers to offer their praise to the Lord. He closes by suggesting a prayer for salvation in order that God may be praised. In calling for the worship of God, David reminds the people of two reasons why God is worthy of their praise. God is worthy of praise because of who He is and because of what He has done for His people.

> **PRAYER REFLECTION**
>
> *Break our hearts, Lord God. Set us on fire with incredible hunger until nothing else and nothing less than Your presence will satisfy.*
>
> —*Tommy Tenney*

Who is God that David would request His listeners to offer up praise? He is the One whose name is holy (16:10). He is also mighty in strength (16:11). "Honor and majesty are before Him; strength and gladness are in His place" (16:27). God, in His very being, is worthy of our worship!

However, David did more than call the people to praise God for whom He is. He also points out that God makes Himself worthy of our praise by the many things He has done. David praises God for His wondrous work in creation, in which even land and sea attribute praise to God (16:26–33). David praises God for choosing and protecting His people (16:13), and for establishing a never-ending covenant with them (16:15). History had displayed God's faithfulness to keep this covenant, protecting His people from destruction.

As Christians, we have every reason to praise God for exactly the same reasons. If we have repented of our sins and believed in Jesus Christ for salvation, we can rest assured of our inheritance in God's everlasting covenant. As His people, we ought to praise Him for who He is and for the great things He has done for us. God is more glorious and beautiful than any other, and He alone can satisfy our deepest longings. God's glory has overflowed into His mighty works—in creating us in His image and in restoring that image, which was marred due to our sin. Surely something within us feels compelled to say with David, "For the LORD is great and greatly to be praised." Let your heart sing out a prayer of praise to God for all that He is and all that He has done.

Lord, Creator of all, I sing to You. Along with Your very creation I proclaim the good news of Your salvation from day to day. Thank You for all You have done for me. Thank You for saving me and promising eternal life. Thank You for watching over the pathways of my life and guiding me in Your will. Thank You for the many blessings You have bestowed on my life. You are a great God, and greatly to be praised.

Blessed are You, LORD God of Israel, our Father, forever
and ever.
Yours, O LORD, is the greatness,
The power and the glory,
The victory and the majesty;
For all that is in heaven and in earth is Yours;
Yours is the kingdom, O LORD,
And You are exalted as head over all.

—*1 Chronicles 29:10–11*

Our responsibilities can sometimes feel overwhelming. Perhaps it is a job assignment that puts us in over our head, or a church responsibility that we don't think we have the resources to fulfill, or a situation with a friend that we don't know how to handle. Sometimes life feels too big, and we don't think we can do what we know we should do.

Israel's King Solomon inherited a huge responsibility. When the crown was placed on his head, he may have felt in over his head already. His father left him with the awesome task of building a temple. The people of Israel had been longing for the temple, a permanent place to worship God. When they wandered through the wilderness, the tabernacle had traveled with them. The tabernacle stayed with the people through the time of the judges and into the beginning of the kingdom. As king, David had the same desire to build a grand home for God's glory. However, God did not choose David for this task, but his son Solomon: "Nevertheless you shall not build the temple, but your son who will come from your body, he shall build the temple for My name" (1 Kings 8:19).

David rejoiced, even though his son Solomon was young and inexperienced and the task that lay ahead was momentous. David had seen God's greatness and strength in big tasks before. David attributes greatness to God, because he recognizes that all of heaven and earth are His. So he prays for his son: "And give my son Solomon a loyal heart to keep Your commandments and Your testimonies and Your statutes, to do all these things, and to build the temple for which I have made provision" (1 Chronicles 29:19).

The words of David are still true today. God is king over heaven and earth, and we depend on His strength to complete great tasks. Are you standing at the beginning of something new? Are you young and inexperienced, wondering how your tasks will ever be completed? Are you experienced but still wondering how to complete the things God has called you to do? God called Solomon to build the temple and has called you to do His will. Unlike Solomon, you are not building the temple. You are now the temple, where the Spirit dwells within you.

Practice praying as David did, with confidence and asserting God's goodness. "In Your hand is power and might; in Your hand it is to make great and to give strength to all" (29:12). Have confidence that God will give you strength for the great tasks He calls you to complete.

I have a big responsibility before me, Lord, and I know that I don't have the strength, ability, or resources to do it. But I know that You do. You have the power and the glory, the victory and the majesty. You have called me to this task, and I know that You will be with me to do it. Help me today to do what You have called me to do.

A PRAYER OF PRAISE FOR GOD'S STRENGTH
LUKE 1:46-55

My soul magnifies the Lord,
And my spirit has rejoiced in God my Savior.
He has shown strength with His arm;
He has scattered the proud in the imagination of their
    hearts.
—*Luke 1:46–47, 51*

At times the tasks God calls us to do are not exactly what we would have chosen. We often don't comprehend God's desire to use willing servants in various tasks—tasks to which we may not at all feel suited. But God knows us intimately, down to the very core of our being. He knows those who are best suited for doing a certain part of building His glorious kingdom.

Mary was a young woman with a plan. She was engaged to be married, and she probably expected her life to continue much as the lives of her family and friends had. But God interrupted her plan with a plan of His own—a plan bigger and grander than Mary's teenage mind could ever have considered on her own. God knew she was a willing servant with a faithful heart. When the angel came, Mary was ready.

Mary's prayer in Luke 1 is one of the great biblical prayers used by Christians throughout the centuries. Its traditional title is *Magnificat,* taken from the first word of the prayer in Latin. Mary prays this prayer with wonder and amazement at the works of the Lord. After receiving the message that she is pregnant with God's Messiah, she visits her relative, Elizabeth, who is pregnant in her old age with John the Baptist, who will prepare the way for Mary's child. When Mary arrived at Elizabeth's home, Elizabeth honored her as "the mother of my Lord"—an amazing honor considering that Mary is younger, unmarried, and pregnant under apparently dubious circumstances. In response to Elizabeth's praise, and perhaps overwhelmed by these amazing events, Mary bursts into her prayer of praise to God.

Mary's prayer is primarily praise for God's bringing about salvation. She recognizes the pivotal role she will play as the mother of the Messiah and connects her role to God's history of involvement with Israel. Mary characterizes God as the strong God who turns the patterns of the world upside down—He raises the lowly and brings down the proud. At the end of the prayer, she recognizes that this coming salvation is the fulfillment of God's promises to Abraham and Israel.

> ### PRAYER REFLECTION
>
> *O Lord, the Scripture says "there is a time for silence and a time for speech." Savior, teach me the silence of humility, the silence of wisdom, the silence of love, the silence of perfection, the silence that speaks without words, the silence of faith.*
> *Lord, teach me to silence my own heart that I may listen to the gentle movement of the Holy Spirit within me and sense the depths which are of God.*
>
> —*Frankfurt Prayer,*
> sixteenth century

Along with Christians throughout history, we can pray this prayer with Mary as an exuberant prayer of praise to God for the experience of His salvation through Jesus Christ. Every individual Christian and every Christian community has times when the wonder of God's mercy and salvation are overwhelming to them.

Take a cue from young Mary. Be ready for God to use you.

God, You are my strength when I am weak. I don't know that I can do this task You have given me. But I want to trust that You know I can do it. I magnify You, Lord, and my spirit rejoices in You. You give me Your strength to accomplish Your will. Thank You for the provision of Your strength for the task ahead.

A PRAYER OF PRAISE FOR OUR RELATIONSHIP WITH GOD
LUKE 1:68-79

To give knowledge of salvation to His people

By the remission of their sins,

Through the tender mercy of our God,

With which the Dayspring from on high has visited us;

To give light to those who sit in darkness and the shadow
of death,

To guide our feet into the way of peace.

—*Luke 1:77–79*

By far the greatest relationship we have is our relationship with the Sovereign Lord. Christians are set apart as people who have intimacy with God. No other religious faith allows such a concept. Yet the Bible tells us that we can call God our Father and that we are His children. Such intimacy was bought at a price. God wanted it so much that He sent His only Son to die in order to give it to us. When we accept that sacrifice on our behalf, we walk into the throne room of God as His dearly beloved children.

Zacharias stood at the intersection of two covenants. He was raised in the world of the Old Testament with its promises of a coming Savior. The angel that met him in the temple revealed that a momentous time had come. The promised Savior would soon enter the world, and Zacharias himself would be a part of the process, fathering the child who would grow to be the promised forerunner of the Messiah. The words of Zacharias's prayer in Luke 1 are the first to cross his lips after his muteness during his wife Elizabeth's pregnancy. He was struck dumb because of his disbelief when the angel proclaimed the pregnancy to him. He regained his speech after the child had been named.

PRAYER REFLECTION

When I think of prayer, the image that comes to mind is that of a small child, reaching up in trust to grasp the hand of a tall adult. The adult smiles, bends down, and gently takes the tiny hand in his own. The image, one of utter intimacy, is one I return to again and again. For I know that I am the child, and the adult is God, my Heavenly Father.

—*Larry Richards*

Like the other prayers in the opening chapters of Luke's Gospel, Zacharias's prayer recognizes that what has happened to him is part of God's great scheme of salvation and the history of God's care for His people. Zacharias praises God for fulfilling His promises to Israel and redeeming Israel from its enemies.

But his prayer then turns to blessing his new son's role in the coming of the Messiah. John, he says, will be able to go directly before the Lord and prepare the way for Him. This was an amazing privilege at the time. Zacharias was a priest, one of very few people in Israel with the most direct access to God. But his son John would have an even closer way to encounter God—he would prepare all the people of Israel for a direct encounter with God and speak to Christ face to face.

While Zacharias's prayer for his son John expresses something of John's unique role in Christ's coming, we too can echo themes of this prayer. Christ has opened our access to God. Each of us is, like John, brought into a direct encounter with the living God. We are also called to follow in John's footsteps to prepare others for an encounter with Christ. We should praise God for His mercy and praise Him publicly so that everyone may hear of "the tender mercy of our God" and see the light of the Daystar. Zacharias praised God for his son's role as prophet to prepare the way for Jesus. We can praise God for using us and other Christians to spread the gospel of Jesus Christ. Praise Him for giving you a personal, intimate relationship with Him. That gift alone is worthy of our highest praise.

Thank You, Father, for saving me, cleansing my sin, and bringing me into an intimate relationship with You. Thank You that I can come before You with my needs and requests and that, like a loving Father, You hear and answer. Thank You for the privilege of sharing this message with others so that they, too, might come into a personal relationship with You.

PRAYERS FOR FORGIVENESS

A REQUEST FOR GOD TO HEAR AND FORGIVE
I KINGS 8:23–53

Lord God of Israel, there is no God in heaven above or on earth below like You, who keep Your covenant and mercy with Your servants who walk before You with all their hearts. . . . And may You hear the supplication of Your servant and of Your people Israel, when they pray toward this place. Hear in heaven Your dwelling place; and when You hear, forgive.

—*1 Kings 8:23, 30*

When Solomon completed the Lord's temple and prayed this prayer of dedication, he rejoiced that God had fulfilled the promise that was made to his father, King David. In 2 Samuel 7, the Lord promises that David's line will rule forever before God, and that God will make his final dwelling through this line. David, and Solomon after him, saw that fulfillment in the building of the temple in Jerusalem. God had accompanied His people in the tabernacle, but that was only a tent, a temporary structure. Now, God finally had a permanent dwelling on earth, with His people Israel.

But in his prayer, Solomon acknowledges that it is inconceivable to think of the God and Creator of heaven and earth contained within the walls of a building (8:27). In awe of this thought, he continues his prayer with humility. He recognizes that the temple is not some sort of magic that guarantees answers to prayer. So he continues the prayer by asking that God will hear those who approach the temple in prayer. And he asks first that God will hear the most important petitions brought to Him—petitions for God's forgiveness (8:30).

As New Testament believers, we may see even deeper meanings in this prayer. David's line did not establish an endless earthly monarchy. But Jesus, his descendant, whom we confess as King of all the earth, is the ultimate fulfillment of God's promises to David. He is not only our King but also the temple of God's presence with us on earth. In Jesus, God does dwell on earth. God is contained in the body of a human being. And Solomon's petition in 8:30, for God to hear our prayers and forgive our sins, becomes the promise of the new covenant in Christ. In our prayers, we should pray to God with appropriate humility but also with the assurance that through Jesus Christ, God will hear us and forgive our sins.

> *Forgiving Father, thank You that You are also my King. Thank You that You chose to send Your Son to earth so that we could see You. I praise You that You are larger than the highest heavens yet You live within my heart. Thank You that You hear my prayers. And when I confess my sins, I pray that You will hear and forgive.*

A PRAYER OF SORROW FOR SIN
EZRA 9:6–15

O my God, I am too ashamed and humiliated to lift up my
face to You, my God; for our iniquities have risen higher
than our heads, and our guilt has grown up to the heavens.
—*Ezra 9:6*

God had been gracious to Israel and had delivered some of the people from their captivity in Babylon. In spite of this, the hearts of His people indulged in the pagan practices of the Canaanites. They had been instructed in the law not to become like the Gentiles (Deuteronomy 7:1–3), and the prophets were certain to preach this very message (Malachi 2:10–16). Yet the people had failed. They just could not keep the simplest and most important commandment. So Ezra prayed this confession of sin.

We notice immediately the deep sense of shame expressed in this prayer. Ezra approached the God of all mercy yet found it difficult even to show his face. He recognized how ungrateful the people were, for they had forsaken the One who delivered them. This intense sense of shame was a driving force in the heart of Ezra. The

PRAYER REFLECTION

Prayer made the difference between Peter denying his Lord and the same Peter preaching with great power and incredible results on the Day of Pentecost.

—*Paul Cedar*

people had become a disgrace, so Ezra was down on his knees before God. Ezra gives us an example of how "godly sorrow produces repentance leading to salvation, not to be regretted" (2 Corinthians 7:10).

Have we also fallen victim to such worldliness as the Israelites did? Often we allow ourselves to be satisfied with pagan things of this world. We live in a highly immoral society and see it displayed on a daily basis. You can turn on your television tonight and in less that thirty minutes, you will observe one or more of the Ten Commandments broken in a blatant fashion several times. You are most likely not able to go a day without noticing someone who flaunts his or her perversions carelessly. One sad thing is that we have become so immune to it. We must ask ourselves, "When I encounter these things, do they grieve my heart?" Sadly, most of the time we are not fazed. Sometimes we even indulge in it. We have become calloused to actions dishonoring God because we have allowed them to rub up against us too long. We desperately need God to cut away these calloused portions of our hearts so that we might be more sensitive to His ways. We need forgiveness. Although we are called to live in the world, we should not become like it. Let us admit our shame before the Lord so that His healing balm may soothe our sin-sick souls. Let us seek His forgiveness so that we might once again be satisfied wholly in Him. To continue taking our cues from the values of a shame-filled world will only produce disgrace. Following God with an open heart will enable us to feel His love flowing once again.

Dear Lord, there is sin all around me—and sadly, sin within me. I know I have been saved from sin, and I praise You for that salvation. Yet You have left us in this sin-sick world to make a difference. Give me the strength and courage to stand strong for You against the sin that surrounds me. Help me not to be tempted by it, but to see it for what it is. Forgive my sin. Purify my heart that I might once again serve You.

A PRAYER OF CONFESSION
NEHEMIAH 1:5-11

Please let Your ear be attentive and Your eyes open, that
You may hear the prayer of Your servant which I pray
before You now, day and night, for the children of Israel
Your servants, and confess the sins of the children of Israel
which we have sinned against You. Both my father's house

and I have sinned. We have acted very corruptly against You, and have not kept the commandments, the statutes, nor the ordinances which You commanded Your servant Moses.

—*Nehemiah 1:6–7*

When Nehemiah was in Babylon, he heard a report of the great distress and ruin that still remained in Jerusalem, the beloved capital city of his homeland. Immediately, he cried out to God, asking for forgiveness and restoration. He called upon God to be faithful to the covenant, especially to the promise of restoration as the people repented (Deuteronomy 12:5; 30:1–5). It's not that God needed the reminder; the people did. This prayer, like many others, is the pray-er's way of begging people to seek God, to turn to God.

Anyone who seeks forgiveness of sins will discover much comfort in this passage. In seeking forgiveness from God, Nehemiah admitted Israel's and his own unworthiness before God. Nehemiah knows that the people have shown disrespect and indifference toward God. It was necessary for the Israelites to admit their ill feelings against God and that these attitudes were the very reason why they were in captivity. They must have already been discouraged about the dismay of Jerusalem, and now they had to admit it was their fault! Confession of sin at this point must have been pretty painful.

Pride keeps us from seeking God's forgiveness. We find it difficult to admit that we are wrong, much less that we deserve endless punishment for our rebellion against God. We are like children in this sense, justifying our rebellion, blaming our circumstances, finding fault in every place except our own hearts. However, real confession of sin is exactly what God looks for as He moves to forgive that sin. The apostle John made it clear: "If we confess our sins, He is faithful and just to forgive us our sins and to cleanse us from all unrighteousness" (1 John 1:9). The question is not whether God will forgive us, but whether we will humble ourselves and repent of our wrong. Put away your pride today and humble yourself before the Lord. This is the path to forgiveness, and to all that follows—the abundant life God has promised to you.

Gracious Lord, I know that I have done wrong. I have sinned against You and done evil in Your sight. I have acted corruptly against You and have not kept Your commands. Please hear my prayer today. Please forgive me for my sin against You. Please wash it away and make me clean.

A PRAYER FOR GRACE AND MERCY
NEHEMIAH 9:5–37

Now therefore, our God, the great, the mighty, and
    awesome God,
Who keeps covenant and mercy:
Do not let all the trouble seem small before You that has
    come upon us,
Our kings and our princes, our priests and our prophets,
    our fathers and on all Your people,
From the days of the kings of Assyria until this day.
However You are just in all that has befallen us; for You
    have dealt faithfully,
But we have done wickedly.
—*Nehemiah 9:32–33*

Some of us have to be hit over the head before we get it. Sometimes it takes an extremely difficult situation to cause us to wake up to problems in our lives, in our character, in our attitudes.

The Israelites had been greatly blessed by God, but throughout their history they had constantly been drawn away from Him. The Books of 1 and 2 Kings describe a nation that constantly rebelled against God. Finally, God made good on His promise to punish them and send them away into exile.

Then later, God also made good on a promise to bring them back to their land and to their beloved city of Jerusalem. Many returned from exile and gathered together to rebuild their nation. The place to start, of course, was the reading of the Book of the Law (Nehemiah 9:3).

When the Israelites heard the Law of God proclaimed, they quickly felt guilty and knew it was appropriate to confess their sins. The rest of the chapter recites a song of the Levites, which sums up their confession before God. It recounts the glory of God in creation (9:6), in choosing Abraham as the founder of their nation (9:7), and in making a covenant (9:8) with His people. The song goes on to describe Israel's sinfulness in spite of God's love for them. Furthermore, it seeks restoration from God (9:32), yet acknowledges that the people do not deserve it (9:33).

By drawing upon God's action in creating, electing, and making the covenant, the Levites were describing and illustrating the character of God. This God, the true God, is a God of abundant mercy. Because of this mercy, the people could ask forgiveness, even though they deserved severe judgment for their sins. In fact, they readily acknowledged that they had responded with only wickedness to God's previous acts of grace. In spite of these insults against God, they had good reason to seek forgiveness. Their God was a God of mercy. God's actions and words reveal this truth, so the Israelites held fast to this hope.

Today, like long ago, God's mercy abounds more than our sins (see Romans 5:20). God's desire to show mercy is part of His very being. In spite of our great wickedness, we should never feel unwelcome in seeking God's forgiveness. His grace is greater than anything we can think, say, or do. While we have nothing within us to gain the favor of the Lord, we have good reason to seek God's favor. What a wonderful God we have, that He delights in granting mercy! Is this not the right reason, all the time, whatever the situation, for us to humble ourselves in confession before Him? The ground for forgiveness is solid, a sure solution for our most despicable sins. Let your heart take joy, for God's mercy brings delight to those who seek it.

Merciful God, I know that I don't deserve to come to You. I have sinned again, and once again, I need Your forgiveness. I know that what I deserve is punishment, yet You offer me grace and mercy. I take hold of Your grace and mercy today, Lord, understanding that it comes because of who You are, not who I am. Forgive me, Lord. By Your grace and mercy help me to walk close to You.

A PRAYER OF REPENTANCE
JOB 42:1-6

I know that You can do everything,

And that no purpose of Yours can be withheld

    from You.

Therefore I abhor myself,

And repent in dust and ashes.

—*Job 42:2, 6*

Many people want to have the last word. In a debate, the person giving the final closing argument definitely has the advantage.

The Book of Job is a running debate. We observe the debate between God and Satan over Job's righteousness. We read the debates between Job and his four friends, who seek to convince him that his suffering is due to his sinfulness. Finally, we hear the debate between God and Job—but it's not much of a debate, for God has the last word. All that Job can say is "I abhor myself, and repent in dust and ashes." He repents not of some hidden sin, as his friends had suggested. He repents for doubting God.

For readers of the Book of Job, the prayer in chapter 42 seems especially unusual. All through the book, we have known what Job didn't know—that his suffering was sent by Satan to try to dislodge Job's strong faith. As readers, we saw the drama between God and Satan played out in heaven. And yet, in our own lives, we are in Job's position—suffering without understanding why.

There is nothing wrong with a healthy appetite for further knowledge of God and His ways. Our faith should move us to explore Scripture, theology, and the wisdom of other Christians. Prayers that are honest and express our frustration and even anger are also appropriate. But, like Job, there are times when we simply cannot understand how God is working in our lives. Job's steadfast righteousness is a strength that we should strive for, and underpinning this righteousness there should always be strong trust in God's ways.

Praying Job's prayer from chapter 42 might help us to cultivate trust. When we are struggling and suffering, prayers of lament are an essential part of our communication with God. But lament should always move toward faith. Perhaps God will indeed show us a sin from which we need to repent and turn away. Then sorrow and repentance should follow. Sometimes, no explanation is given, no sin is pointed out, and we need help praying for trust in God's ways. Scripture provides prayers like Job's to give us words when we don't know what to say. Like Job, our acceptance of God's will ought to come from an underlying trust in God's love for us.

Almighty God, I don't understand everything about You—I'll be the first to admit it. Through my suffering show me, Lord, if there is some sin from which I need to repent, and I will do so. "Search me, O God, and know my heart; try me, and know my anxieties; and see if there is any wicked way in me, and lead me in the way everlasting" (Psalm 139:23–24).

A PRAYER OF HOPE IN GOD'S MERCY
ISAIAH 63:15 — 64:12

But now, O LORD,
You are our Father;
We are the clay, and You our potter;
And all we are the work of Your hand.
Do not be furious, O LORD,
Nor remember iniquity forever;
Indeed, please look—we all are Your people!
—*Isaiah 64:8–9*

Clay in the hands of a master potter can become an object of beauty. As the potter turns the wheel and spins the clay, he works the clay to make into reality what he sees in his mind. A vase, a bowl, a cup, a masterpiece—only the potter knows what the clay will become.

In coming to God for forgiveness, Isaiah used two analogies. By mentioning God as "our Father," he states the fact that God adopted the Israelites as His children. Drawing upon the image of a potter and his clay, Isaiah points out the almighty power of God and His plans for His people.

239

Notice that Isaiah did not seek forgiveness of sin on account of anything special done by the Israelites. Indeed, Isaiah was quick to dismiss the people's virtues as false reasons for hope. Thus, he confessed, "all our righteousnesses are like filthy rags" (64:6). Here the confession finds hope in the tender mercies of God. In us, as weak human beings, there is no hope for forgiveness. We are no more than a lump of clay—unable to do anything of value on our own. If we are to receive forgiveness, we must rely wholly upon our tender and merciful Father. We should praise God, because He extends great mercy by adopting sinners to be His own beloved children.

> **PRAYER REFLECTION**
>
> *Prayer is trusting God to do what He knows is best for your life, not just in the short run but also in the long run. The character of God is the anchor for prayer. He loves you. He always works for your best. You can always trust him.*
>
> *—Charles Stanley*

Notice that Isaiah recognized the tendency of people to run from God rather than seek Him for forgiveness. Not only does our sin leave us guilty, but it also leaves us corrupted. Thus, Isaiah said, "There is no one who calls on Your name, who stirs himself up to take hold of You" (64:7). At this point, the confession finds hope in the creative powers of God. Isaiah called upon the Potter to form them anew, being "the work of Your hand" (64:8). If we are to receive forgiveness, we must first turn to the God of all mercy. God is worthy to be praised, for He delights to draw our hearts close to His. When we allow the Potter to mold us, we become all that He intends for us to be.

It is important to see that Isaiah pleaded for forgiveness based upon the actions of God. Equally significant, the prophet recognized that people typically avoid facing their sins and run from God's way of redemption. Christians today can fall into the same trap. Focusing on past blessings from God, we can mistakenly overlook weakness, greed, jealousy, and lust. Let us seek the mercy of God on behalf of our families, our cities, and our churches. Let us pray that God would awake us to our need for forgiveness and grant it to us. Let us allow the Potter to mold us into what He alone envisions for us—then we can make a difference in our world.

> *You are the Potter; I am the clay, Lord. I recognize that without Your creative hand, I am nothing. Forgive me for running from You and in my pride refusing to see the sins You have wanted to cleanse from my life. I confess those sins to You now and yield to Your hand. I trust that You will mold me and shape me into what You want me to be. I trust that as the work of Your hand, I am most precious to You.*

PRAYERS OF THANKSGIVING

A PRAYER OF THANKS FOR ANSWERED PRAYER
I SAMUEL 2:1–11

My heart rejoices in the LORD;

My horn is exalted in the LORD.

I smile at my enemies,

Because I rejoice in Your salvation.

No one is holy like the LORD,

For there is none besides You,

Nor is there any rock like our God.

—1 Samuel 2:1–2

Knowing that God hears and answers prayer is one thing; experiencing it for ourselves is quite another! What a thrill we feel when we fervently pray for something and then God miraculously answers! We rejoice, we praise, we may even shed a few tears. What a joy to experience God's answers to prayer.

Hannah's prayer is one of thanksgiving to God for an answered prayer. Hannah had wanted to have a child, but she couldn't. On a visit to the tabernacle, she decided to lay her request before the Lord. She prayed so fervently for a child that her intensity was mistaken for drunkenness (1 Samuel 1:13–14). In ancient Israelite society, children were a mother's insurance—they gave her worth in the eyes of others, and they ensured that someone would take care of her in her old age.

The Old Testament is filled with stories of women who longed for children, but through barrenness or death of adult children, their situation appeared hopeless. Hannah's prayer for a child echoes the cries of Sarah, Rachel, and Naomi. God answered all of their prayers, exhibiting His special concern for the powerless in society—such as the childless women. And the sons and grandsons of all of these women contributed in important ways to the lineage of the promised Messiah.

Hannah's prayer of thanksgiving shows the proper response of exuberant praise to the God who hears and answers our prayers. It also shows how broad the themes of these prayers can be. Our prayers of thanks for answered prayers frequently focus on the specific situation we were praying about. It may seem odd that Hannah does not make mention of her own answered prayer at the center of this prayer. She does not praise God because Samuel was a beautiful baby who gave her much joy or rejoice because his life will be dedicated to God's service. Instead, Hannah's praise describes a God who hears the prayers of the hungry, the barren, and the beggar. Hannah places her thanksgiving in the context of God's answers to the prayers of Israel throughout its history. There is even a forward-looking aspect to Hannah's prayer—Mary's prayer in Luke 1 is very similar to Hannah's prayer.

We too can place ourselves in the context of God's mighty acts throughout history. For example, a family prayer of thanks for answered prayer might include praise for ways that God has heard the family in the past. Reciting God's faithfulness in prayer praises God and reminds us that God truly is faithful to His people.

Dear God, thank You for answering my prayer! My heart rejoices that You heard my need and came to intervene. I know I shouldn't be surprised, for Your Word says that You hear and answer prayer—but it is such a joy to experience that personally! Thank You for all that You have done for me and continue to do for me.

A PRAYER OF THANKS FOR GOD'S BLESSINGS
2 SAMUEL 7:18–29

Who am I, O Lord GOD? And what is my house, that You have brought me this far? And yet this was a small thing in Your sight, O Lord GOD; and You have also spoken of Your servant's house for a great while to come. Is this the manner of man, O Lord GOD? Now what more can David say to You? For You, Lord GOD, know Your servant. For Your word's sake, and according to Your own heart, You have done all these great things, to make Your servant know them.

—*2 Samuel 7:18–21*

Look around you. Look at your home. Your family. Your possessions. Your job. Your gifts and talents. You are a blessing; you are surrounded by blessings. Consideration of this might cause you to resonate with David's words, "Who am I, Lord, that you have given me all of these blessings?"

God graced David with many blessings. David had not sought to be the king of a great nation—indeed, he probably thought he'd be a shepherd for life. Yet God sought a heart open to serving Him and found it in the young shepherd in Bethlehem (see 1 Samuel 16:7). David became the king of Israel and desired to build a temple for the Lord as a way of thanking Him for all He had done.

But God gave an unexpected answer: He said no.

David was not to build the temple. But David would receive a blessing even bigger: God would honor him by extending his lineage into eternity. What is most remarkable about this promise to David is that it was completely unmerited. David wanted a temple, but God turned around and promised eternity. David was humbled. "Who am I, O Lord GOD?" he prayed, "And what is my house, that You have brought me this far?"

David did nothing to earn this blessing. It was simply God's grace. By the same token, we can never earn our salvation or make any offering or sacrifice to God that would ever match the sacrifice He made for us through Jesus. And we really don't deserve anything else we have either. The blessings you have came to you by God's grace.

David honored God throughout his lifetime, receiving the legacy of being a man after God's own heart. Did he make some mistakes? Of course—in fact, the Bible records some horrible misdeeds. But David had a teachable spirit, and when he sinned, he both learned his lesson and paid the consequences. Still, God worked with His servant and blessed him beyond his wildest imaginations.

Now look again at all that God has given you. Your greatest way to thank Him is to be a person after God's own heart.

You have blessed me so richly, Lord, and I know I don't deserve it. Thank You for all that You have done in my life—for my salvation, my family, my heritage, my job, my possessions. May I use my blessings in order to be a blessing to others. And may I be a person after Your heart, always seeking to follow You.

THE JOY OF OFFERING THANKS TO GOD
ISAIAH 38:10-20

The LORD was ready to save me;

Therefore we will sing my songs with stringed instruments

All the days of our life, in the house of the LORD.

—*Isaiah 38:20*

From our youngest days, our parents taught us to say thank you. When someone does something kind, "Say thank you." When given a gift, "Say thank you." And if we ever forgot, they were ready with the words, "Now what do you say?" Say thank you.

Hezekiah had learned to say thank you. Hezekiah was a king of Judah—a good king who loved the Lord and sought to serve Him. But one day he became ill. God sent the prophet Isaiah to tell him to get ready to die. Hezekiah turned to the Lord and with bitter weeping asked to be spared.

God sent Isaiah back to the king with a new message, "I have heard your prayer, I have seen your tears; surely I will add to your days fifteen years" (Isaiah 38:5).

By God's mercy, King Hezekiah had been delivered from a life-threatening sickness. The Lord heard his prayer and blessed him with recovery of health and granted an additional fifteen years to his life. Upon recovery, Hezekiah proclaimed God's goodness in sparing his life. After recalling his distress, he delivered this great hymn of thanksgiving.

> **PRAYER REFLECTION**
>
> *When you pray, you come to know God in the most practical and personal way possible—His mind, His will, and His character. Knowing God can make a dull life exciting, a doubting life sure, a timid life bold, a wandering life purposeful.*
>
> —*Charles Stanley*

Several features in Hezekiah's offering of gratitude will help us understand what it means to have a prayerful heart of thanksgiving toward God. First, Hezekiah's thanksgiving revealed his sincere appreciation for and delight in God-given grace. God had granted mercy to Hezekiah by pardoning his sin and extending his life. As a result, Hezekiah recognized that God ultimately brought him through the bitter times in order to impart a peace in his soul (38:17). This written record of Hezekiah's joyous response expresses his pleasure in experiencing an amazing grace. If we have not expressed thanksgiving for all that God has done for us, can we really say that we appreciate Him?

A second important feature is that Hezekiah's thanksgiving sought to give due recognition for the good he had received. Hezekiah looked forward to seeing God praised for what had been done, so he declared his intentions to sing songs with stringed instruments all the remaining days of his life (38:20). He found it good for his soul to give God the glory. If God displays His glory for our good, we should take equal pleasure in giving Him the entire honor.

A third feature of his thanksgiving is that Hezekiah desired others to find enjoyment in the goodness of God. He refused to sing God's praises alone. Instead he said, "We will sing." Hezekiah wanted God's blessing conveyed to others. Likewise, our thankfulness ought to enthuse us to persuade others to rejoice in our glorious God.

Will our prayers display our appreciation to God? Will they grant honor to Him rather than us? Will they lead us to excite others to find their delight in the glory of our God? O God, grant us thankful hearts!

I say thank You today, Lord, and desire to thank You every day for the rest of my life. I don't ever want to take Your blessing to me for granted. I want to honor You and remember that all I have comes from Your hand. I desire that others will recognize Your hand on my life and desire to seek You as well. Develop in me a thankful heart.

A PRAYER OF THANKS FOR WISDOM AND GUIDANCE
DANIEL 2:20–23

> Blessed be the name of God forever and ever,
> For wisdom and might are His.
> He gives wisdom to the wise
> And knowledge to those who have understanding.
> I thank You and praise You,
> O God of my fathers;
> You have given me wisdom and might.
>
> —*Daniel 2:20–21, 23*

How scary it is to get lost in an unfamiliar place. Perhaps you're driving in a new city and can't find your way. Then what relief you feel when you see a sign back to the highway and you recognize the route number. At least when you get there, you know where you are. You're not lost anymore.

The great King Nebuchadnezzar was lost—in the unfamiliar land of his dreams. He knew a god was speaking to him through this peculiar dream, but he hadn't the foggiest idea what it meant. So he called in all the wise men of Babylon, but they couldn't figure it out either. So Nebuchadnezzar unwisely decided that all of his wise men should be executed.

Among those wise men was Daniel, a Hebrew who had been brought into the service of the king after his capture of Judah. With a death penalty looming over his head, Daniel gathered his Hebrew friends together to pray for the wisdom to interpret the dream. The Bible tells us that "the secret was revealed to Daniel in a night vision" (2:19). And what did Daniel do next? He praised God!

> **PRAYER REFLECTION**
>
> *Prayer is as essential to a Christian's spiritual life as breathing is to his physical life. All Christians pray. How they pray, however, is almost as varied as people. Some people never develop a deep or disciplined prayer life because they have never seen one modeled for them. How you pray will influence how others pray.*
>
> —*Tim LaHaye and Ed Hindson*

Like Joseph before him, who had interpreted dreams for Egypt's Pharaoh, Daniel knew that kings with troubling dreams appreciate wise answers. This prayer in chapter 2 is Daniel's response to God and the wisdom He had revealed. Later, Nebuchadnezzar was so delighted with Daniel and his friends' wisdom that he gave them great posts of power in the kingdom.

Even as Daniel prayed this prayer of praise, he was unsure of his future, but he was sure of his God. He prayed this great prayer of thanks before he knew how the king would respond, before he knew if he'd even get a chance to speak to the king. Yet he had been confident of God's ability to reveal hidden secrets, and God had done so. Daniel thanked God for this wisdom and insight that had been given to him. Nebuchadnezzar would later recognize that the God of Israel reveals the hidden things.

Wisdom is one of the most precious gifts that God gives. Solomon asked God for wisdom and received immeasurable wisdom to rule his nation wisely (1 Kings 3:9). To anyone who asks, God gives wisdom. James reminds us, "If any of you lacks wisdom, let him ask of God, who gives to all liberally and without reproach, and it will be given to him" (James 1:5). God can see through the darkness, and His wisdom gives us direction and provides the boundaries for a healthy life.

Are you lost today? On the wrong path? Unsure of where to go next? God knows the best path for you to take, even when you do not. He is generous to answer prayers for wisdom. Ask God for the wisdom and guidance You need today. You can be sure He will give it. Then, along with Daniel, thank Him for all He has done.

God of all wisdom, I know that You promise wisdom to anyone who lacks it, and I'm definitely lacking it in this situation. I need Your wisdom and guidance to do the right thing and to honor You. Thank You for Your promise. Thank You for giving wisdom and understanding. I praise You, Lord, along with Daniel, for showing me the way to go.

A PRAYER OF THANKS FOR SALVATION
LUKE 2:29–32

Lord, now You are letting Your servant depart in peace,
According to Your word;
For my eyes have seen Your salvation
Which You have prepared before the face of all peoples,
A light to bring revelation to the Gentiles,
And the glory of Your people Israel.

—*Luke 2:29–32*

"My eyes have seen Your salvation." What a joy it is to step into grace when we receive Christ as Savior. What rejoicing we do when we watch others find salvation as well. The transformation may not be visible to our eyes, but in our hearts we know that we are observing the miracle of a life changed from the inside out.

Simeon had devoted his entire life to waiting for the Messiah to appear. When Jesus arrived with Mary and Joseph at the temple, Simeon took the baby in his arms and praised God—he was praising the very God whom he was holding! The prayer Simeon prayed acknowledged that the infant Jesus was the fulfillment of all of God's promises to Israel. He was a revelation to the Gentiles and the glory of His people, Israel.

The church has used Simeon's prayer for centuries, calling it the *Nunc Dimittis,* for the first words of the prayer in Latin meaning, "Now dismiss." Traditionally, it has been used at the end of worship services, expressing thanks to God because, once again, we have heard the Good News of Jesus Christ and witnessed God's salvation.

This beautiful prayer can be used at any time we want to thank God for His amazing work of salvation. Every time we witness the transformation of another person through Christ's work, this is an appropriate way to thank God. We can use this prayer any time we witness a sign of God's salvation, such as a baptism or a commitment to Christ. Whenever we are overcome with joy because of our own salvation, we should thank God.

But we shouldn't forget that the original meaning of the prayer was not dismissal from worship, but dismissal from this life. We can also use this prayer to honor and praise God for a saint who has died or is dying. It could be a comforting prayer for the dying and the mourning at a hospital bedside. When one of God's children has gone home to Him, we know that his or her eyes will see God's salvation even more clearly than was ever possible in this life.

Thank God today for Your salvation in Jesus Christ. Thank Him for those around You who are believers. In a very real sense, when you look at them, you are seeing salvation—and what a beautiful sight it is!

Thank You, my Savior, for saving me. Thank You for the moment You touched my life and made me Your own. I thank You for friends and family who are also believers. Thank You for making us so different, yet drawing us to Yourself. I praise You that my eyes, too, have seen Your salvation.

A PRAYER OF THANKS FOR OTHERS' GIFTS AND ABILITIES
I CORINTHIANS 1 : 4 – 9

I thank my God always concerning you for the grace of
God which was given to you by Christ Jesus.
—*1 Corinthians 1:4*

Too often, we discover deficiencies in others and fail to appreciate the good in them. When was the last time you actually pointed out the good in someone else instead of complaining about the bad? How would our church fellowships be transformed if we all thanked God for one another's gifts instead of complaining about one another's imperfections?

It is precisely at this point where Paul's prayer gives us guidance. Paul was writing to a church that had experienced its fair share of problems. In the letter of 1 Corinthians,

Paul rebuked the church several times for their poor conduct. Nevertheless, Paul remained genuinely grateful to God for what He had done for this struggling church.

Notice that Paul's thankfulness was habitual, not momentary. His prayers of gratitude were "always" rising up to God. Moreover, he was thankful that God abundantly enriched them with spiritual gifts. This is especially striking, since Paul reprimanded them later in the letter for their abuse of their spiritual gifts. Paul showed a maturity that we desperately need in our churches today. While he was certainly not afraid to address the problems of the church, he could see that the Corinthians were still God's grace-gifted people. It was this foundational gratitude for God's work in the church in Corinth that allowed Paul's corrective measures to be recognized as redemptive, rather than taken as empty and bitter scolding.

PRAYER REFLECTION

God is not a cosmic bellboy for whom we can press a button to get things.

—*Anonymous*

How we need to take heed of this important lesson! We must examine ourselves to see if we display this abiding sense of gratitude for God's work in other Christians. Can you think of the last time you stopped to thank God for the grace He has given to others? Has gratitude penetrated your heart so that you express thankfulness for God's work in the lives of Christians who may be causing you grief? This soul-searching is not meant to cause us to overlook difficulties in the church. Rather, it should help to undergird our delight to see God's glory manifest among His people. When we recognize the grace of God in those believers who give us trouble, it will be easier for us to be redemptive agents like Paul. If we truly take pleasure in God's presence among His people, we will savor it in gratefulness wherever we find it.

Our gracious God who never ceases to give good gifts, grant us the sight to see Your grace in others. Make us truly thankful for Your work among Your people. Let not the tarnish of abused grace keep us from recognizing the shining glory of Your blessings in the church.

A PRAYER OF THANKS FOR OTHERS' FAITHFULNESS
I THESSALONIANS 1:2–3

We give thanks to God always for you all, making mention of you in our prayers, remembering without ceasing your

work of faith, labor of love, and patience of hope in our
Lord Jesus Christ in the sight of our God and Father.
—*1 Thessalonians 1:2–3*

Faithfulness is a valuable quality. Faithful friends are hard to find. Faithful spouses seem to be in a minority (at least from Hollywood's vantage point). And faithful believers? They are vital to the growth of the church and the ministry of God's message. It takes faithful believers to make a difference in a world of unfaithfulness.

PRAYER REFLECTION

O what peace we often forfeit,
O what needless pain we bear,
All because we do not carry
Everything to God in prayer.
—*Joseph Scriven*

One of God's greatest gifts to his children is the church. Our relationship with God happens in the context of a large group of brothers and sisters who support each other in our walk with God. When Paul began his first letter to the Thessalonians, he wrote with affection, telling them that he thanked God for their faithfulness. The church at Thessalonica was a young church, filled with recent converts. But the youth of the congregation did not stop them from being a vital force for good.

Paul recognized their "work of faith, labor of love, and patience of hope." These young believers had a lot more maturity than many older believers. They apparently weren't arguing over the color of the church carpet or the style of church music. They were busy with the work of the faith, laboring in love for the sake of the gospel. No wonder Paul never ceased to give thanks for them. Surely they were a joy to his heart. Such faithfulness in his "children" gave new strength to Paul's own ministry.

Paul's prayer was genuine. He was not just playing up the positive aspects of the Thessalonian church merely to encourage them—although his words surely did that for this young congregation. He was thankful for their early faithfulness. But by telling them openly of his thanks for them, Paul also encouraged the Thessalonians to continue in their faithfulness.

Our gratefulness for faithful brothers and sisters in Jesus Christ should also be apparent in our prayer lives. We shouldn't hesitate to publicly thank God for their faithfulness. When you look around and see people working to share their faith, laboring in unlovely circumstances with love, or struggling through difficulty with patient hope, you are watching faithfulness in action. Let them know that you are making mention of them in your prayers, thanking God for them.

Thank You, Lord, for the faithfulness I see in my fellow believers. I see many in my church who are working hard to share their faith with others, and I thank You for their work of faith. I see others showing love in unlovely places, and I thank You for their compassion. I know many are struggling with some kind of difficulty, yet their patient hope is such an encouragement to me. Help us to continue to be faithful followers and servants of You.

A PRAYER OF THANKS FOR THE JOY OTHERS GIVE US
1 THESSALONIANS 3:9–13

> For what thanks can we render to God for you, for all the
> joy with which we rejoice for your sake before our God,
> night and day praying exceedingly that we may see your
> face and perfect what is lacking in your faith?
>
> —*1 Thessalonians 3:9–10*

Who brings you joy? Are there believers in your life who are a delight to you? Like a crystal clear fountain, they flow into your life for a few moments and refresh you. Are you that type of person, spreading joy wherever you go?

Unfortunately, too many believers spend their days either worrying, judging, or complaining. No wonder the church sometimes gets bad press. We have the power to make a change—first, by spreading joy; second, by thanking and encouraging those who bring joy to us.

The Thessalonian believers brought joy to the apostle Paul. They were a young church, and they had a few misconceptions that Paul addressed in this letter, but mostly Paul wanted to thank them for being such an encouragement. They had accepted the gospel message and had even faced persecution because of it. Yet they had stood strong, providing an example for others. The very first line of his letter says, "We give thanks to God always for you all" (1:2).

Time passed and Paul had not heard from these believers. Wouldn't Paul have loved e-mail! Instead, he had to depend on fellow travelers to bring him news of his newly-planted congregations. He admitted that he had started to worry about these young believers. Would they stay strong in the faith? Would they be able to face persecution without wavering? Would trials eventually get the better of them? So Timothy went to encourage the church, and as it turned out, he was encouraged by them. His positive

251

report came back to Paul, and in these verses in chapter 3, Paul gave thanks for the joy the Thessalonian Christians were bringing him. They had indeed been standing strong, and this brought great joy to the apostle's heart.

Who gives you joy? Tell that person, and thank God for having him or her in your life. Are you a joy giver? When people see you coming, do they know that they will find refreshment from your words, your attitudes, your actions?

God, You are the source of all joy. Thank You for my fellow believers who bring joy into my life. I pray that You will help me to become a joy giver. I want to refresh people with the joy that You have given me through Your Holy Spirit. Grow the fruit of joy in my life.

A PRAYER OF THANKS FOR FELLOW BELIEVERS
2 THESSALONIANS 1:3

We are bound to thank God always for you, brethren, as it
is fitting, because your faith grows exceedingly, and the
love of every one of you all abounds toward each other.
—*2 Thessalonians 1:3*

How often do people hear you say thank you? How often does God hear it? Oh, you may thank God when a prayer is specifically answered or when you finally feel overwhelmed by blessings you have received.

But how often do you thank God for your fellow believers? You know, the ones at church who have taught you so much, been such a support, cared for your children? How about those fellow believers who sometimes drive you crazy, who at times are difficult or immature, or even those who have hurt you (perhaps without meaning to)?

Surely the Thessalonian church was filled with all kinds of believers—mature and immature, helpful and needy, supportive and not so supportive, kind and hurtful. And like every church today, the body of believers is replete with all kinds of people at all different levels of spiritual growth and maturity with different opinions and hot buttons. This sends some believers on a quest for a perfect church where none of this occurs. The problem is, if they find such a church, they probably shouldn't join it lest they spoil it.

So what do we do? Like Paul, we're "bound to thank God always" for our brothers and sisters in Christ. The Thessalonian believers weren't perfect. In fact, this letter was written because it came to Paul's attention that they needed correction and admonition.

However, Paul begins by expressing his thanks to God for them. The church and its members were not perfect, but they were blessed, and for that, thanks was due to God. There is always room for improvement in our churches. But we should also remember how much we have been blessed and be thankful. This gratitude keeps us from becoming antagonistic in our efforts for improvement.

For what can we give thanks? We can thank God for growing faith and abounding love. These are two measures of the health of a church—not statistics of total membership or contributions or buildings or programs, but growth in faith and in love for one another.

Growth in faith is the first mark of church vitality. Any growth in membership, contributions, and outreach has to start with the deepening of faith. This faith is a relationship of trust in and love for God. This relationship with God in Christ is the foundation on which the church is built.

Love for one another is the second mark of church vitality. Love for God is exercised in love for others. Life in Christ unites us with all who are in Christ. This unity in Christ will be demonstrated in the life of the Christian community. Where there is dissension, the body of Christ is fractured and its influence weakened.

Faith and love are results of the transforming work of the Spirit in us. Thank God for this fruit of the Spirit grown in the church. Yield yourself to the inner work of the Spirit. And when the Spirit prompts you to offer constructive criticism to brothers and sisters in Christ, also express your gratitude to God for their faith and love.

I thank You, God, for my church. Thank You that it is Your body here on earth. Even with all of their imperfections, I thank You for these believers who are growing in their faith and learning to love one another. May this continue, to Your honor and glory.

A PRAYER OF THANKS FOR LOVE AMONG THE BELIEVERS
PHILEMON 4 – 6

I thank my God, making mention of you always in my prayers, hearing of your love and faith which you have toward the Lord Jesus and toward all the saints, that the sharing of your faith may become effective by the acknowledgment of every good thing which is in you in Christ Jesus.

—*Philemon 4–6*

The Holy Spirit grows "fruit" in our lives, and the first one listed for us in the Bible is the fruit of love (Galatians 5:22). We may think that love should come naturally, but if you spend time with any group of people for very long (especially in your church), you'll find a few people for whom the attitude of love doesn't come naturally. To grow in love, we need the help of the Holy Spirit. The kind of love He grows in our lives is not the emotional warm feeling that we have for our dearest friends. While that love is important, the love He demands begins with a decision. This is the love Jesus said we are to have even for our enemies (Matthew 5:44). We may not feel like loving, but we choose to do so because we have been commanded to do so.

> **PRAYER REFLECTION**
>
> *I am not worthy, Master and Lord . . . yet since You in your love . . . wish to dwell in me, in boldness I come. Open the gates which You alone have forged; and You will come in . . . and enlighten my darkened reason. I believe that You will do this: for . . . all of those who came to You in repentance, were counted in the band of Your friends, who alone abide blessed forever, . . . unto the endless ages.*
>
> —*St. Chrysostom*

Philemon was a well-to-do Christian who hosted the Colossian church at his home. Paul wrote to Philemon, Apphia, and Archippus that he was praying to God on their behalf. Paul thanked God for the great love that these three had for God's people, the saints. Philemon was gifted by the Spirit to show love to God's people and to share his faith with those who were not yet part of the family of God.

But there was one person he probably wasn't too keen on loving at the moment. That person was his servant, Onesimus, who had run away (and probably stolen some money in the process to finance his journey). As God would have it, Onesimus ran smack into the apostle Paul, who led him to Christ. Thus, both Philemon and his servant were Christians. Paul knew that Onesimus needed to make things right with his master by returning to him. Onesimus was understandably afraid, so Paul interceded, writing a letter to send along with him as he returned to Philemon. Paul requested that Philemon forgive Onesimus and receive him as a brother in Christ, loving him as he loved all the other saints.

With this kind of love, we draw others to us. Jesus understood the power of such love when he explained to His disciples, "By this all will know that you are My disciples, if you have love for one another" (John 13:35). Say a word of thanks for the love in your church and among the Christians you know. That love binds us together even with Christians we've never met. That love is a taste of heaven.

God of love, I praise You for growing the fruit of love in Your people. Thank You for the love I experience from my Christian friends. Thank You for the love that binds us with believers around the globe. Help me to love even those I don't naturally feel love toward. May this love show the whole world that we are Your disciples.

PRAYERS FOR HELP

A PRAYER FOR SUCCESS IN A TASK
GENESIS 24:12-14

O Lord God of my master Abraham, please give me success this day, and show kindness to my master Abraham.

—*Genesis 24:12*

It might feel a bit awkward to pray for success, but Abraham's servant didn't feel that way.
He had an important task to fulfill, so he pulled out all the stops and asked God Himself
to intervene. We can take a cue from the wise servant—don't be afraid to ask God to help
you succeed.

Genesis 24 presents us with Abraham's oldest servant on a journey to the city of
Nahor in Mesopotamia. Abraham sent him there to find a wife for his son Isaac. The fact
that Abraham sent him away from Canaan for this mission shows that Abraham was not
willing to settle on just any woman for his son. The servant knew full well the weight of
his responsibility, and he must have felt its enormous pressure. Upon reaching his desti-
nation, the servant cried out to God for help in the task of finding Isaac a wife. The Lord
heard and answered.

The significance of this prayer goes beyond the fact that God provided a wife for
Isaac. What stands out is that God had promised Abraham that he would bless his family
abundantly. Only Isaac, among Abraham's sons, could legitimately extend the line of his
family, so finding a wife for this "young man of promise" was crucial. God's answer to this
prayer provided a means for the family of Abraham to continue, a family that was to bless
the nations through the coming of the Messiah.

While the prayer maintains a special place in the history of redemption, it also gives
us hope for our everyday life of faith. The loving-kindness of the Lord for his children
continues. Jesus said that God takes care of His children and provides for their every need
(Matthew 6:25–34; Philippians 4:19). If God was faithful to preserve the promised

lineage that would produce a Savior for His people, He will surely be faithful to His promise to supply the daily needs of those who call Him Lord.

We can take great comfort in this. Do you have a need that is central to your future? Seek the Lord! Are there pressing needs in your life that cause you distress? Take them to the Lord in prayer. He awaits the prayers of His loved ones, desiring to demonstrate His glory in their lives and for their good. The Lord seeks to triumph majestically in your situation either by removing the difficulty or by sustaining you by His grace so that you might overcome in the midst of adversity. He delights in bringing success to His people in their endeavors for Him. Be encouraged by the example of Abraham's servant, and make your petition to God for the help you need. The one who depends on God will not be disappointed.

The task before me is difficult, Lord, but I know You have called me to do it. I know how important it is, and the responsibility weighs heavily on me. I pray that You will bring me success this day, Lord, and that You will receive all the glory.

A PRAYER FOR CHANGE
I SAMUEL I:II

O LORD of hosts, if You will indeed look on the affliction of Your maidservant and remember me, and not forget Your maidservant, but will give Your maidservant a male child, then I will give him to the LORD all the days of his life, and no razor shall come upon his head.

—*1 Samuel 1:11*

The Book of 1 Samuel opens with the story of a woman who was barren. Hannah desperately wanted a child and had been unable to conceive. Many can identify with her tears of yearning and desire. Her barren status made her a person of lesser value in ancient Israel, but she was not satisfied to remain in her current status. Yet as poignant as this is, the story of Hannah's prayer and the birth of Samuel is about more than personal fulfillment.

Peeking behind the obvious story of God's hearing the cries of the outcast, we find another layer of meaning. From a divine perspective, all of Israel was barren. The various judges who had been trying to keep the invading Canaanites and Philistines out of Israel's new land had left the people of Israel confused, disorganized, and sliding into moral decay. The nation was not healthy and therefore could not yield good fruit. Israel was destitute while dwelling in the land of promise. Israel should not have been satisfied with its current state of affairs.

PRAYER REFLECTION

Prayer is the breath of the soul.
—O. Hallesby

Hannah took her desire for new life to the only one who could provide this miraculous gift—the Lord. She asked God, not just for a child, but for a son whom she would dedicate to the LORD. Hannah provided the model for Israel. Israel needed a son, a leader dedicated to the LORD, who would provide security and leadership. But notice the reciprocal nature of the agreement that Hannah understood so clearly: if the Lord will give a son, then that son will be given back to the Lord to serve Him.

The son given to Hannah and Elkanah was Samuel, who became the last of the judges, a priest, and a prophet. It is Samuel whom God called to anoint Saul, the first king in Israel, in order to pull the nation out of moral decay. Ultimately, Samuel also anointed David as the next king of Israel, and during his reign, the land and the people experienced rest from their enemies for the first time in their history.

One who would venture to pray this prayer today must first pause. Hannah was asking for more than a child; she was asking for a savior. To pray with Hannah today is to be unsatisfied with the way things are, to long and yearn for better days. To pray with Hannah is to pray for revival, for strong leadership, for greater discipleship. We pray that we all might bring the kingdom of God one step closer to its consummation. We pray asking for boldness and courage so that God can use us as a part of His plan to bring many others to Him.

Lord, I want to see a change—in my life, in others' lives, in my nation. Look on the troubles we have faced and remember us. I am ready to serve You and do whatever You need me to do to make a difference. Give me conviction of Your will and courage to carry it out.

A PRAYER TO DISCERN RIGHT FROM WRONG
I KINGS 3:6–9

> Therefore give to Your servant an understanding heart to
> judge Your people, that I may discern between good and
> evil. For who is able to judge this great people of Yours?
>
> —*1 Kings 3:9*

The lines between right and wrong get blurred sometimes. We want to do God's will and act rightly, but it can be so easy to rationalize, to cover up, to say that the end justifies the means. Even harder are those situations in which both sides have compelling arguments and good people presenting them. How can we sort through competing claims? We need righteous discernment. We need to clearly hear God's will through all the surrounding static. We need to pray for understanding hearts.

Israel's beloved King David died, and his son Solomon ascended to the throne. David left Solomon with a peaceful, stable kingdom. He was indeed a hard act to follow! While this prayer of Solomon's casts him in the most favorable light, the preceding parts of the story reveal that Solomon was just like everyone else—a flawed human being in greater need of wisdom than he realized. The opening verses of chapter 3 tell us that Solomon took a foreign wife, the princess of Egypt, a marriage outlawed by Israelite law but politically expedient. She was the first of many foreign wives. In later chapters, we read that these women led him into idolatry. He had already revealed a tendency to depend on his own cunning, rather than on God, to guide and protect the nation. But God had promised to watch over David's throne, so He appeared to Solomon and said, "Ask! What shall I give you?" (3:5). It was then that Solomon made his famous request.

Here we see Solomon at his best. Much like all of us, Solomon vacillates between self and God in his priorities. But here he asks for one thing: wisdom to rule God's people rightly. Verses 10–15 reveal that, because Solomon put God and God's people first in his prayer, God granted his request. In fact, because Solomon put God's kingdom first, many other things were given to him as well (see Matthew 6:33).

We all want good things in life. Like Solomon, we want comfortable and enjoyable relationships with friends and family. We want material prosperity to offer us security in times of uncertainty. We want a name that is recognized in the common culture. Yet, Solomon also loved the Lord. It is when Solomon placed his love for the Lord and the

Lord's people first that he got it right. Like Solomon, we too need turn to God for wisdom in being able to discern between good and evil. Yet we must strive to make it a way of life, not just a moment in time, not just because we have been thrust into some kind of leadership position. We are to have the same mind as Christ, praying for the glory of God, the wise leading of God's people (in whatever role we may have), and the advancement of God's kingdom. Jesus assured us that God is willing and ready to provide for our bodily needs. But what God wants is our determination to chase after the kingdom to which we belong.

In Solomon's life, God took the initiative to mold a selfish, sinful man into a wise ruler of God's people. So too in our lives, God has been revealed to us in the person of Jesus Christ, in whom we have our salvation. And now we are called to pray, along with Solomon, for the wisdom to know the right from the wrong in our lives. This prayer calls us from our selfishness and sinfulness to ponder anew a sanctified set of priorities we are invited to make our own, for the glory and extension of God's great kingdom.

Lord, I need an understanding heart. It takes great wisdom to be able to discern right from wrong, good from evil, and then to have the courage to do what is right and good. You say in Your Word that if we lack wisdom, all we have to do is ask (James 1:5). I ask for wisdom and an understanding heart so that I may live rightly before You.

A PRAYER THAT GOD WILL MAKE HIMSELF KNOWN
1 KINGS 18:36–37

LORD God of Abraham, Isaac, and Israel, let it be known this day that You are God in Israel and I am Your servant, and that I have done all these things at Your word. Hear me, O LORD, hear me, that this people may know that You are the LORD God, and that You have turned their hearts back to You again.

—*1 Kings 18:36–37*

This prayer of Elijah's is one of the most "in-your-face" prayers of the Bible. It comes at the climax of 1 Kings 18—the dramatic confrontation between this vagabond prophet and the powerful pagan king of wayward Israel. In fact, the Bible describes Ahab as the fiercest king of Israel. Crossing Ahab meant putting one's life in certain jeopardy. And yet

Elijah taunted and teased Ahab and the prophets of Baal on the summit of Mount Carmel. He mockingly stacked the deck against himself and his God to ridicule Ahab and Baal all the more. And then, with this short and to-the-point prayer, Elijah made way for the Lord to reveal Himself as the only true God in the universe.

That's definitely a prayer of faith! But even Elijah's towering faith and astounding victory on the mountain didn't mean his life was easy. In fact, 1 Kings 19 reveals that after this great victory, Elijah ran for his life. He became a wanted fugitive for the way he had been bold for the Lord. But that's often the shape of true faith in a fallen world. Elijah had shown his faith and called upon God to intervene and reveal Himself to His wayward people—and God heard and answered.

As Christians sent by this same God who desires to be revealed to all people (Romans 16:25–27), we must pray this same prayer in bold faith. And yet this prayer of bold faith can only emerge from a life of bold faith. To pray this prayer, we must make way for God to reveal Himself through us—in our families, on the job, at church, in the neighborhood. This is not a prayer to be prayed in hopes that someone else will do the job. Elijah prayed this prayer from the mountaintop, before the hostile crowd. This prayer, combined with a life of evangelistic boldness, is to be prayed (in words and actions) before the nations of the world and the neighbors of our lives.

Living this prayer may begin in our worship centers on Sunday, but it demands that, Monday through Saturday, our Christian convictions will affect our lifestyle and transform our world. Whatever we do in life—as an employee, a boss, a politician, a teacher, a parent, whatever our other roles—we are first and foremost disciples of Christ. We are to pray for God to send down His healing fire, the gospel that binds up broken hearts, proclaims freedom to prisoners, and dawns a new day of light in Christ (Isaiah 61:1–2). Pray that God will help the people around you to know that He is the Lord God, and pray that He will turn their hearts back to Him. That's the prayer of faith today!

My heart breaks for those around me who don't know You, Lord. Yet I also realized that You have placed me in their lives for a reason. Give me the courage to live out my faith before them. And I pray that You will make Yourself known to them, Lord, so that they will turn to You and be saved.

A PRAYER FOR HELP AGAINST IMPOSSIBLE ODDS
2 KINGS 19:14–19

Now therefore, O LORD our God, I pray, save us from his
hand, that all the kingdoms of the earth may know that
You are the LORD God, You alone.

—*2 Kings 19:19*

In the year 701 B.C., Assyria attempted to conquer the tiny southern kingdom of Judah. It had been twenty years since the northern kingdom of Israel was plundered and deport-ed into exile. Now, King Sennacherib of Assyria was pounding on Judah's gate, threatening to overtake Jerusalem. And he was quite sure of himself, sending messengers to Judah's King Hezekiah with the ominous threat, "Do not let your God in whom you trust deceive you, saying, 'Jerusalem shall not be given into the hand of the king of Assyria.' Look! You have heard what the kings of Assyria have done to all lands by utterly destroying them; and shall you be delivered? Have the gods of the nations delivered those whom my fathers have destroyed . . . ?" (2 Kings 19:10–12).

> **PRAYER REFLECTION**
>
> *Prayer is not a magical formula to be repeated, but the personal communication, awed and adoring, of the redeemed creature who stands in the presence of the Saviour God.*
>
> —*Edmund Clowney*

Hezekiah had already turned down a bloodless opportunity for surrender (18:13—19:7). So, in 19:8–37, Sennacherib challenged Hezekiah a second time—this time blas-phemously questioning the Lord's power and His sovereignty over Judah.

Hezekiah responded by personally praying to the Lord in the temple. He knew that his army was vastly outnumbered. He knew that Sennacherib had already been victori-ous in many cities, laying them to waste. He knew that nothing he could do would stop him.

However, Hezekiah did know something that Sennacherib didn't. Hezekiah knew that the God of Israel was not like the powerless gods of the other nations. Hezekiah declared that the Lord is sovereign and that He alone created this world and all nations. He confessed that all other gods were "but the work of men's hands" (19:18) and totally unable to save. It is to this God that Hezekiah prayed for deliverance. He asked for help from the Lord "that all the kingdoms of the earth may know that You are the LORD God, You alone" (19:19). Hezekiah asked the Lord to display divine power and sovereignty as well as His covenant faithfulness to Judah.

The Lord answered Hezekiah's prayer in a miraculous manner. The prophet Isaiah proclaimed victory (19:20–34), and Sennacherib's army was obliterated by the angel of the Lord, demonstrating that the victory was accomplished not by humans but by God. Sennacherib himself was assassinated by two of his sons upon his return home to Nineveh (19:35–37).

At times we are in situations that, to us, appear impossible. We can see no way out. We are outnumbered, we have no resources, we are weak, we are afraid. But we do have a recourse—and that recourse is prayer. When the impossible comes, we turn to the God for whom nothing is impossible (Mark 10:7). To pray this prayer today is to stand firmly on the Lord's side. We acknowledge the sovereign rule of God, and we acknowledge our own powerlessness. We lay the impossible request before God and ask Him to show us the way. Then we exclusively trust in the Lord's power to save us. And in the end, He will receive the glory.

I lay before You a request today that to me is impossible. I can't see a way out; I am overwhelmed and afraid. But I know that what seems impossible to me is possible with You. I ask that You will protect me today, show me Your will, and make the impossible possible.

A PRAYER FOR HELP IN TIME OF NEED
ISAIAH 25:1–5

For You have been a strength to the poor,
A strength to the needy in his distress,
A refuge from the storm,
A shade from the heat;
For the blast of the terrible ones is as a storm against the
wall.

—*Isaiah 25:4*

As a prophet, Isaiah reminded the people about God. Standing in the gap between God and His people, Isaiah delivered the Word of God to the people and the complaints of the people to God. But, this prayer to God was more personal. Isaiah addressed this prayer to the Lord, his God.

Ever mindful that God keeps His promises, the prophet looked to the past to reassert what God had already done among His people. God gives strength to the poor and needy, and He answers their calls of distress. Isaiah went on to describe specific instances of the needs of the poor being met. God had provided a refuge from the driving rain and shade in times of heat.

The final sentence of this prayer refers to the enemies of God—the "terrible ones," as used in Hebrew, in reference to the ruthless enemies of God, especially those of the nations surrounding the promised land. They made a lot of noise, like rain hitting the wall of the city, but in the end, the rain could not destroy the fortified wall.

The promises that Isaiah recalled are quite similar to those Jesus recited during the Sermon on the Mount. God will meet our basic needs, and nothing will foil us. Jesus reminded his listeners, "Therefore do not worry, saying, 'What shall we eat?' or 'What shall we drink?' or 'What shall we wear?' For after all these things the Gentiles seek. For your heavenly Father knows that you need all these things" (Matthew 6:31–32).

As Isaiah did, Jesus explained that God promises to sustain and provide for His people. While the fulfillment of this promise may be different from how we imagine, God is faithful. During hard times, it is helpful to remember these promises. It both assures us of the reality of God's provision for our lives and reminds us that God is our strength when we are poor and needy, our refuge from the storm, and our shade from the heat.

He is all we need.

Lord, things are tough right now, and I am in need. You have promised in Your Word that You delight to care for Your people. You are my strength, refuge, and shade. You are a powerful Protector and Provider. I need Your provision today. You promise to care for our needs, so I claim that promise today and thank You now for Your answer.

A PRAYER FOR HELP IN DIFFICULTY
JEREMIAH 20:7–18

But the LORD is with me as a mighty, awesome One.

Therefore my persecutors will stumble, and will not prevail.

They will be greatly ashamed, for they will not prosper.

Their everlasting confusion will never be forgotten.

But, O LORD of hosts,

You who test the righteous,

And see the mind and heart,

Let me see Your vengeance on them;

For I have pleaded my cause before You.

—*Jeremiah 20:11–12*

Many faithful Christians can understand Jeremiah's complaint in these verses. How many have come to Christ because of the offer of the abundant life (John 10:10), only to find that that Christian life is often a battle—spiritual, and sometimes even physical? That was Jeremiah's situation when he cried out to God in these verses.

Jeremiah had answered God's call to serve Him as a prophet, but it didn't turn out to be what Jeremiah expected. It is understandable that Jeremiah said that God induced, or persuaded, him (20:7). God's call is compelling; it is a call that we cannot refuse to answer. But God never promises a comfortable life. Instead, He promises a life of truth.

This life of truth, though sometimes discouraging, is a life of complete enjoyment of God's presence. In that, Jeremiah rejoiced despite his frustrating circumstances (20:11). No matter how much Jeremiah's friends (and foes) teased and taunted him, Jeremiah knew that God, one day, would bring stumbling, shame, and confusion to those who set themselves against God and His kingdom.

> **PRAYER REFLECTION**
>
> *There was a famous preacher years ago who had many unusual expressions. One of them was this: "When a man prays for a corn crop, God expects him to say 'Amen' with a hoe." You can't just stay on your knees all the time and pray for a corn crop. That's pious nonsense.*
>
> —*J. Vernon McGee*

Jeremiah saw far beyond his own need to the very end of time. God would one day win. On that day, God's enemies will stumble; they will not prevail. On that day, those against God will perish, and those on God's side will enter into the victory celebration for which history has been waiting.

And that's the message for the church today. In a world in which evil seems always to have the upper hand, Christians, like Jeremiah, constantly face the taunts of those around us who belittle our faith and Christian lives. Many Christians face severe persecution.

Yet in the midst of this, we know that the Lord is with us. We know that one day the tables will be turned, and we will enter into the victory celebration that has been arranged for God's faithful messengers.

Whatever difficulty you may be facing today, seek God. Call to Him. He is the mighty, awesome One. He is on Your side, ready to intervene. When you think about that, you realize that there is really no contest!

Almighty God, I am facing a difficult time today. My faith is being ridiculed; my life for You is misunderstood. I know that I am in the right, but it sure is hard to stay there. You are the mighty, awesome One. You promise that those who are against Your kingdom will not prevail. I pray that they will not prevail over me today. I plead my cause before You and trust that You will come to my aid.

A PRAYER FOR HOPE IN HOPELESS TIMES
JEREMIAH 32:17-25

> Ah, Lord GOD! Behold, You have made the heavens and the
> earth by Your great power and outstretched arm. There is
> nothing too hard for You.
> —*Jeremiah 32:17*

Whenever we need hope in a time of hopelessness, we must keep God's faithfulness in mind as we pray. The prophet Jeremiah had repeatedly warned his people that God would allow the Babylonians to destroy Jerusalem as punishment for their sins. Now the time of judgment had come. The siege ramps were being laid against the city walls. The situation was indeed hopeless. Israel was about to be removed from the promised land because of her history of sin (32:23).

Then God did something very strange. He recommended that Jeremiah invest in some real estate—in Israel! The city was about to be handed over to the Babylonians, and God recommended that Jeremiah buy a field and make sure that the transaction was witnessed and made legal. Jeremiah probably thought God should stay out of the real estate market! Why buy land you'll never be able to own?

Well, that was God's point. This was the spark of hope in the hopeless darkness. God was assuring His prophet that He would indeed one day return His people to their land and that His holy city would be rebuilt. The real estate transaction was not pointless; it made a vivid point to Jeremiah and to the people. Punishment would come, but the promise would endure.

The Lord holds us accountable for our sin—the Israelites went into exile because of their sin. But our God is also a God whose thoughts toward us are "thoughts of peace and not of evil, to give you a future and a hope" (29:11). We can rely on our God of faithful hope even when our outlook seems hopeless. When our circumstances seem to be going against us, we have hope

that they are for a purpose that will benefit us. The New Testament promises that "all things work together for good to those who love God, to those who are the called according to His purpose" (Romans 8:28). When we encounter trouble in our lives, we must remember God's faithfulness and have hope for the future.

But it's not enough just to hope in the faithfulness of God. God wants us to put our hope into action. Remembering what it took to make our salvation possible, we can be confident that God is with us, God is faithful, and God can be our source of hope. Therefore, each day is a new opportunity to live life in hope; to live life grounded in God's faithfulness; to live life keenly aware that God goes with us wherever we go. God's faithfulness and our hope move us to live bold Christian lives. We don't need to fear. God is with us, and the future with this faithful God is one in which the bright rays of hope are already shining from beyond the horizon.

God of hope, I claim the promise that Your plans for me are for good and will give me a future and a hope. I don't feel very hopeful about the future right now, but I know that You can work all things together for good. You made the heavens and the earth by Your great power; there is nothing too hard for You. I give You my hopelessness and ask You to replace it with Your hope.

A PRAYER WHEN GOD SEEMS SILENT
LAMENTATIONS 1 – 4

Remember my affliction and roaming,
The wormwood and the gall.
My soul still remembers

And sinks within me.

This I recall to my mind,

Therefore I have hope.

Through the LORD's mercies we are not consumed,

Because His compassions fail not.

They are new every morning;

Great is Your faithfulness.

—*Lamentations 3:19–23*

With tears in his eyes, Jeremiah looked at Jerusalem, the city he loved. "He has done violence to His tabernacle, as if it were a garden; He has destroyed His place of assembly" (2:6). The temple was gone—the place where God said He would meet His people. Gone. All of Jerusalem was nothing but rubble.

The destruction was so extensive that the city itself was expressing the loss—the walls were forlorn with tears, the ramparts lamented, and the gates slouched in the sand, depressed. These were supposed to be the children of the promise of God. But the nation had slipped into ruin and exile! The glory gone! Even the law and the prophets were finished—sure signs of God's severe judgment.

> PRAYER REFLECTION
>
> *Remember that intercessory prayer is the sweetest prayer God ever hears . . . and is exceedingly prevalent. What wonders it has wrought!*
>
> —*Charles Spurgeon*

Jeremiah watched it all with his knees on the ground, hands in the air, tears in his eyes. All ruined. The judgment was terrible against Jerusalem and the sins of its people, but Jeremiah felt that God had an agenda against him as well. "He has also broken my teeth with gravel, and covered me with ashes. You have moved my soul far from peace; I have forgotten prosperity" (2:16–17). The prophet yelled to the heavens. His world had come crashing down upon him.

We can feel that way too—as if the world is so hard and our "luck" so lean that nothing right can ever happen again. Sometimes we take it even deeper. We may feel that God just doesn't care about us—that we can't find a job, or that we're neck-deep in debt, or that we are grieving over a loss. Why even pray for help? Like Jeremiah, we want to yell, "Where is God now?"

But Jeremiah knew better, and his faith pulled him through. Even as he saw and grieved over Israel's affliction, Jeremiah remembered the hope of God's promises.

Through prayer, we come to know God deeper, to understand that God's mercy is new every morning. Great is His faithfulness, for He remembers us. In our prayers for help, God hears and comes down. Not only has God kept His promises to us, but He has also come down Himself for us, taking our judgment upon Himself. He came down and died for us on the cross. No matter what, we have hope in Christ and in the promises of God. For His mercies are new every morning; great is His faithfulness.

Lord, I feel afflicted and alone. This problem is too great for me to bear. My soul is sinking in fear. I feel like You don't care about me anymore. But I know better. I know that You are a loving and merciful God who cares intimately about me. Therefore I have hope. Because of Your mercy, this situation will not consume me. Your compassion will never fail; in fact, it is new every morning. Great is Your faithfulness. Show me Your compassion; make it new as the morning.

A PRAYER FOR RENEWAL
LAMENTATIONS 5

You, O LORD, remain forever;
Your throne from generation to generation.
Why do You forget us forever,
And forsake us for so long a time?
Turn us back to You, O LORD, and we will be restored;
Renew our days as of old.

—*Lamentations 5:19–21*

We all have a common fear of rejection. That's why in high school many of us wore certain unusual fashions—so we could fit in. That's why many of us remain silent at times when we know we should speak up. That's why many of us hesitate to try something too risky. We don't want to be rejected, to be pushed aside or written off. Rejection hurts. It hurts us deeply.

Jeremiah was worried about the ultimate rejection—rejection from God. And he was feeling it. Jeremiah is sometimes called the weeping prophet because he wept over the people of Israel. He worried—and for good reason—that the people of the promise, the people of Israel, had been rejected by God forever. Their capital city was destroyed, and the people were taken into exile. God had said if the people rejected Him, He would reject them. He had given that warning through countless prophets—including Jeremiah—but the people had refused to listen. Their rejection led to God's rejection—and punishment.

Jeremiah asked in 5:20, "Why do You forget us forever, and forsake us for so long a time?" He knew the answer. He knew that God was merely carrying out the punishment that He had warned would come. The people had been more worried about rejection by their pagan neighbors than about rejection by God. They had been worshiping other idols, doing what it took to "fit in." By focusing on what others were worshiping and doing, they lost their focus on God.

> **PRAYER REFLECTION**
>
> *There are three basic ingredients that have been key in our crusades. The first is prayer. The second is prayer. And the third and final ingredient is prayer!*
>
> —Billy Graham

Jeremiah begged God to come and turn the people once more back to His ways. He wanted renewal, not rejection. He knew that could only come from God. "Turn us back to You, O Lord, and we will be restored; renew our days as of old" (5:21). He prayed that God would lead the people into a new state of mind, a clean heart, a devotion to the truth so complete that it would become again a witness to all nations of the greatness of God.

When we pray for such renewal, we must understand that such a process happens because of God's grace, one person at a time, starting with you. When we pray for renewal in the church, in the community, or in the nation, we must also pray for renewal in our own lives, in our walk with God. We have been cleansed of sin through Jesus Christ, yet we still live with old appetites and old loyalties. In our prayer for renewal, we must ask God to teach us to live a godly life, giving us new joy in following and serving Him, so that we can help renew others.

We need renewal, Lord. I pray for renewal in my church, in my community, in my nation. But most of all, I pray for it in my own life. Show me what I need to do to follow You more closely. Renew me, refresh me, make me Your willing servant so that I might help renew others.

A PRAYER FOR DELIVERANCE
JONAH 2:1-10

I cried out to the LORD because of my affliction,
And He answered me.
Out of the belly of Sheol I cried,
And You heard my voice.
When my soul fainted within me,
I remembered the LORD;
And my prayer went up to You,
Into Your holy temple.

—Jonah 2:2, 7

When we read Jonah's prayer, we read a frightening description of the plight of a drowning man. But when those in ancient Israel read this prayer, they read the prayer of a man who had descended as deep as he could go and had entered into a situation of complete horror. In ancient Israel, water, and especially the ocean, represented absolute chaos. This chaos threatened to overtake the world unless a merciful God continued to hold it back. When Jonah sank into the depths of the sea, he sank to the very foundations of the world.

It is striking that Jonah prayed this prayer while he was in the belly of the great fish. If we are familiar with the story of Jonah, but unfamiliar with the placement of this prayer within the book, we might assume that Jonah prayed this prayer as praise to God after the fish had delivered him safely to shore. But that wasn't the case. Jonah was still in the belly of the fish, in a frightening and desperate situation. His prayer showed his absolute trust that God would deliver him.

This prayer is appropriate at any time when we feel like we have sunk to the depths of life—when we feel like we are so far from God's mercy and providence that we are beyond His reach. Our lives are filled with times of desperation—depression, illness, loneliness. Like Jonah, we can acknowledge how God has already been faithful even as we hope for further deliverance. Prayer can spur our hearts on to further trust in God's mercy and faithfulness. When we are as desperate as Jonah, it can be difficult to pray a prayer of trust. Praying a prayer like this one, even if it feels like going through the motions, allows the Holy Spirit to help us in our prayers and builds our trust in God.

Lord, I am sinking fast. I need You to reach down and rescue me. I don't even feel worthy to pray this prayer, for I know that, like Jonah, at times I get myself into my own difficult situations. Yet I acknowledge that You alone can help me, so I humbly pray for You to deliver me.

A PRAYER FOR GOD'S MERCY
HABAKKUK 3:1–19

O LORD, I have heard your speech and was afraid;

O LORD, revive Your work in the midst of the years!

In the midst of the years make it known;

In wrath remember mercy.

—*Habakkuk 3:2*

Are you ever afraid of God? Some have strayed so far from Him that they're afraid to come back—even when they want to. Will they face ridicule? Harsh punishment? Even rejection? What if they want to come back and He says no?

The prophet Habakkuk lived in Judah before the nation was destroyed by Babylon. Troubled, he watched as the wicked Babylonians became the dominant world power. He wondered why God would allow wickedness to flourish. He recited the prophecy that God gave him to deliver to the people. The burden contained woes and judgment to those who chased after idols and shed blood. The prophet sensed the gravity of this prophecy and knew the strength and judgment of God. Still, he was able to respond to God with this prayer.

This prayer is phrased like a psalm, beginning with musical direction. He addressed God, willing to ask the tough questions. "O LORD, how long shall I cry, and You will not hear? Even cry out to You, 'Violence!' and You will not save" (1:2). But God was not put off by the questions. He answered Habakkuk.

Habakkuk's then replied, "O LORD, I have heard Your speech and was afraid." Yet, he wanted to see God's work continue among His people. The prophet prayed for God's mercy to come amidst judgment.

In the midst of your turmoil, ask God to remember mercy. If you're scared of God or of His judgment, or doubt that He loves you because you have failed to meet His standards, this is an important prayer to remember. "I am afraid, but I know that judgment is not the last word. God, please remember mercy." God is gracious and will continue His work in us even when we have failed Him.

There was a lot of work to be done, and as Habakuk prayed, God began it again. As part of God's generosity, He prospered His people's works. Indeed, He is a mighty and awesome God, worthy to be feared. But He also is a loving Father who calls people to Himself because of His grace and mercy. He wants to be merciful, so come.

Lord, I am afraid. I have strayed so far, and I'm not even sure You want me to come back. I need Your mercy, for I know that You are a merciful God. I don't deserve it, but I need it. Remember Your mercy toward me, I pray. Renew and restore me to fellowship with You.

HEARTFELT PRAYERS

focus on prayer starters to help you pray
for many kinds of needs and situations

PRAYERS FOR . . .

CHURCH

O God, You have come to us in Jesus Christ, and You call us to represent Christ to the world. Guide and empower my church in its ministry. I pray that You will protect and inspire the leaders of my church. . . .

Lord, the church is where Your people meet to worship. When I go, help me to be more prepared to worship You by . . .

FAMILY

Precious Savior, we live in Your love. Encircle my family with Your love. Be near to each member today . . .

Father God, in our family, love is not all it could be. Help me with . . .

FRIENDS

Dearest Friend, thank You for the gift of friendship. I hold each of my friends in the light of Your love. You know their needs. . . .

Lord, when Your friends disappointed You, You forgave. I need to forgive someone today. Help me to forgive; show me how to forgive . . .

To my unbelieving friends, I pray, Lord, that You will let me be a clear and shining light for You. Reach into their hearts and show them their need to know You. . . .

FUTURE

God of hope, I do not know what the future holds. But You know. I entrust myself to Your care and ask You to uphold and guide me. . . .

Your promise of guidance to our heavenly home is all I need today, Lord. Thank You for giving me the hope of a future forever with You. In the meantime, Lord, I want to do all that You have planned for me during my time here. Show me Your will. . . .

MARRIAGE

O Lord, You blessed the wedding at Cana so that a couple's marriage began with You. So also in our marriage, may Your presence bring new life out of the everyday routines we find ourselves in. May our conflicts be seen as opportunities for personal and marital growth as we seek to follow You as husband and wife. Today help me to . . .

Lord, help me to look upon my spouse as a partner in the journey of life. May our relationship be a refuge for both of us. Show me how I can encourage my spouse today . . .

PRAISING GOD

God of creativity, You created the world to clap and sing Your praises. You fashioned humanity with all its various gifts to give voice to all the praise Your creation is ceaselessly proclaiming to You. I praise You today for . . .

"Continually offer the sacrifice of praise to God" (Hebrews 13:15). *Lord, enable me to praise You and remember You in the mundane. Remind me that all good things in this life are blessings from You. I praise You today for giving me . . .*

PURITY

Holy God, You have called us to be holy. Through Jesus Christ and by His Spirit, You have set us apart for Yourself. Inspire within me that devotion to Your holiness to set myself apart for You. Today, help me to remain pure. . . .

Lord, help me set aside all the demands and people that populate my life. May I enter Your presence with a purity of mind and singleness of heart, believing that in seeking Your face I will find peace. Focus my mind away from . . .

RELATIONSHIPS

O God, You must grieve over the fractured relationships You see in the world. Grant me forgiveness and grace to seek reconciliation. Help me to create relationships that mirror Your self-giving love. I need to mend a relationship with . . .

Lord, I know that the only one I can control is myself. Fill me with Your grace as I deal with a particular relationship. Show me what to do. . . .

REPUTATION

"A good name is to be chosen rather than great riches" (Proverbs 22:1). *Lord, keep me ever mindful of my name. Protect me from doing anything that would disappoint You or hurt my reputation as a believer. . . .*

Lord, people are trying to hurt my reputation with lies and slander. I need Your help to know what to do to speak the truth. I ask for Your help as I . . .

SALVATION

No matter how far I've fallen, how much I've strayed, how badly I'm stained, Your love reaches me. Savior, I turn to You in my need . . .

God, I am so grateful that Jesus holds my life in His hand. I want to thank You for saving me. I praise You today for the changes in my life. . . .

SUCCESS

Lord of power, without You I can do nothing. I pray that you will abundantly bless this effort that it may give glory to You. . . .

Whatever I do today, Lord, the credit is Yours. To serve You well, please give me success in this endeavor. . . .

THANKING GOD

Gracious God, all I am and all I have is from You. Today, I want to thank You for . . .

Dear God, I want to thank You for putting this person in my life. He/she is a gift from Your hand to my heart. Bless him/her today. . . .

USE OF SPIRITUAL GIFTS

Holy Spirit, You equip me for the ministries to which I am called. Show me how You want me to use the gifts You have given me. Guide me as I . . .

I know You have gifted me with the ability to do this job. Heavenly Father, today's responsibilities are reason to ask for Your special help with . . . .

PRAYERS FOR WHEN I NEED . . .

ASSURANCE

Thank You, God, that my salvation does not depend on my own efforts. It is by Your grace, given freely to us in Christ, that I am Yours forever. I know this is true, but sometimes I just need reassurance from You. Assure me today, Lord, that . . .

Lord, Your Word tells me that Your love will never fail. Press that promise into my heart, especially when . . .

BALANCED LIFE

Lord Jesus Christ, full of grace and truth, too often I fail to strike the balance between those two necessary things. It is too easy to be all grace and no truth. It is also too easy to be all truth but no grace. Grant me the wisdom and balance to be both truthful grace and gracious truth. . . .

Lord, help me to strike the balance in my life between prayer and action, and faith and planning. I want to be doing Your will, not mine. I want to know that I am serving You, not being busy to serve myself. Show me what I need to do to be balanced. . . .

BLESSING

Lord, I constantly feel like I'm struggling against You, against life. Like Jacob, Lord, I can't stop wrestling unless You bless me. So show Your face to me and bless me that I might have peace. . . .

"God be merciful to us and bless us" (Psalm 67:1). I pray along with the psalmist for Your blessings. Lord, I thank You for the blessings in my life. I recognize that all good things come from You. I ask for Your continued blessing in the area of . . .

COMFORT

O Lord, my soul thirsts for You. I hunger after Your righteousness. Comfort me with the assurance of Your presence with me. Feed me by Your Word and Spirit that I might rest in Your love, grace, and care. I need Your help today as I face . . .

Lord, You promise in Your Word that You heal the brokenhearted and bind up their wounds (Psalm 147:3). My heart is broken today, Lord. I need Your presence. I seek Your comfort. . . .

COMPASSION

Lord Jesus, You looked with compassion on the broken places in our world. You reached out Your hands to touch and heal. In the end, You reached out Your hands upon the Cross to display Your compassion to the world. Help me to show compassion to those I meet today. . . .

Lord, it is so easy to get bogged down in my own life. Let me remember those around me in prayer and action today. . . .

CONFIDENCE

O Lord my God, the prophet Isaiah said that in rest we will be saved, in confidence we will find strength (Isaiah 30:15). Enable me to rest in Your power to save me from whatever I face. I need confidence as I go today to . . .

Help me to be confident in Your love, Lord, the love of a strong and powerful God Who conquers the world and yet still loves me. Give me that confidence as I . . .

CONTENTMENT

Lord, I recognize that all good things come from You. I praise You and thank You for the good things in my life, especially . . .

Lord, You remind us to keep our lives free from the love of money and to be content with what we have (Hebrews 13:5). Lord, at times I look around at others, and I feel discontent about what I have. I don't want to do that. Take away those feelings, and grant me Your contentment with all that You have given me. . . .

COURAGE

Lord, give me courage to do the things that You put in front of me. I am particularly concerned about . . .

Lord, You sent an angel to comfort Jesus in the Garden of Gethsemane and have given Your servants courage when they most needed it. Grant me courage and strength today. I am fearful of . . .

ENDURANCE

Lord, Paul regarded this life as a race. You have stood by me in training; now help me to press on toward the goal. I need Your encouragement to keep going with . . .

In Galatians 6:9, we are encouraged to not become weary in doing good, for at the proper time we will reap a harvest if we do not give up. Help me to push on and keep my eyes focused on You. I feel like giving up, Lord, but I know You want me to keep going with . . .

FAITH

Your Word describes faith as "the substance of things hoped for, the evidence of things not seen" (Hebrews 11:1). Lord, most of the time I don't know what this verse means, let alone how I am supposed to be convicted of things unseen. Yet I know that You have given me the faith to believe in You. Strengthen my faith, Lord, so that I may . . .

You promise in Your Word that our faith can move mountains. I have a mountain that needs moving, Lord, and I don't know if my faith can do it. But I do know that I have faith in a great God Who can do anything. So I pray today that . . .

FORGIVENESS

I know I am supposed to forgive as You have forgiven Lord, but that's really difficult. When I am angry, help me to forgive, keeping in mind that the debt You forgave me is much greater. I need to forgive . . .

Lord, I humbly come to You, asking Your forgiveness. I have sinned by doing . . . and I ask that You will forgive me and help me to experience victory over this sin in the future.

FREEDOM

You promise, Lord, that when we know the truth, the truth will set us free (John 8:32). Lord, help me to enjoy the freedom I have in You . . .

I know that I am free in You, Lord, but I also know that I must handle that freedom in a responsible manner. May I always be aware of those whose faith is young so that I do not use my freedom in ways that would hurt their new faith in You. . . .

GOD'S PRESENCE

The Bible says that in Your presence there are "pleasures forevermore" (Psalm 16:11). I want to be in Your presence, Lord. I want to get a taste of heaven every day. So I come into Your presence now. . . .

I want to be aware of Your presence with me, Lord. I humbly ask that You will make Yourself real to me today as I must . . .

GOD'S WILL

I really need to know Your will in a decision I have to make, Lord. I don't ever want to step outside of Your will, so I need Your guidance about . . .

Lord, I trust that the plans You have for me are good and right. Help me to . . .

GRACE

Lord, I still find it hard to comprehend that You love me so much that You give me the undeserved gift of Your grace. Help me to see Your grace in my life, especially when I have to deal with . . .

I need Your grace today so that I am gracious toward . . .

GUIDANCE

I don't know which way to turn. I have a choice to make and both of my options seem right and good. What should I do, Lord? I ask You to show me which path is the right one for me. I can't see the future, but You can. Set my foot in the right direction. . . .

Lord, You know what is weighing on my heart. You ask us to come to You with everything. I seek Your guidance and wisdom to do the right thing about . . .

HEALING

Lord, I know that You are capable of anything, but discerning Your will is another matter. I pray for healing for my friend. But if it is not Your will to heal, than give me the grace to cope. . . .

You are a great God. Thank You for Your power to heal in our lives. I need healing, not for a physical need, but for an emotional need. I ask for healing of my mind and heart because of . . .

HOLINESS

Lord, You call Your people to be holy. I know that I can't do that in my own strength. No matter how much I try to do, I can never be holy enough for You. Thank You that You have made me holy. Now help me to live to honor You today as I . . .

Lord, You permeate my life. There is nothing I can keep from You. Help me in this area of my life where I struggle . . .

HONESTY

Lord, give me the strength to be honest about who I am. You know me inside out, so I might as well not try to hide anything from You. Lord, I need to confess . . .

Lord, I want to live my life in honesty before You and before others. Teach me to walk in Your ways and to be who You created me to be. I need to be honest about . . .

HOPE

Lord, my hopes are unsure; what I hope for in You is a certainty. Thank You for the hope of eternity, the hope of life forever with You. . . .

Lord, I am feeling hopeless about a situation right now. I don't see any way through it. I ask You to give me hope. Even though I can't see You or hear You right now, I know You're with me and I trust You. Give me a sense of Your hope about . . .

HUMILITY

Lord God, sometimes my head gets too big, my heart gets too proud, and my will strays from Yours. Give me the humility of Jesus Christ. He was God, but He stooped to earth to love us. Remind me that my only glory is in being Your child. . . .

Everywhere I turn, Lord, there's a temptation to be proud, or at least to act proudly. Save me from thinking that the world centers on me. Help me to remember today that You are the source of everything good. Remind me that everything I have comes from Your gracious hand. . . .

INTEGRITY

Holy God, You are the source of truth. You desire truth from Your people. Give me the strength to follow Your will. Help me to be honest in my words, thoughts, and deeds. Let Your truth shine through everything that I do. Keep my integrity intact today as I . . .

I get angry, Lord, when people lie to me. Yet when I face the chance to help myself with a lie, it's hard not to just do it. Help me to show integrity as I face . . .

JOY

Lord God, all Your gifts are so wonderful, and I want to rejoice in them. Thank You for the blessings You have given. I am joyous today because . . .

Today is going to be difficult, Lord. I must deal with the pain of . . . Yet Your Word promises joy even in the most difficult circumstances. Give me that joy today as I face . . .

JUSTICE

Father God, You are the great Judge of all the earth. But there are things that are unfair—people have wronged me, and I don't see justice yet. Help me to lay every hurt and wrong in Your hands and trust You to be the perfect Judge. Bring justice regarding . . .

Near me, Lord, maybe in a place I cannot see, someone is abused and doesn't know what to do. Give me a passion for justice, dear God, so I am never casual in the presence of people so aggrieved. Show me what I can do today. . . .

LOVE

Lord Jesus, You are the best picture of love. Your love for me is so deep, so constant. Please fill me with Your love, and let it overflow to all those around me. Help me to love my dear family and friends. . . .

I've got someone in my life today, Lord, who I don't really feel like loving at all. Help me to understand that love is a choice, and then help me to make that choice in Your strength today. Help me to love . . . and to show it by . . .

MERCY

God, You are merciful to me every day. You forgive my sins and give me everything I need. I know I don't deserve it. Teach me to be merciful, to give people what they don't deserve in gratitude for Your great mercy to me. Help me to be merciful toward . . .

Help me, Lord, to know the right time for mercy and the right time for anger. Because anger is easier for me, tilt me toward mercy. I feel angry about . . . so show me how I can show mercy in this situation. . . .

OBEDIENCE

Lord, I want to obey You, but what I know I should do is going to be very difficult. Please give me the strength to obey You today about . . .

Lord, You have called me to be right where I am. Help me to be obedient not only in the great things for the kingdom, but in the small things, too. . . .

PATIENCE

Lord, You are patient with us, forgiving when we ask. You tell us that trials in our lives produce endurance, and endurance leads to patience. Please give me the strength to endure the trials that I am facing, and teach me patience so that I may make it through all of the hard times in life, especially this situation. . . .

It's hard to wait, Lord. There is so much I want to do for You, and I feel like I am in a holding pattern. Help me to learn what You want to teach me today, Lord, so that I am ready to move into the future with You. Give me patience today. . . .

PEACE

Jesus, Prince of Peace, I long for wholeness and peace. I feel like a mess. Send Your Spirit, be close to me, and guard my heart and mind from the trouble and lies of this world. Please give me peace as I deal with . . .

The world is in so much turmoil, Lord. I pray for peace for . . .

PERSPECTIVE

Jesus, You taught us about the wisest and best way to live, just as You lived. Prayer is the best way to gain the right perspective, so I come to You to ask for a renewed perspective. Open my eyes to see Your truth, to look at things the way I should, especially regarding . . .

I am really confused about . . . I don't understand what is happening. It doesn't make sense to me, so I need Your perspective, Lord. Show me what I need to see in this situation. . . .

PRIORITIES

Lord, my life is too busy. Please show me what is most important, and teach me to wait on You. Give me the strength to deal with the people in my life and the ability to complete the tasks that I need to finish. Most of all, be my number one priority today, as I struggle to balance . . .

I think I've been getting my priorities mixed up, Lord. I am not taking time for You, so I am finding that nothing else is making much sense. Help me to schedule an appointment with You. I want to seek Your face every day . . .

PROTECTION

Loving God who keeps my feet from slipping, protect me by Your power. Send Your angels to surround me and keep me safe. Provide protection for me in this time of . . .

The psalmist wrote, "Deliver me from my enemies O my God; defend me from those who rise up against me" (Psalm 59:1). Help me, Lord! I need Your protection because I fear . . .

PROVISION

Loving and generous Father, how greatly You provide for Your children, sustaining us like the birds in the air and clothing us as the lilies of the field. Please provide for me in this time of need. You know that I need . . .

Lord, You ask us to seek first Your kingdom and tell us that You will care for our needs. Lord, You know my needs before I ask, but I come to You in faith to ask for Your provision for . . .

SELF–CONTROL

Holy Spirit, please tend to my spirit and grow the fruit of self-control, helping me to learn restraint. Give me the strength and the ability to control myself when . . .

Lord, You know that I struggle with . . . Give me Your strength to conquer it today. And if I conquer it today, give me more strength to do it again tomorrow.

SELF–WORTH

Good Creator, You created me in Your image, making me the splendor and crown of Your creation. Help me to recognize my value and worth despite what others may tell me. . . .

Lord, some days it's hard to believe You love me when I don't even like myself. Lift me from this empty place. Help me not to isolate myself when I need community the most! Give me the courage to . . .

STRENGTH

Lord of power, You possess all strength. Recognizing my weakness, I pray that You uphold me, giving me strength to face the battles in my life. Give me the strength today to . . .

Lord, I need to lean on Your strength to help me through this time. I feel weak and insecure. Please give me courage as I . . .

TRUTH

God, who is truth, Your Word is truth; Jesus is truth. Guide me into the truth, and give me eyes to see what is true in this world of so many lies and differing voices. Give me wisdom and open my eyes to see the truth in . . .

Lord, John 16:13 reminds me that the Spirit of truth will guide me into all truth. Lord, please send me the Spirit of truth. I need Your guidance because I am unsure about . . .

TRUST

Almighty God, trust is so difficult, especially when I remember past hurts, and the future seems so uncertain. But You are steadfast, strong, and caring, so help me trust in Your provision and care. Please help me to trust You in this time of need. . . .

Give me discernment to make good judgments about trustworthy people. Give me Your wisdom to place my trust in the right people. I'm not sure who I can trust in this situation, so I need Your guidance, Lord. . .

VINDICATION

God, You are righteous and just. You must get pretty angry when people hurt Your children. Protect me today from . . . Save me by Your righteousness, and vindicate me by Your power. Support and defend me in this situation.

You are a God of truth, and I am facing lies today. I need Your help to know what to say and what to do to reveal the truth . . .

WISDOM

Father of Light, You delight in Your children and are generous to give wisdom to whoever asks. Please fill me with Your wisdom. Help me to discern what is best and how to deal with hurts and wrongs. Help me to make good choices and to grow in wisdom every day, especially in this situation of . . .

You promise in Your Word that if we feel we lack wisdom, all we have to do is ask (James 1:5). So I am asking for wisdom today, Lord. I need Your wisdom in order to discern . . .

PRAYERS IN TIMES OF . . .

CHANGE

O God Who does not change, You are the same yesterday, today, and forever. There is no place I can go to escape Your presence with me. Though my circumstances may change, Your love, protection, grace, and peace never will. Help me as I face this change. . . .

Lord, during this time of change, help me to find Your peace in the midst of everything. I am afraid, but I trust in Your plans for me. . . .

CHOICES

O Lord, You are my light and my salvation. I pray that Jesus Christ, Light of the world, will illuminate my path. While there is no shadow of turning in You, there is too much shadow of turning in me. Grant me Your wisdom and courage. I have a choice to make about . . .

Lord, life is full of difficult choices. I know the choice I must make, but I don't want to do it. Give me the courage to choose rightly, even if it is not the easiest path. . . .

CRITICISM

Jesus, You stood before the criticisms and assaults of Your torturers and did not strike back. Now I feel the sting of criticism. Lord, grant me the grace to not strike back, but to return good. Grow in me love for those who criticize me about . . .

Lord, I am being criticized about . . . Help me to know, Lord, if there is truth in the criticism so that I might learn from it. . . .

DANGER

Lord Jesus, there is nothing—not even danger—that can separate me from You. Even danger You have conquered by Your blood. As I live in You, bring me closer to You in love, and grant to me a vision of the victory I have in You. I am going into a place of danger. . . .

Lord, I trust that the worst thing that can happen to me is death, and You have triumphed over that as well. Give me all of Your strength and courage to go into this dangerous situation. . . .

DECISIONS

God of present, past, and future, I have important decisions to make. My future lies before me, on the other side of deciding. Walk with me, send Your Spirit to me with wisdom and strength to honor You in this decision about . . .

"Be anxious for nothing, but in everything by prayer and supplication, with thanksgiving, let your requests be made known to God" (Philippians 4:6). Lord, I seek Your peace as the confirmation in this decision. I made this decision in keeping with what I sense as Your will, so now guide me to . . .

DISAPPOINTMENT

God of peace, You guide my life and lift my spirit. I pray for Your will to be done in my life during this time of disappointment. Please guide my steps, make clear to me Your path, and send Your Holy Spirit to be near to me as I am disappointed about . . .

Lord, I keep knocking on doors and not getting any answers! Where are You in my disappointment? I felt I was following Your will, but was I wrong? I trust in Your guidance; please guide me! I need Your help as I . . .

DISCOURAGEMENT

Father, You are my glory and the lifter of my head. May You give me peace and direction in this time of discouragement. Lord, place those in my path who can provide encouragement and give me a new focus toward You in this time of discouragement over . . .

Lord, I am having a hard time seeing You in anything right now. Please make Yourself known to me again even through this discouragement. . . .

DOUBT

Lord, You are patient and true. As I wrestle with doubt, show me Your truth and confirm Your reality. Use this time of doubt to draw me closer to You and answer my doubts about . . .

Lord, help my unbelief! I want to believe You are there, but I don't see You or feel You. I doubt You love me. I doubt You're there. Help me believe in You again. . . .

FAILURE

Father, I long to do the right thing and to follow Your will, yet I acknowledge that I am weak and broken. I have fallen short this time and pray that You are near. Help me to recoup and follow Your will next time. Forgive me for my sins, and bind up my broken heart as I have failed to . . .

Lord, forgive me. I have failed to do the things that I ought to do and have done the things I ought not to have done. Help me to get it right next time. I'm sorry for . . .

GUILT

Father, through Jesus Christ, You've forgiven all my sins. My head knows this, but sometimes my heart forgets. I feel very guilty about . . . Show me what I need to do today to rectify the situation. If there is nothing more I can do, graciously take my guilt away, and assure me of Your forgiveness and salvation.

I ask for Your forgiveness today, Lord. You have used the guilt I feel to drive me toward You. Please forgive me for . . .

HURT

Lord, there is so much hurt in our world. Right now, You seem very far away. Remind me that You are very present even in the pain facing our world. Make Your presence known to . . .

My pain is very intense today, Father. I am hurting deeply. Draw me closer to You today. Take this pain of . . . and carry it because I can't. Then put Your loving arms around me.

JEALOUSY

Father, You promise to provide everything I need. But sometimes I am distracted by what You've given to others. I feel jealous about . . . Help me to be content with what You've given me, to praise You for Your gifts to others, and to trust You for all my needs.

Lord, I know that You have gifted me in some very special ways. Help me to use my gifts—not to make others jealous, but to glorify You. Keep my motives pure as I serve You in . . .

LEADERSHIP

Holy God, You've entrusted me with the responsibility to lead others. As I take this leadership over . . . , give me love, strength, integrity, and a servant's heart. Send Your Holy Spirit to be with me so that everything I do as a leader may glorify You.

Lord, help me with the details today, and the big plan, as well. I want my impact on others to be a witness of Your care for all of us. As I lead, help me today to . . .

LONELINESS

Lord, I am lonely. Everyone seems far away. Sometimes I even wonder where You are. Walk alongside me and remind me that You are my closest companion. Surround me with Your love and fellowship. Be with me even in my loneliness. . . .

I know in my head, Lord, that as lonely as I feel, around me are a lot of people who feel the same way. If You will put me in their way today, I'll do something to relieve their loneliness, even if it's just a word. . . .

MONEY PROBLEMS

Father of Light, You delight in Your children and provide for them even more generously than You do the birds or the flowers. Lord, provide for me in this time of financial trouble; please give me the ability to work and discernment for using my resources wisely. Bless me that I may bless others. . . .

Lord, I know we need to choose to serve either You or money. Help me to serve You and submit my finances to You. I am in trouble and I need Your help. . . .

PAIN

Lord Jesus, being fully human, You suffered and endured our pain at the Cross. I pray that Your strength will be made perfect in my weakness. By Your stripes I am healed, so bring me peace and healing in this time of pain. . . .

Lord, I hurt and I carry all of it myself. Help me to give the pain to You, the willing bearer of my burdens! Take this pain I am facing today. . . .

PERSECUTION

Good Shepherd, You care for Your children and provide for them in times of persecution and suffering. Please be with Your children in this time of suffering. We remember our brothers and sisters around the world who are not free to worship You; protect them and be near to them. Be with me in this time of persecution. . . .

Lord, I feel persecuted because I believe in You. I'm trying to remain true to You, but it is hard. Please protect me, and work in the hearts of those who are hurting me. . . .

PRESSURE

Lord of eternity, remind me of the everlasting, and help me to discern what is truly important. At the same time, give me the ability to meet the demands that have been placed on me. Give me rest and peace in this time of pressure. . . .

Lord, I'm feeling overwhelmed. I know that You don't give us more than we can handle, but I'm at my breaking point! Help me through this time to complete . . .

REJECTION

Jesus, You faced rejection from Your family, religious leaders, and the government, yet You never strayed from Your mission. Please be with me as those around me misunderstand me. Send Your Holy Spirit to bear fruit in my life and to assure me of Your love. Draw me to You in this time of rejection by . . .

Lord, I am so lonely. I feel isolated and misunderstood. I know that Jesus was rejected, but He was the Messiah! Comfort the lowly and bless me with a friend who can encourage me . . .

RESPONSIBILITY

Loving Father, You sustain me and guide me through life. You give me tasks to do, a calling to follow, and a vocation to fill. I pray that whatever my hands find to do, they do it in Your name. Help me to meet my responsibilities in . . .

Lord, thank You for trusting me with . . . I feel overwhelmed by the responsibilities sometimes, but I recognize that all good things come from You. Help me to do this job well and to Your glory. . . .

SORROW

Jesus, the Man of Sorrow, You are like us in every way except for sin. I ask You to send the Spirit, the Comforter, to bring rest to my soul, to bind my sorrow, to bring peace. Please be near to me now and bring joy in this time of sorrow over . . .

Lord, You know the sorrow I carry with me. Paul learned to live with the thorn in his life as a reminder of Your love. Help me to see You in my sorrow, and give me peace in the midst of it. . . .

STRESS

God, You give me peace, not confusion, in times of great struggle. Please be near to me in this time of heightened stress. Show me how to deal with this stress in my life, and provide the means to deal with it. Steady trembling hands and fluttering hearts and give me peace in this time of . . .

Lord, I pray during this time of overwhelming demands that I can maintain a level head. Help me to remember that You are an oasis in the storm of life, and I can always turn my mind toward You for peace, no matter what I'm doing. . . .

SUFFERING

Jesus, in Your ministry on earth You reached out to those who were suffering and downcast. Be near to me, touch my suffering body, and bring Your strengthening presence to my dispirited mind. . . .

"We are hard pressed on every side, yet not crushed; we are perplexed, but not in despair; persecuted, but not forsaken; struck down, but not destroyed" (2 Corinthians 4:8–9). Lord, give me hope through this time of suffering and grant me Your peace. . . .

TEMPTATION

Lord Jesus, You know temptation because You were tempted in every way, but You did not sin. Increase my resolve to follow You, determined to resist this temptation. Keep sin from me but Your love close. I am facing temptation about . . .

You promise, Lord, that You will not allow me to be tempted beyond what I am able to handle, but with the temptation You will also provide a way of escape (1 Corinthians 10:13). I need to see that way of escape! Lord, show me the way out! I am feeling like I can't handle it anymore. . . .

TROUBLE

O God, I am troubled. And my troubles turn my eyes away from You. Calm the storms that swirl around me, and set my feet on the solid rock of Your love. Teach me to trust You, and block out those things that distract me from You. I am troubled by . . .

"Cast your burden on the LORD, and He shall sustain you; he shall never permit the righteous to be moved" (Psalm 55:22). Lord, I feel so alone and overwhelmed. Please take my burden and lead me through the storm. I need You to sustain me in this difficult time. . . .

WITNESSING

Lord Jesus, all power and authority belong to You, and You have sent out Your disciples to proclaim the faith, hope, and love of the gospel message. Give to me a gentleness of heart and a respect for those I meet that I may give a true account of the hope I have in You. . . .

I am sometimes so afraid to share my faith. I don't know what to say, and I'm afraid that someone will have a difficult question that I can't answer. How can I witness for You today, Lord? Give me the right words to say to . . .

WORRY

Lord Jesus, forgive me for not believing Your words that life is more important than food or drink and that my body is more important than clothing. Forgive me for not truly considering Your care of the lilies of the field or the birds of the air. Take this worry from me and remind me of Your care, concern, and provision. . . .

Lord, You tell me not to be anxious about anything but to give all of my concerns to You (Philippians 4:6). Lord, I am worried about . . .

PRAYERS TO OVERCOME . . .

ANGER

Lord God, don't let my anger take control of me. Give me strength to resist my temper. Fill me with love and gentleness toward the people around me. I am angry today about . . . so help me . . .

I need three breaths today, Lord, to give me pause before I say in anger what I will later regret. Peace, love, joy. Give me those three words, in three breaths, when my anger boils. Today, when I have to face . . . help me to breathe in the peace of Your Spirit, and give me the right words to say. . . .

BACKSLIDING

Father God, I feel like I am slipping away from You. When my hands are too weak to hang on, hold onto me. When I stray from Your path, guide me back. I trust You because You are faithful to Your children. I think the problem is . . . , so show me what to do to get back on the right track.

I've been away from You, Lord. I'd like to come back home. I am knocking at Your door, and I confess my sin of . . . and humbly ask that You will open the door and receive me. . . .

COMPLACENCY

Holy Spirit, fill me with Your fire—keep me from becoming complacent. Remind me of the warmth of Your love for me and of my love for You. Encourage me to love the things that You love and to work for the benefit of Your kingdom. Give me an opportunity today to live out my faith. Guide me today. . . .

Sometimes it gets so easy to sit back and enjoy all Your gifts to me without thanking You or realizing the responsibility You have given along with those gifts. Show me what to do today to use what You have given me to build Your kingdom. . . .

DEATH

Lord Jesus, You conquered sin and death for us, but death still threatens our present lives. I am hurting today over the death of someone I love. I need You today, Father, more than ever. Give me Your peace as I grieve this loss. Walk with me today as I must . . .

I know that everyone must die, Lord, but I'll admit I'm just not ready. It doesn't seem fair. Watch over those around me who must deal with losing me. Protect their hearts and their faith. Help them not to doubt Your goodness. And help me to go into Your presence with joy and grace. . . .

DEPRESSION

Father God, I've hit the bottom—life is dark and I am out of hope. Raise me up, God, and show me the light of Your love. Remind me of the joy of serving You. Heal me and comfort me with Your Holy Spirit. Today, give me the strength to . . .

Peace, hope, and joy are Yours to give, Lord, but I can't even reach out for them. Remind me, despite myself, that You never give up, that Your gifts never run out. I need Your peace, hope, and joy today, for I must . . .

DISCRIMINATION

God, Creator of humanity, You respect and love all of Your children. Give me the strength to love all who bear Your image, and help me to forgive those who persecute Your children. Reveal my heart to me and show me if I am discriminating in any way. . . .

Lord, You created a world of beauty and diversity. Yet there are plenty of people who don't understand that. I feel discriminated against because of . . . Give me the strength to do Your will even as I face this injustice. . . .

ENEMIES

Jesus, You faced many enemies while You were here on earth, yet You loved them. I pray for those who are oppressing me, that they may find Your love and change their ways. Lord, be with those who persecute me, and show me love during this persecution. . . .

You told us to pray for our enemies. Today, I am trying to follow Your command and pray for . . .

EVIL PEOPLE

Lord, some people stand against Your ways and all that is good. Please keep Your children safe from their evil schemes. Send Your angels to surround all of those who stand in danger. Give me courage to stand for Your truth against this evil person. . . .

It is difficult when evil stares me in the face, but that is what is before me. How do I deal with this obvious evil, Lord? What do I do about . . . ?

FEAR

Father, You care for Your children in times in trouble. You are light and salvation to us. Help me have the courage to not be afraid about . . . , knowing that You protect me wherever I go. Thank You that You are so trustworthy and loving. Give me grace to face my fear. . . .

I know that I am worrying and then facing fear over things I'm worrying about. I know that You want me to trust You. So take my burden of fear today. . . .

GOSSIP

Jesus, You were the object of many cruel words, but You never opened Your mouth in gossip. I know that it is wrong to say cruel things about the people around me. Please forgive me for the gossiping I have done. I don't want to speak it or hear it any more. The next time I'm tempted to gossip, help me to . . .

Lord, what do I do when people are gossiping around me? How can I be a good influence on them? When I'm with these gossiping people today, help me to . . .

GREED

Father, You give us so many blessings, but it is easy to want more. I get greedy, wanting more than I have. And most of it I can easily do without. Today, I'd rather be a little hungry and get closer to You, than distracted by . . .

Lord, I am dealing with greed. I want more, but I realize that I might easily cross the line and be unethical in order to get more. Protect me from that, Lord. Keep me from letting greed blind me to what is right. . . .

HABITS

Lord, some habits in my life are not healthy, habits that developed when I did not know You so well. Please take away those old habits that are seeking to control me again. . . .

I want to develop good habits, Lord. I want to get into the habit of having a regular quiet time and of praying to You. Show me how to begin those good habits today. . . .

HATRED

God of love, I forget that other people are made in Your image, especially when I don't like them. Sometimes I start to hate them and my head gets filled up with destructive thoughts. I can't deny my anger and hatred, so I bring it to You, asking for Your help to deal with these emotions. Please help me today to . . .

Someone really hates me, Lord, and I don't know why. I can sense it when I am with that person. Show me what to do and how to act in ways that will glorify You. . . .

LEGALISM

Jesus, our Master and Teacher, You said that to follow You is like rest for our souls. Sometimes, I am tempted to follow rules, maybe because it makes me feel righteous. Too many rules bind me and cut me off from people I love and from You. Today, free me from . . .

Lord, I have a past that is filled with rules that have driven me away from You. Now I understand that I am saved by Your grace and not by those rules. Show me how to live in the light of Your truth, Your freedom, and Your grace. Rid me of the legalism that has bound me in fear for so many years. . . .

LIES

Jesus, Your name is Truth. Protect me by Your truth. Strengthen my discernment to find the truth among the lies, and strengthen my resolve to tell the truth when the lies seem more appealing. Help me to speak the truth about . . .

I am being lied about, Lord. What do I do? How can I set the record straight? Show me what I should say and to whom I should say it. . . .

MATERIALISM

Loving Father, You pour out Your blessings on us, yet it is so easy to elevate those material things to places higher than they deserve. Help me see that the stuff is not eternally important. Teach me to be generous with all I have, and thank You for all good things in my life. . . .

I look at all that I have, Lord, and I am ashamed that I sometimes want even more. Free me from being materialistic. Change my focus today from . . . to . . .

PRIDE

Father, You love us and have created us in Your image, but sometimes I overestimate my abilities. Pride is so easy, even when that pride hurts others. Forgive my pride and fill me with Your Spirit to develop a humble heart and mind. Teach me that all that I have comes from You. . . .

Lord, if in any way I am letting pride get out of control, show me. . . .

SELFISHNESS

Jesus, You are King and Lord and deserve all honor, glory, and praise. If I try to be the center of the universe, I only hurt myself and others, like I did when . . . Help me to serve others with a loving servant's heart.

Today take away my selfishness regarding . . . and help me to . . .

SLANDER

Lord of truth and love, I am hurting today because of lies people are saying about me. This is hurting my reputation. What can I do, Lord? Show me how to bring the truth to light and to continue to be Your humble servant in the process. Today I need Your help as I face . . .

Teach me to speak the truth always, Lord. I don't want to get caught in the web of gossip, lies, and slander. Teach me to seek the truth and then speak the truth about . . .

SPIRITUAL WARFARE

God of victory, You will win the final victory over sin and Satan, yet we still fight the battle. Help me to put on Your armor to defeat the schemes of the wicked one, and protect me as I fight for You. Give me eyes to see beyond the physical and give me the strength to overcome . . .

Lord, help me cling to You and keep my eyes fixed upon You. I trust that You are Master of the spirit world, too. Today I am facing spiritual warfare, and I dare not fight alone. Be with me as I deal with . . .

TOPICAL INDEX

SCRIPTURE INDEX

297

NOTES AND FURTHER READING
ON PRAYER

Introduction
1. P. T. Forsyth, *The Soul of Prayer* (Grand Rapids: W. B. Eerdmans Pub. Co., 1916), 11.
2. Ibid., 78.

The Person to Whom We Pray
1. *Prayers To Move Your Mountains* (Nashville: Thomas Nelson Publishers, 2000), 12–13.
2. Max Lucado, *The Great House of God* (Nashville: W Publishing Group, 1997), 33.
3. Dave Veerman, "Talking to a Holy God," in *Practical Christianity,* ed. LaVonne Neff, Ron Beers, Bruce Barton, Linda Taylor, Dave Veerman, and Jim Galvin (Wheaton, Ill.: Tyndale House Publishers, Inc., 1987), 422–3.
4. Randy Southern, *Fuel: Igniting Your Life with Passionate Prayer* (Nashville: Thomas Nelson Publishers, 2001), 22–24.
5. Robert J. Morgan. ed., *Nelson's Annual Preacher's Sourcebook,* "The Kneeling Christian" (Nashville, Thomas Nelson Publishers, 2001), 384–85.
6. Evelyn Christenson, *What God Does When Women Pray* (Nashville: Word Publishing, 2000), 27–29.
7. Larry Christenson, "The Spirit's Prayer for His People," in *Practical Christianity,* eds., LaVonne Neff, Ron Beers, Bruce Barton, Linda Taylor, Dave Veerman, and Jim Galvin (Wheaton, IL: Tyndale House Publishers, Inc., 1987), 418–19.
8. Michael Youssef, *The Prayer That God Answers* (Nashville: Thomas Nelson Publishers, 2000), 8–11.
9. Max Lucado, *The Great House of God* (Nashville: Thomas Nelson Publishers, 1997), 61–62.
10. J. Vernon McGee, *On Prayer: Praying and Living in the Father's Will* (Nashville: Thomas Nelson Publishers, 2002), 6–10.
11. J. Vernon McGee, *On Prayer: Praying and Living in the Father's Will* (Nashville: Thomas Nelson Publishers, 2002), 10–13.
12. J. Vernon McGee, *On Prayer: Praying and Living in the Father's Will* (Nashville: Thomas Nelson Publishers, 2002), 13–16.
13. J. Vernon McGee, *On Prayer: Praying and Living in the Father's Will* (Nashville: Thomas Nelson Publishers, 2002), 16–20.
14. St. Francis of Sales, *Introduction to the Devout Life* (London, Oxford, Cambridge: Rivingtons, 1876), 69–71.
15. Ronnie W. Floyd, *How To Pray* (Nashville: W Publishing Group, 1999), 107–11.
16. Charles Stanley, *How to Handle Adversity* (Nashville: Thomas Nelson Publishers, 1989), 132–34.
17. George MacDonald, *Unspoken Sermons, Second Series,* "The Words of Jesus on Prayer" (London: Longmans, Green and Co., 1885).
18. Stormie Omartian, *Lord, I Want to Be Whole* (Nashville: Thomas Nelson Publishers, 2000), 217–18, 221–23.
19. Paul Cedar, *A Life of Prayer,* ed. Charles R. Swindoll (Nashville: Word Publishing, 1998), 122–24.
20. Randy Southern, *Fuel: Igniting Your Life With Passionate Prayer* (Nashville: Thomas Nelson Publishers, 2001), 161–64.
21. Randy Southern, *Fuel: Igniting Your Life With Passionate Prayer* (Nashville: Thomas Nelson Publishers, 2001), 163–64.

22. *The Word In Life Study Bible* (Nashville: Thomas Nelson Publishers, 1996), 446.
23. Paul Cedar, *A Life of Prayer,* ed. Charles R. Swindoll (Nashville: Word Publishing, 1998), 57–59.

The Person

 1. Cynthia Heald, *When the Father Holds You Close* (Nashville: Thomas Nelson Publishers, 1999), 74–75.
 2. Charles Stanley, *How to Listen to God* (Nashville: Thomas Nelson Publishers, 1985), 106–7.
 3. Cynthia Heald, *When The Father Holds You Close* (Nashville: Thomas Nelson Publishers, 1999), 71–72.
 4. Andrew Murray, *With Christ in the School of Prayer* (New York, Chicago, Toronto: Fleming H. Revell, 1885), 16–20.
 5. Cynthia Heald, *Becoming a Woman of Faith* (Nashville: Thomas Nelson Publishers, 2000), 69–70.
 6. Charles Stanley, *How To Listen To God* (Nashville: Thomas Nelson Publishers, 1985), 160–162.
 7. *The Kneeling Christian* (Grand Rapids: Zondervan, between 1924 and 1947), Chapter Seven.
 8. Ronnie W. Floyd, *How To Pray* (Nashville: W Publishing Group, 1999), 21–28.
 9. Martin Luther, "Treatise on Good Works," in *Works of Martin Luther, Vol. 1,* ed. Adolph Spaeth, L. D. Reed, Henry Eyster Jacobs (Philadelphia: A. J. Holman, 1915), 173–285.
10. John Maxwell, ed., *Partners in Prayer* (Nashville: Thomas Nelson Publishers, 1996), 52–63.
11. George MacDonald, "The Words of Jesus on Prayer," in *Unspoken Sermons,* Second Series (London: Longmans, Green, and Co., 1885).
12. Cynthia Heald, *When the Father Holds You Close* (Nashville: Thomas Nelson Publishers, 1999), 63–64.
13. Charles Stanley, *How to Listen to God* (Nashville: Thomas Nelson Publishers, 1985), 107–8.
14. John Bevere, *A Heart Ablaze: Igniting A Passion For God* (Nashville: Thomas Nelson Publishers, 1999), 68–70.
15. Anne Graham Lotz, *Just Give Me Jesus* (Nashville: W Publishing Group, 2000), 51–55.
16. Evelyn Christenson, "How Sin Affects Prayer," in *Practical Christianity,* ed. LaVonne Neff, Ron Beers, 17. Bruce Barton, Linda Taylor, Dave Veerman, and Jim Galvin (Wheaton, Ill.: Tyndale House Publishers, Inc., 1987), 424–5.
18. Tim LaHaye and Ed Hindson, *Seduction of the Heart* (Nashville: W Publishing Group, 2001), 42–45, 49, 56, 280–1.
19. *The Kneeling Christian* (Grand Rapids: Zondervan, between 1924 and 1947), Chapter Seven.
20. Tommy Tenney, *The God Catchers* (Nashville: Thomas Nelson Publishers, 2000), 186–87, 189, 190–91.
21. P.T. Forsyth, *The Soul of Prayer* (Grand Rapids: Eerdmans, 1916), Chapter One.
22. P.T. Forsyth, *The Soul of Prayer* (Grand Rapids: Eerdmans, 1916), Chapter One.
23. Randy Southern, *Fuel: Igniting Your Life With Passionate Prayer* (Nashville: Thomas Nelson Publishers, 2001), 139–41.
24. Stormie Omartian, "Powerful Prayer," in *The Soul Care Bible,* ed. Tim Clinton (Nashville: Thomas Nelson Publishers, 2001) 1238–39.

The Power

 1. J. Vernon McGee, *On Prayer: Praying And Living In The Father's Will* (Nashville: Thomas Nelson Publishers, 2002), 49–50, 57–58.
 2. Charles Stanley, *Into His Presence* (Nashville: Thomas Nelson Publishers, 2000) 156.
 3. Max Lucado, *The Great House of God* (Nashville: Thomas Nelson Publishers, 1997), 2–4.
 4. Paul Cedar, *A Life Of Prayer,* ed. Charles R. Swindoll (Nashville: Word Publishing, 1998), 159–61.
 5. Becky Tirabassi, *Let Prayer Change Your Life* (Nashville: Thomas Nelson Publishers, 2000), 133–5.
 6. Paul Cedar, *A Life of Prayer,* ed. Charles R. Swindoll (Nashville: Word Publishing, 1998), 157–9.

7. Joan H. Young, "Why Should I Pray If God Knows Everything?" in *Practical Christianity,* ed. LaVonne Neff, Ron Beers, Bruce Barton, Linda Taylor, Dave Veerman, and Jim Galvin (Wheaton, Ill.: Tyndale House Publishers, Inc., 1987), 437–9.

8. Augustine, "Commentary on the Sermon on the Mount" in *The Ante-Nicene Fathers,* vol. 6, ed. Alexander Roberts and James Donaldson (Grand Rapids: Eerdmans, 1950–51. Orig. 1885–96), Book II, Chapter III, Sections 13–14.

9. Paul Cedar, *A Life of Prayer,* ed. Charles R. Swindoll (Nashville: Word Publishing, 1998), 104–6.

10. Becky Tirabassi, *Let Prayer Change Your Life* (Nashville: Thomas Nelson Publishers, 2000), 21–23.

11. Becky Tirabassi, *Let Prayer Change Your Life Workbook* (Nashville: Thomas Nelson Publishers, 1995), 178–84.

12. Evelyn Christenson, *What God Does When Women Pray* (Nashville: Word Publishing, 2000), 21–27.

13. Paul Cedar, *A Life of Prayer,* ed. Charles R. Swindoll (Nashville: Word Publishing, 1998), 101–3.

14. Stormie Omartian, *Praying God's Will for Your Life* (Nashville: Thomas Nelson Publishers, 2001), 77–80.

15. J. Vernon McGee, *On Prayer: Praying and Living in The Father's Will* (Nashville: Thomas Nelson Publishers, 2002), 129–31.

16. Larry Ward, "Are Some Prayers Insignificant?" in *Practical Christianity,* ed. LaVonne Neff, Ron Beers, Bruce Barton, Linda Taylor, Dave Veerman, and Jim Galvin (Wheaton, Ill.: Tyndale House Publishers, Inc., 1987), 430–1.

17. Ronnie W. Floyd, *How To Pray* (Nashville: W Publishing Group, 1999), 131, 133–7.

18. John Calvin, *Institutes of the Christian Religion,* Book III, Chapter Twenty, Section 46.

19. Bill Bright, "Releasing God's Power Through Fasting," in *Partners in Prayer,* ed. John Maxwell (Nashville: Thomas Nelson Publishers, 1996), 125–6.

20. Bill Bright, "Releasing God's Power Through Fasting," in *Partners in Prayer,* ed. John Maxwell (Nashville: Thomas Nelson Publishers, 1996), 137–9.

21. Linda K. Taylor, *Does God Care If I Can't Pay My Bills?* (Wheaton, Ill.: Tyndale House Publishers, 1995), 21–29.

22. "The Shepherd of Hermas" in *The Ante-Nicene Fathers,* vol. 1: The Apostolic Fathers With Justin Martyr and Irenaeus, ed. Alexander Roberts and James Donaldson (Grand Rapids: Eerdmans, 1950–51. Orig. 1885–96), Similitude Second.

23. Harold Myra, "The Joy of Intercessory Prayer," in *Practical Christianity,* ed. LaVonne Neff, Ron Beers, Bruce Barton, Linda Taylor, Dave Veerman, and Jim Galvin (Wheaton, Ill.: Tyndale House Publishers, Inc., 1987), 434–5.

24. Ronnie W. Floyd, *How To Pray* (Nashville: W Publishing Group, 1999), 116–17.

25. Charles Stanley, *Into His Presence* (Nashville: Thomas Nelson Publishers, 2000), 317.

26. Paul Cedar, *A Life of Prayer,* ed. Charles Swindoll (Nashville: Word Publishing, 1998), 209–11.

27. Stormie Omartian, *Lord, I Want to Be Whole* (Nashville: Thomas Nelson Publishers, 2000), 28–30.

28. J. Vernon McGee, *On Prayer: Praying And Living In The Father's Will* (Nashville: Thomas Nelson Publishers, 2002), 84–85.

29. Paul Cedar, *A Life Of Prayer,* ed. Charles R. Swindoll (Nashville: Word Publishing, 1998), 4.

30. E. M. Bounds, Power Through Prayer (London: Oliphants, 1964), Chapter Six.

31. J. Vernon McGee, *On Prayer: Praying And Living In The Father's Will* (Nashville: Thomas Nelson Publishers, 2002), 99–102.

32. Evelyn Christenson, *What God Does When Women Pray* (Nashville: Word Publishing, 2000), 266–9.

33. *The Kneeling Christian* (Grand Rapids: Zondervan, between 1924 and 1947), Chapter Seven.

34. Reginald Cherry, *Healing Prayer* (Nashville: Thomas Nelson Publishers, 1999), 73–76.

35. Vernon Grounds, "Can My Prayers Influence World Leaders?" in *Practical Christianity,* ed. LaVonne Neff, Ron Beers, Bruce Barton, Linda Taylor, Dave Veerman, and Jim Galvin (Wheaton, Ill.: Tyndale House Publishers, Inc., 1987), 435–7.

36. Paul Cedar, *A Life of Prayer,* ed. Charles R. Swindoll (Nashville: Word Publishing, 1998), 201–3.
37. John Maxwell, *Partners In Prayer* (Nashville: Thomas Nelson Publishers, 1996), 123–24.
38. *The Word in Life Study Bible* (Nashville: Thomas Nelson Publishers, 1996), 55.

The Process
1. Ken Anderson, *Bible-Based Prayer Power* (Nashville: Thomas Nelson Publishers, 2000), 203–6.
2. Becky Tirabassi, *Let Prayer Change Your Life* (Nashville: Thomas Nelson Publishers, 2000), 142–8.
3. Max Lucado, *Just Like Jesus* (Nashville: Word Publishing, 1998), 43–45.
4. Max Lucado, *In the Eye of the Storm* (Nashville: W Publishing Group, 1991), 136–7.
5. Max Lucado, *In The Eye of the Storm* (Nashville: W Publishing Group, 1991), 202–5.
6. Stormie Omartian, *Lord, I Want To Be Whole* (Nashville: Thomas Nelson Publishers, 2000), 19–21.
7. Stormie Omartian, *Praying God's Will For Your Life* (Nashville: Thomas Nelson Publishers, 2001), 35–39.
8. Ronnie W. Floyd, *How To Pray* (Nashville: W Publishing Group, 1999), 76–79.
9. J. Vernon McGee, *On Prayer: Praying and Living in the Father's Will* (Nashville: Thomas Nelson Publishers, 2002), 21–24.
10. Randy Southern, *Fuel: Igniting Your Life With Passionate Prayer* (Nashville: Thomas Nelson Publishers, 2001), 53–55.
11 Dave Bastedo, "Constant Prayer: A Natural Response to God," in *Practical Christianity,* ed. LaVonne Neff, Ron Beers, Bruce Barton, Linda Taylor, Dave Veerman, and Jim Galvin (Wheaton, Ill.: Tyndale House Publishers, Inc., 1987), 426–28.
12. John Calvin, *Institutes of the Christian Religion* Book III, Chapter Twenty, Section Fifty.
13. Hank Hanegraaff, *The Prayer of Jesus.* (Nashville: W Publishing Group, 2001), 92–93.
14. *Prayers To Move Your Mountains* (Nashville: Thomas Nelson Publishers, 2000), 154–5.
15. From *Prayers To Move Your Mountains* (Nashville: Thomas Nelson Publishers, 2000), 170–1.
16. Terri Gibbs, ed., *Praying God's Promises for Your Husband* (Nashville: J. Countryman, 2002). 8–10, 12.
17. *The Word in Life Study Bible* (Nashville: Thomas Nelson Publishers, 1996), 869.
18. *Prayers to Move Your Mountains* (Nashville: Thomas Nelson Publishers, 2000), 132–3.
19. Hank Hanegraaff, *The Prayer of Jesus* (Nashville: W Publishing Group, 2001), 21–27.
20. Charles Stanley, *How to Handle Adversity* (Nashville: Oliver-Nelson Books, 1989), 22–25.
21. Paul Cedar, *A Life of Prayer,* ed. Charles R. Swindoll (Nashville: Word Publishing, 1998), 197–9.
22. Ronnie W. Floyd, *How To Pray* (Nashville: W Publishing Group, 1999), 220–1.
23. Paul Cedar, *A Life of Prayer,* ed. Charles Swindoll (Nashville: Word Publishing, 1998), 184–6.
24. Jennifer O'Neill, *From Fallen to Forgiven* (Nashville: W Publishing Group, 2001), 141–2.
25. Ronnie W. Floyd, *How to Pray* (Nashville: W Publishing Group, 1999) 63–66.
26. Endnote: *The Word In Life Study Bible* (Nashville: Thomas Nelson Publishers, 1996), 1046.
27. Thomas à Kempis, *The Imitation of Christ.*
28. William Law, The Spirit of Prayer (London: 1749), Part II.
29. Max Lucado, *The Great House of God* (Nashville: W Publishing Group, 1997), 50, 54–55.
30. Randy Southern, *Fuel: Igniting Your Life With Passionate Prayer* (Nashville: Thomas Nelson Publishers, 2001), 172.

PRAYERS OF THE BIBLE

[selected biblical prayers to help you pray]

Genesis 15:2	Abraham prays for an heir
Genesis 18:22–33	Abraham intercedes for Sodom
Genesis 24:12–14	Abraham's servant prays for success
Genesis 27:28–29	Isaac gives his son a blessing
Genesis 32:9–12	Jacob prays for protection
Exodus 15:1–17	Moses praises God for delivering the people
Exodus 32:31–32	Moses intercedes for the people
Exodus 33:18	Moses prays to see God's glory
Numbers 6:24–26	Aaron blesses the nation
Numbers 14:11–19	Moses pleads for the Israelites
Numbers 27:15–17	Moses prays for a new leader for Israel
Deuteronomy3:23–25	Moses pleads with God to visit Canaan
Deuteronomy 32:1–43	Moses praises God for all He has done
Deuteronomy 33:1–29	Moses blesses the tribes
Joshua 10:12	Joshua prays for a miracle
Judges 5:1–31	Deborah praises God for victory
Judges 6:36–40	Gideon asks for a sign
Judges 10:10	The people confess their sin
Judges 16:28–31	Samson prays for strength
1 Samuel 1:11	Hannah prays for a son
1 Samuel 2:1–11	Hannah praises God
2 Samuel 7:18–29	David thanks God for His covenant promise
2 Samuel 22:1–51	David praises God for deliverance
2 Samuel 24:10	David asks for forgiveness
1 Kings 3:6–9	Solomon asks for wisdom
1 Kings 8:23–53	Solomon blesses the temple
1 Kings 18:36–37	Elijah asks for God's presence
2 Kings 6:17	Elijah prays for his servant to see
2 Kings 19:14–19	Hezekiah asks God for deliverance
2 Kings 20:1–3	Hezekiah prays for healing
1 Chronicles 4:10	Jabez prays for prosperity
1 Chronicles 16:8–36	David thanks God as he brings the ark to Jerusalem
1 Chronicles 29:10–19	David prays for Solomon
Ezra 9:6–16	Ezra confesses the nation's sin
Nehemiah 1:5–11	Nehemiah prays for his nation
Nehemiah 9:5–37	The Israelites confess their sins
Job 42:1–6	Job acknowledges God's sovereignty
Psalms 1, 5, 15, 19, 25, 32, 48	Prayers for guidance
Psalms 2, 7, 14, 26, 37, 49, 58, 82	Prayers for justice
Psalms 3, 4, 7, 16, 17, 18, 23, 27, 31, 57, 91, 121, 125, 142	Prayers for protection from danger

Psalms 6, 32, 38, 40, 51, 69, 86, 103, 130	Prayers for forgiveness
Psalms 5, 6, 23, 34, 44, 74, 120, 137	Prayers of sorrow
Psalms 11, 16, 23	Prayers of faith
Psalms 18, 30, 32, 67, 75, 118, 136, 138	Prayers of thanks
Psalms 100, 103, 106, 107, 113, 117, 119	Prayers of praise
Isaiah 25:1–5	Isaiah praises God's faithfulness
Isaiah 38:10–20	Hezekiah thanks God for healing him
Isaiah 63:7—64:12	Isaiah prays and praises
Jeremiah 20:7–18	Jeremiah brings his complaint to God
Jeremiah 32:17–25	Jeremiah expresses his trust in God
Lamentations 1–4	Jeremiah laments over the fall of Jerusalem
Lamentations 5	Jeremiah prays for Jerusalem's restoration
Daniel 2:20–23	Daniel thanks God for wisdom
Jonah 2:1–10	Jonah prays in his distress
Habakkuk 3:1–19	Habakkuk expresses his awe of God
Matthew 6:9–13; Luke 11:2–4	Jesus gives His disciples a special prayer
Matthew 11:25–26; Luke 10:21	Jesus praises God for His revelation
Matthew 26:36–44	Jesus agonizes in the Garden
Luke 1:46–55	Mary praises God (*Magnificat*)
Luke 1:68–79	Zacharias praises God (*Benedictus*)
Luke 2:29–35	Simeon praises God (*Nunc Dimittis*)
John 11:41–42	Jesus praises God before raising Lazarus
John 12:27–28	Jesus expresses His troubled heart
John 17:1–5	Jesus prays for Himself
John 17:6–19	Jesus prays for His followers
John 17:20–26	Jesus prays for all future believers
Acts 1:24–25	The apostles pray for guidance
Acts 7:59–60	Stephen prays as he is martyred
Romans 1:8–10	Paul prays for the Roman believers
Romans 10:1	Paul prays for the Jewish people
Romans 16:25–27	Paul gives glory to God
1 Corinthians 1:4–9	Paul thanks God for the Corinthian believers
2 Corinthians 1:3–4	Paul praises God for His comfort
2 Corinthians 13:7–9	Paul prays for spiritual growth
Ephesians 1:16–23	Paul prays for the Ephesian believers
Ephesians 3:14–21	Paul prays that the Ephesians will grow spiritually
Philippians 1:9–11	Paul prays for the Philippian believers to have wisdom
Colossians 1:3–14	Paul prays for the Colossian believers
1 Thessalonians 1:2–3	Paul remembers the Thessalonian believers in prayer
1 Thessalonians 2:13	Paul gives thanks to God
1 Thessalonians 3:9–13	Paul prays for the believers to have strength
1 Thessalonians 5:23	Paul prays that the believers will be sanctified
2 Thessalonians 1:3	Paul thanks God for the believers
2 Thessalonians 2:13, 16–17	Paul prays for the believers to be encouraged
2 Thessalonians 3:16	Paul prays for the believers to have peace
2 Timothy 1:3–4	Paul remembers Timothy in his prayers
Philemon 4–6	Paul expresses appreciation for Philemon
1 Peter 1:3–5	Peter gives thanks to God
Jude 24–25	Jude praises God
Revelation 19:1–8	All of heaven praises God